HAK-9768

Varieties of Thinking

Philosophy of Education Research Library

Series editors
V. A. Howard and Israel Scheffler
Harvard Graduate School of Education

Recent decades have witnessed the decline of distinctively philosophical thinking about education. Practitioners and the public alike have increasingly turned rather to psychology, the social sciences and to technology in search of basic knowledge and direction. However, philosophical problems continue to surface at the center of educational concerns, confronting educators and citizens as well with inescapable questions of value, meaning, purpose, and justification.

PERL will publish works addressed to teachers, school administrators and researchers in every branch of education, as well as to philosophers and the reflective public. The series will illuminate the philosophical and historical bases of educational practice, and assess new educational trends as they emerge.

Already published

The Uses of Schooling
Harry S. Broudy

Educating Reason: Rationality, Critical Thinking and Education
Harvey Siegel

Thinking in School and Society
Francis Schrag

Plato's Metaphysics of Education
Samuel Scolnicov

The Sense of Art: A Study in Aesthetic Education
Ralph A. Smith

The Teacher: Theory and Practice in Education
Allen Pearson

Liberal Justice and the Marxist Critique of Education
Kenneth A. Strike

Philosophical Foundations of Health Education
Ronald S. Laura and Sandra Heaney

Teaching Critical Thinking
John E. McPeck

Accountability in Education: A Philosophical Inquiry
Robert B. Wagner

Varieties of Thinking

Essays from Harvard's Philosophy of Education Research Center

Edited with an Introduction
by V. A. Howard

Foreword by Howard Gardner

Routledge
New York   London

Published in 1990 by

Routledge
An imprint of Routledge, Chapman and Hall, Inc.
29 West 35 Street
New York, NY 10001

Published in Great Britain by

Routledge
11 New Fetter Lane
London EC4P 4EE

Library of Congress Cataloging in Publication Data

Varieties of thinking : essays from Harvard's Philosophy of Education
    Research Center / edited with an introduction by V. A. Howard.
        p.   cm.—(Philosophy of education research library)
    Includes bibliographical references.
    ISBN 0-415-90085-9
    1. Thought and thinking—Study and teaching.   2. Cognition in
children.   I. Howard, V. A., 1937–   .   II. Harvard University.
Philosophy of Education Research Center.   III. Series.
LB1590.3.V37   1990
370.15′2—dc20   89-29530

British Library cataloguing in publication data also available.

Contents

Foreword
Howard Gardner

Even for those superannuated educators who remember the aftermath of
the launching of Sputnik, these are exciting times. Hardly a month goes
by without the issuing of a new—and typically quite critical—report on
some aspect of education. Mayors, governors, chief executive officers,
and many private citizens are entering freshly into the debates about
the quality of education. Schools of education are undergoing careful
scrutiny, and there are serious efforts afoot to create professional standards for teachers. Sometimes, these initiatives involve the commitment
of sizeable sums of money, but even when the resources are spiritual
rather than pecuniary, consciousness is raised about important educational issues.

To the extent that educational content has achieved more than lip-
service, I discern two principal calls. On the "right," so to speak, there
is a cry for return to basic skills—to an assurance that those who have
passed through the American school system will know how to read,
write, calculate, and perhaps compute—so that they can, at a minimum,
hold a job, and, at a loftier level, be informed citizens. On the "left,"
there are parallel calls for attention to higher-level skills—and, in particular, for an enhanced attention to the fostering of "thinking."

Only an individual whose cynicism exceeded his patriotism could
oppose either of these implorations—to oppose the three "Rs" or the
teaching of thinking is akin to questioning motherhood or the flag.
Moreover, and in any event, the three "Rs" speak for themselves and
do not require additional justification. When it comes to fresh attention
to thinking, however, there is again an uncomfortably high ratio of noise
to signal. There are many new programs which purport to teach thinking,
countless weekend workshops and conferences which bring advocates
(more rarely critics) together, a never-ending stream of nostrums and
"quick fixes" designed to transform a nation of cognitive illiterates.
What is virtually absent are serious considerations of the nature of
thinking and its place in the philosophical, psychological, and educational firmaments of today.

And this is why the volume which you hold in your hands is so timely
and so welcome. Eight talented scholars associated with the Philosophy
of Education Research Center at the Harvard Graduate School of Education have turned their attention to diverse facets and processes of think-

ing—they have thought long and they have thought well about thinking. Among them, they have approached the issue of thinking from major analytical perspectives—conceptual, empirical, applied. They have considered thinking in the arts and the sciences, the worlds of theory as well as the worlds of practice. Spurning facile formulations and easy answers, they have uniformly opted to confront the intricate, delicate, and multifaceted aspects of thought, and to pose difficult and often unfamiliar questions. The resulting collection is a feast for the mind—at times hard going but in the end illuminating and not infrequently fun to read as well.

Intended or not, the title of the book itself signals its trove of treasures. I take it as a *treble entendre:* there are many kinds of thinking—if you will, multiple intelligences—ranging from that of the poet to that of the philosopher; each form of thinking itself is multi-faceted, involving problem-definition or -finding, design features, processes of evaluation, and the like; and thinking itself is exemplified in multifarious ways in the pages of this book. I am confident that readers will encounter yet further varieties in this book and will be persuaded that there is more to thinking than is dreamt of in most philosophies.

The book begins, as V. A. Howard's essay begins, rooted in philosophy, and in the classical philosophical tradition. It is no accident, however, that many sciences and arts are called upon in the course of the book, and that the book ends with an aspiring new science, cognitive science, the science of the mind. One of the most valid reasons for the contemporary excitement about matters educational is the emergence of this new field, which draws on a range of scientific perspectives to answer questions about the nature of thought.

Cognitive science has its "pure" aspects, but to my mind, one of its chief appeals is its possible contributions to educational practice. As we learn more about the mind, and about thinking, we ought to be able to bring this knowledge to bear in diverse educational settings. While much of this knowledge will be empirical in nature, its proper deployment will demand constant and careful scrutiny with reference to issues of purpose, means, effectiveness, and consequences. In short, it will need the highest level of thinking about thinking processes, as they are realized (or thwarted) in educational settings. I see *Varieties of Thinking* as the harbinger of a new and indispensable tool in education—a philosophically informed analysis of the cognitive scientific approach to education. May there be many others, of comparable high quality, in the future.

Preface

The papers comprising this volume grew out of discussions of the continuing Research Seminar of the Philosophy of Education Research Center (PERC) in the Harvard Graduate School of Education. In different ways, all of them focus on the general topic of thinking in educational perspective. As such, these essays represent a selection from among a series of Seminar topics, public lectures, and publications emanating from PERC since its beginning in July 1983. Three of the following nine papers were published previously; all have profited from the scrutiny of the regular Seminar participants, most of whom appear here.

Funded initially by the EXXON Education Foundation and lately by the Latsis Foundation, PERC was founded by Co-directors V. A. Howard and Israel Scheffler to promote philosphical inquiry into the processes, practices, and purposes of education, domestically and abroad. Much of PERC's current work explores the relations between curriculum and mental process with focus upon "the understanding of understanding"—that is, analysis of the creative and critical activities of mind ingredient to teaching, learning, and schooling generally. Complementary inquiries probe the historical and cultural origins of curriculum, wherein traditional school subjects are viewed as continuous with the heritage of achievements in art and performance, science and history, craft and technology, literature and language. Central to PERC's inquiries into the mental and cultural processes of education is the role of symbolic systems as instruments at once of invention, discovery, and communication.

Beyond these commonalities, the authors gathered here display resolute independence of mind in thinking about thinking, thereby exemplifying, even as they explore, the diversity of thinking to be found in educational settings. While we feel that the results justify publication under one cover, these papers mostly represent work in progress and a cross-section of PERC inquiries into the many facets of thinking.

I am grateful to my colleague and co-director, Israel Scheffler, for his encouragement and critical help in planning and preparing the volume. Heartfelt thanks are due to the other contributing authors for their originality, patience, and many hours of edifying conversation. Harry Haskell deserves special mention for a yeoman's job of copy editing. Grateful acknowledgment is also due to the journal editors of *Social Research,* of *Machine-Mediated Learning,* and of *Teachers College Record* for permission to reprint the essays by Elgin, Schwartz, and Scheffler, respectively.

Introduction
V. A. Howard

Thinking up a tree

Not long ago, I decided to look for the old logging trail to Davidson's Head, a promontory overlooking Passamaquoddy Bay on Deer Island where I maintain a house. The trail is marked by a dotted line on the old island map, long out of date. I left the main road walking up a track that led in the direction of the Head. About a quarter of a mile into the woods the track divided in a "Y," either branch being plausible, perhaps leading to opposite sides of the peninsula. I chose the right branch as the best bet because of its being uphill and seeming to lead more directly to the Head. Another quarter of a mile brought me to a cul-de-sac and abandoned sandpit strewn with the usual rusting automobile parts and evidence of teenage trysts. No discernible trail led beyond the sandpit. Likely, the old trail had grown over. Retracing my steps, I tramped down the left branch smiling in remembrance of Frost's "Road Not Taken," only to find myself yet another quarter-mile too far to the left and downhill from the Head in a vast clearing of cut-and-slash. Obviously the area was a rich source of birch and spruce for island stoves, which explained the road. Apparently, the old trail pushed on beyond the sandpit but no longer existed. I climbed a tall spruce tree to take my bearings. Off to the northeast was the Head already sinking into the fog. It would be a damp, chill trek through dense undergrowth to get out there, and risky in the waning light of later afternoon. Smiling again at *both* roads taken to no avail, I paused long enough in my perch to observe the graceful tracery of the fog as it crept from the sea towards me through the woods below. Shivering, I climbed down and trudged on back to the warmth of my kitchen stove fired, no doubt, by birch cut from that very clearing.

Imagine my surprise some weeks later while perusing the latest edition (1986) of Dewey's *How We Think* to find the following passage under the heading of "The Importance of Uncertainty and of Inquiry [for reflective thinking]."

A man traveling in an unfamiliar region comes to a branching of the road. Having no sure knowledge to fall back upon, he is brought to a standstill of hesitation and suspense. Which road is right? And how shall his perplexity be resolved? There are but two alternatives: he must either blindly and arbitrarily take his course, trusting to luck for the outcome, or he must discover grounds for the conclusion that a given road is right. Any attempt to decide the matter by thinking will involve inquiring into other facts, whether brought to mind by memory, or by further observation, or both. The perplexed wayfarer must carefully scrutinize what is before him and he must cudgel his memory. He looks for evidence that will support belief in favor of either of the roads—for evidence that will weight down one suggestion. He may climb a tree; he may go first in this direction, then in that, looking, in either case, for signs, clues, indications. He wants something in the nature of a signboard or a map, and *his reflection is aimed at the discovery of facts that will serve this purpose* (pp. 121–22).

Dewey "generalizes" his illustration for what he calls "reflective" thinking (as opposed to fancy or the unfocused "stream of conscious- ness"). "Thinking," he says,

begins in what may fairly enough be called a *forked-road* situation, a situation that is ambiguous, that presents a dilemma, that proposes alternatives. . . . In the suspense of uncertainty, we metaphorically climb a tree; we try to find some standpoint from which we [may get] a more commanding view of the situation, decide how the facts stand related to one another. . . . *Demand for the solution of a perplexity is the steadying and guiding factor in the entire process of reflection* (p. 122).

And again, "Thinking is not a case of spontaneous combustion; it does not occur just on 'general principles.' There is something that occasions and evokes it" (p. 123).

Further reflections on thinking up a tree

Recovering from the *déjà vu* of Dewey's illustration, I was equally struck by the accuracy of his "generalization"—so far as it went. I did indeed literally and metaphorically "climb a tree" to get a better sense of the lay of the land; and I did assess "how the facts stand related to one another." And the perplexity of locating the old trail was in fact guiding my thinking. Still, Dewey's man thinking up a tree seems to lack something of the richness of thinking *in foro interno;* that is, if we are able to take Dewey's account at face value. Or, to put it another way, Dewey's "forked-road situation" seems simpler, somehow too pat, lacking in color and allusion, perhaps because more urgent, than my own.

To be fair, Dewey is focusing on "reflective" (i.e., critical) thought which "involves not simply a sequence of ideas, but a *con*-sequence— a consecutive ordering in such a way that each determines the next as a proper outcome, while each outcome in turn leans back on, or refers to, its predecessors" (p. 114). Even so, and notwithstanding the urgency of many of the problems we face, there is more to thinking than directly meets the "demands for the solution of a perplexity." Here, anyway, Dewey, along with some recent champions of "critical thinking," distrusts the mind's divagations. I cannot see why. In my own thinking above, Frost's poem, as well as the scene viewed from my "aesthetic perch" high in the spruce tree, helped to elaborate the situation in ways useful, poignant, and pleasing. Moreover, I see no reason why reflection should not be a case of "spontaneous combustion" or occur "just on 'general principles'."

For example, my ironic allusions to Frost's "Road Not Taken," though associative, run fore and aft, as it were, adding allegorical perspective to my present search for the old trail while projecting that search against the backdrop of other choice points in my life. Such imagery may be spontaneous enough, but no less *thinking* or consequential in ways that could only be described as "reflective." Further, such ruminations do often occur "on general principles"—if by that phrase we mean certain habits of mind and perception, special sensitivities, or a disposition to reflect upon things in characteristic ways, say, as a painter, a geologist, or a psychiatrist might do.

To that extent, many of our "perplexities" are prehensile, so to say, reaching out on their own along channels of imagination and perception, of experience and discipline, and of hope and fear. Even for the same individual many construals of a situation are possible depending upon one's aims, interests, passing moods, or recollections. My own experience of thinking up a tree in the forest was a patterned quilt of many designs—some literal, some metaphorical—amongst the branching roads, the poem, the creeping fog, fear of injury in a dark forest, the old map, and the birch logs in my kitchen stove. They cohered in what Dewey elsewhere describes as *"an* experience"—something beyond the humdrum and involving many thoughts, imaginings, perceptions, facts, and interpretations. (Dewey, 1980, ch. 3: "Having an Experience," pp. 35–57).

A truer picture of Dewey's man, or myself, thinking up a tree would avoid reduction of the varieties of thinking that give coherence to an experience to one, albeit important, kind. Or conversely, perhaps there is more to reflective thinking than the assessment of given facts and the drawing of conclusions relative to a preconceived objective or obstructive problem. Depending upon our training and interests, we learn to observe and to select some facts while ignoring others. Facts are not just "there" waiting to be picked up (Hanson, 1961, ch. 2, pp. 31–49). Moreover, we are not always *goaded* into thinking by unwanted problems; rather, we often think precisely to *find* problems we do not yet have—for the sheer fun of it, for the joy of making discoveries, to exercise acquired powers, or, as we might well say, "on general principles." In short, there is more to thinking in general and to reflection in particular than noting facts, and relating evidence and premises to conclusions, important as they may be.

Taking that as a theme, the main purpose of this collection is to widen the educationally prevalent notion of reflective thought as fully circumscribed by rules of deductive and inductive inference—or variants thereof—to include its equally important manifestations in performance, aesthetic perception, deliberation, inquiry, and imagination.

Some features of thinking

The effort to understand thinking in its broader aspects is an ancient enterprise in Western philosophy having its first systematic culmination in the work of Aristotle. Originator of the idea of logic as an *organon* (or general "instrument") of thought, Aristotle was keenly aware of the varieties of thinking involved in specifically different pursuits. Thus, in Book VI of the *Nicomachean Ethics,* he subdivides knowledge (construed as the products of thinking) into three basic kinds: theoretical, practical, and productive. (For simplicity's sake, I am ignoring "intelligence"—knowledge of first principles—and other details of Aristotle's analysis.)

Theoretical knowledge *(epistémé)* is "contemplative," aiming at explanations of a sort that we should nowadays describe as "scientific" or "philosophical." Practical knowledge *(politiké)* concerns deliberation, decision, and action, particularly in the social and moral domains where the consequences of what we do are measured against their effects upon the interests and welfare of others. Productive knowledge *(techné)* has to do with the elements of craft, design, and know-how involved in the exercise of trained skills, say, of building, agriculture, or even of the composition of poetry and music (the concepts of art and of craft being the same in Aristotle's time).

For each form of knowledge, there is an appropriate activity of thinking and an outcome: contemplation results in a conclusion—an explanation or belief; deliberation in a decision or resolution for action; design or skill in works of art or artisanry. Each kind of thinking can be done well or badly, carefully or carelessly, intelligently or foolishly depending upon the training, judgment, and the character of the person presuming to have such knowledge.

The wisdom of Aristotle's scheme, whatever its shortcomings, is that it recognizes that no one set of rules or procedures can do for all practical, let alone intellectual pursuits. No one model of the mind's workings can capture the rich variety of its activities, whether thinking is sound or misguided. No one standard of how to think can possibly represent *the* way of satisfying the natural curiosity with which, he felt, we are born.

Further, Aristotle posits a close (but contingent) relation between character and knowledge in the sense that thinking, both sound and silly, may be in the service of virtue or of evil. For Aristotle, it is never quite enough to *know* in order to *do* well; it is also required to *be* virtuous (partly out of knowledge of the good, partly out of habit); that one have the disposition or predeliction, as we would now say, to contemplate, to deliberate, or to design well and for good ends. (cf. Passmore, 1980, ch. 1). Whatever the connections between thinking and values, Aristotle thought of them in the same breath, realizing that knowledge can be turned to action for good or ill. The reflective and the moral life are thus allied for him through the development of character.

How does Aristotle's approach to thinking differ from contemporary efforts to teach thinking skills in schools? Mainly in this: that education nowadays pays scant attention to the *applications* of thinking. In the rush to introduce programs of "critical thinking" into schools, educators all too frequently conceive of thinking narrowly, as an all-purpose computational skill, as an algorithm rather than an *organon,* in effect, as a "bag of tricks." The same criticism can be made of some efforts to cultivate general skills of "creativity" for artistic or problem-solving tasks.[1] Meanwhile, moral or character education tends to be taught separately from intellectual or artistic subjects in ways that overlook the value-laden aspects of the latter. Honesty, after all, is as much a value in science or art as it is in daily life.

Such curricular myopia loses sight of the many varieties and crosscurrents of thinking appropriate to different pursuits, as well as of thinking as a disposition—a trained predeliction—relevant to every domain of life. Accordingly, a second objective of the papers in this collection is to restore the imbalance in our thinking about thinking relative to learning and schooling by exhibiting some of its varieties, interrelations, and values.

Thinking exhibited

How shall we take our bearings on such a vexing topic as the nature of thinking? No sooner do we raise the question than further questions of the relations of thinking to reasoning, to judgment and understanding, to imagination and supposition, to feeling and emotion, to perception, to consciousness itself also arise. Indeed they are precisely the ones that interest us. However, construed as categorical questions of definition, the task of answering them appears singularly quixotic. We get along

---

[1]This is an understandable tendency among practicioners and policy-makers pressured by issues of daily urgency and public accountability. Notable exceptions to the "bag of tricks" approach to the teaching of critical thinking and creativity include Lipman, Sharp, Oscanyan (1980), Perkins (1981 and 1986), McPeck (1981), and Nickerson, Perkins, and Smith (1985).

quite comfortably in daily life without the older faculties of Intellect, Sensibility, and Will; and it is likewise doubtful that 'reasoning,' 'judging,' 'imagining,' 'feeling,' and the like, stand for any univocal, identifiable mental processes. As Gilbert Ryle remarked, "We do not always know when to apply, and when not to apply, the trade-names of epistemology" (Ryle, 1949, p. 284). Certainly they are not the tag labels for runners in a mental race.

Taxonomies of thinking are historically rife and theoretically controversial in philosophy as well as psychology (cf. Aune 1967); and hard-edged definitions tend more to conceptual fixity than to clarity of function. A more practical approach, useful for present purposes, might be to ask, how is thinking ordinarily exhibited? That is, how does a person show whether, what, and how he or she is thinking? Such an approach directs attention to the particulars of thinking, from idle musings to insistent doubtings to intent makings, while freeing up the ways of characterizing them philosophically or psychologically. This approach also reflects the "experimental" spirit, even if it ignores the letter of Aristotle's and Dewey's efforts to examine different activities and states of thought as they occur in real life.

Having abandoned the cookie-cutter mentality toward mental concepts, we are free to begin just about anywhere. Without any pretense to definition or completeness, we can say that thinking is exhibited in *at least* the following ways: first, in a person's *opinions*—in what one says, believes, or asserts to be the case and why; second, in a person's *deliberations*—in how one weighs alternatives in trying to reach a decision or make a choice; third, in a person's *skills*—in how one attends to, heeds, and performs at tasks or other actions; what Ryle describes as "thinking what one is doing while doing it" (Ryle, 1963, p. 29); and fourth, in a person's *imaginings*—in one's penchant for imagery (real or fictive), ability to use imagery to guide action, to entertain possibilities with or without imagery, and to envision their consequences.

Thoughtfulness, or the lack of it, is displayed in how one comports oneself in any and all of these ways, in different combinations, and in varying degrees of success. These patterns of comportment are also reflected in our ordinary talk about thoughtful activities, in such prepositional phrases as 'thinking *that*,' 'thinking *whether*,' 'thinking *how*,' and 'thinking *of*.'

Still, we do well to remember that ordinary language is no slave to taxonomy. Not every occurrence of 'thinking' or its cognates picks out all four of the thoughtful activities aforementioned. Rather, different occurrences of the term select different aspects of thinking within specific contexts. For example, on one use, the verb 'thinks' is a synonym of 'believes,' 'supposes,' or 'imagines'; so that in this sense one may think the most incredible things while in another sense—that of 'heeding,' 'reasoning,' or 'inquiring'—hardly be thinking at all.[2] In yet another sense, one may be thinking very hard what one is doing, say, in attending closely to the drawing of a portrait, without 'deducing,' 'abstracting,' or 'concluding' anything (Ryle, 1949, pp. 282–83). Similarly, one may think carefully what one is doing climbing a tall tree in deep woods without using words in any explicit way to draw conclusions (even if we do occasionally imagine dire consequences or remind ourselves to be careful). Finally, one may imagine (think *of*) the most fantastic of fictional beings or worlds without ever believing (thinking *that*) they exist. Or, out of hope or delusion, one may begin to believe in them, thereby blurring the difference between imagination and belief.

By asking how a person's thinking, whatever its merits, is *exhibited*, we leave open such questions as: how many kinds of thinking are there? how are they related? how may they be learned, practiced, and taught? by what means, technology, or special training? how do they combine, interract, which are dominant, in particular disciplines, professions, arts, science, sports, or crafts? what are the most common or damaging obstacles to correct (or effective) thinking in any given domain? These and many kindred questions are broached in the following papers in ways that bear upon artistic and design training (Schon), problem-solving in mathematics, poetry, and games (Perkins), different conceptions of science education (Schwartz), the place of computers in schools (Scheffler, Schwartz), the role of cognitive emotions in inquiry (Wagner), writing skills (Howard), symbolic comprehension and competence (Elgin), and critical thinking as an aim of education (Hawes)—to mention only the main topics.

Teaching thinking

Which of the aforementioned activities of thinking concern us most as teachers and learners? The answer is all of the above and more, but from a certain standpoint. That standpoint is demarcated by a distinction, again in Ryle's words,

> between the sense in which we say that someone is engaged in thinking something out from the sense in which we say that so and so is what he thinks, i.e. between the sense of "thought" in which thought can be hard, protracted, interrupted, careless, successful or unavailing from the sense in which a person's thoughts are true, false, valid, fallacious, abstract, rejected, shared, published or unpublished (Ryle, 1949, p. 285).

---

[2]This contrast reflects the broad contrast that Ryle draws between dispositional verbs and occurrence verbs: 1963, p. 116ff.

This distinction marks the difference between thought processes and the products of thought.

As pure critics, unconcerned about pedagogy, we are primarily concerned with the products of thinking things out—what finally a person thinks or does. For example, thinking *that*, as in "Felix thinks that measles are caused by sun spots," generally takes a full sentence after the preposition in such a way that neither the sentence ascribing such a belief to Felix nor its negation implies the truth or falsity of the embedded expression. It is simply what Felix thinks or believes. His belief is not so much a mental process as a *state* or propensity to respond verbally or in action to questions about the causes and prevention of measles. Now as critics, we reserve the right to accept or to reject Felix's belief on the basis of whatever grounds he or anyone else can provide for or against it. As teachers, however, we are concerned not only with the truth or falsity, validity or fallaciousness, of his belief but with how *he* thought through to such a conclusion and with how such *matters* are to be thought through. The teacher is thus a diagnostician of thinking, not only of its products but of its processes as measured by public standards (cf. Perkins, 1986, esp. pp. 153–54 on the uses of "mental models").

In becoming such a diagnostician, the teacher assumes responsibility for being acquainted with the most reliable knowledge available about the causes of measles and for guiding Felix's thinking along both valid and truthful paths. In short, "the teacher" is a coach of both the methods and the contents of thinking in all its varieties, from the classroom to the playing field, from books to Bach.

Thinking things through is, therefore, the domain of education and *eo ipso* of what goes under the labels of so-called critical or reflective thinking; but no sooner said than it needs also be stressed again that 'thinking things through' is no one thing but many. It encompasses all the activities of contemplation, deliberation, production, and imagination aforementioned, including sometimes the idle idiocies to which we are all subject. In off moments we can afford to ignore the latter, but as teachers and responsible learners, there is no respite. From the educational standpoint, that of thinking *anything* through, it is important not only what but how people think, how they make decisions, how they perform and produce, and how they use their imaginations.

This underscores yet another theme of the present collection; namely, that one mark of intelligent capacities is their susceptibility to improvement by instruction, including self-instruction. Such instruction typically proceeds by example and direction, by rule and routine, by insight and foresight, by acknowledged success and failure, by criticism and encouragement, whether it be self-instruction or by another person, in a school or elsewhere. Moreover, the many routes of instruction are paved by different kinds of symbols: words, pictures, diagrams, gestures, and demonstrations, to mention only a few. Certain of the following papers emphasize the varieties of verbal and nonverbal symbolism comprising "didactic discourse" in mathematical problem-solving (Perkins), in models of mind (Elgin), in writing instruction (Howard), and in architectural design (Schon).

Ways of thinking things through

Having seen how different uses of the verb 'think' may carry different references according to context, let us now briefly examine how they interact in four commonplace instances of thoughtful activity drawn from the papers to follow. (By no means am I suggesting a ready typology of the papers, still less of the authors, represented below; rather, I am suggesting a philosophical perspective from which they or others writing about thinking may be read.)

First, a case of opinion or thinking *that*. A typical example of what D. N. Perkins calls a "formal problem" might run as follows. Bea thinks José dances the samba because he is Brazilian. Is she right? Yes, if all Brazilians dance the samba; no, if some do not.

The reply of Bea's critic suggests some knowledge of classical logic, in particular the relations on the Square of Opposition between "A" (universal affirmation) and "O" (particular negative) assertions. Knowing that much, the critic can supply either premise, one of which makes the inference valid, while the other makes it invalid. The outcome would seem to be mechanical given such background. However, it takes *some* imagination to realize that not only could José be in the class of non-samba dancing Brazilians, but that even if he is not, the *inference* is still invalid so long as 'Some Brazilians do not dance the samba' is true. What is more, elements of know-how and of deliberation are also involved: the first in knowing how to apply the rules of syllogistic inference to cases, usually through much practice, and the second in knowing when to reverse the decision about Bea's conclusion one way or the other. As Perkins says, "the problem solver typically has plenty of time to think about them [problems] and never makes a move that constitutes an absolute commitment. For example, theorem provers who take a step they regret can take it back."

Second, an example of deliberative thinking *whether*. Design, as Donald A. Schon argues, is essentially a matter of "rational decision" proceeding serially from possibility to decision to possibility to decision, and so on, "where new options are versions of earlier ones, their differences from earlier ones growing out of the thinking that went into the rejection of earlier ones." In effect, one learns (*'that'* and *'how'*) from one trial to the next. Moreover, the designer must select which elements of a structure are fundamental and which "peripheral" or susceptible of alteration. Clearly, both sorts of decision require the designer to weigh past successes and failures (perceived as such) against envisioned outcomes and consequences, not to mention considerable technical know-how to connect means to ends. Viewed in this light, a design or plan, be it of a building or a social service, is compounded of rational (informed) choices of means to imagined future ends.

Third, two examples of skilled thinking *how*. Basic computational skills in mathematics offer good examples of *how to*: add, subtract, multiply, divide, etc. But as Israel Scheffler observes, a side effect of the use of computers to teach such skills is to enhance performance at routine skills with little or no improvement at higher levels of mathematical understanding or the uses of mathematics. "The moral seems to be that while basic skills need to be learned, higher skills also require nurture." A similar complaint is raised by Judah L. Schwartz in his examination of the use of computers in physics and mathematics education. "If we were to teach language the way we teach mathematics, we would continually be asking students to learn a short story by Poe, an essay by Emerson, or a sonnet by Donne. At no point would we ask students to compose a story of their own." Again, imagination is ingredient to such nurture, providing a growing vision both of what *can* be done at higher levels of capacity and of how such capacities may be used inventively to set and to solve a wide range of problems in other areas.

Another kind of skilled thinking, discussed by Schon, is exhibited in the executive phases of the design process, where, after planning, things must be built or done. Such executive action, like athletic or musical performance, has its own "intelligence" compounded of practical judgment, craft, and foresight.

Finally, an example of imaginative thinking *of*. Metaphor is a fertile source of examples of the imaginative use of language. In her study of symbolic (in this instance, linguistic) competence, Catherine Z. Elgin raises the question what one needs to know (*'that'*) to catch the drift of the statement, "Descartes is the Robinson Crusoe of the mind." She says,

> I need to know something about who Descartes is and what he accomplished, about who the fictional character Robinson Crusoe is and the story in which he appears, about how fictive terms can be applied metaphorically to characterize actual individuals, and about how a proper name prefaced by an article functions metaphorically as a general term.

What these hefty conditions of comprehension well show is that flights of imagination are not always flighty. Even as imagination permeates our "contemplative" thinking, so also many of our wildest imaginings in art or science are guided by considerations of consistency, relevance, significant contrast, or appropriate fit.

Even these few examples of thinking activity are enough to show that whatever the dominant mode of thought, others inevitably get involved in surrounding and supporting ways. Such interaction belies simplistic, categorical conceptions of mental process in any one mode. Because the verb 'think' straddles both the processes and the products of thought, it is easy to confound the two: to treat a propositional outcome as the product of purely "propositional" thought; to treat a decision as the result of purely "deliberative" thinking, and so on: as if each outcome were the result of a *single* corresponding process. Nothing could be further from actuality or more theoretically distorting of the complex ways mental processes interact. (Neither, incidentally, was that any part of Aristotle's message.) The effect on teaching of the one-product/one-process fallacy is to encourage overreliance on one or other "bag of tricks" as representing *the* core of "critical," "creative," "moral," or "artistic" thought. Thinking is more like an onion than an apple, and it does no good to insist that an onion, like an apple, *must* have a core. As with misconceptions of writing process misconceptions of thinking readily engender narrow, one-sided instructional practices.

Inside learning

The latter point raises the question of how a broader, more interactive conception of thinking processes might better serve the purposes of instruction. Consider, for instance, a novice at the violin whose progress appears to be stalled. Beyond the details of technique, discovering what the fledgling player attends to, cares about or loathes, or is attracted or repelled by tells a lot about the manner and the content of his thinking about the task at hand. Finding out what is salient to him in his studies and practice includes attention to emotional and cognitive states of mind: to what he notices, fails to notice, is indifferent to, is discouraged by, and so on. Such estimates of another's thinking are equivalent to judging how that person himself *appraises* matters, how his reasoning and evaluations work, including their grounds in his musical ambitions and practice habits. Such estimates may also be equivalent to a *diagnosis* of difficulties or strengths that cut across questions of technical proficiency, musical potential, stage of development, personality traits, and values. In the end, it is a question of how one heeds or attends to one's business, or whether one cares at all—all of which broaches the Aristotelian concern for the relations between thought, action, and the growth of character and personal standards of performance.

In such circumstances as these, thinking what one is doing while doing it is inevitably a trial-and-error affair, an experiment, as it were, in being (or becoming) a violinist. At the very least, it is learning to think with one's hands on a stringed instrument, and also to think critically *about* that effort in ways that will enhance future performances. That may not suit everyone musically or at all; but however the issue gets resolved, whether by a technical "quick fix" or by a long talk about practice habits and ambitions, no rule book exists to carry the learner through. Neither is there any way the teacher can intervene merely "by the book"; for even technical advice is a delicate matter of timing, trying, telling, and tact.

Viewed in this light, critical thinking in any of the modes discussed above emerges less as a prescribed algorithm than as an *attitude* of constructive self-criticism; which is to say, 'critical' for learners means 'self-critical' in ways that reach quite beyond cookbook rules or pat procedures, as necessary or useful as they may be. Tactics and tricks of the trade need to be absorbed into the whole fabric of one's thought and action, "taken in," so to say, in ways that convert *the* procedures to *my* procedures (cf. Howard, 1982, p. 96).

This is no simple action of following recipes, except in the simplest of cases, but rather of transmuting second- or third-person "technical" advice into the first-person perspective from which things are learned, practiced, and done. Michael Polanyi calls this "personal knowledge," encompassing for him everything that qualifies as "knowledge" from high theory to skilled practice (Polanyi 1958). By whatever name, the cautioning question for any teacher is this: who is to say exactly how— by what routes—anyone will acquire such knowledge except as they are actually observed and encouraged to do so? Instead of *the* way, there may be several ways even where the procedures involved are highly specifiable, as in doing long division; finally there is *your* way and *my* way. All the more reason, then, for educators to be aware of the many ways of thinking things through.

Thinking in the round

In emphasizing the breadth of the concept of thinking, the papers in this volume draw attention to its imaginative, evaluative, and performative as well as computational aspects. Accordingly, they share a common bias against simplistic or overly narrow conceptions of thinking.

For example, on the negative side, one finds here arguments against reductive computer models of mind and symbolic competence; against the notion of thinking as an exclusively verbal activity; against the hasty substitution of computer software for personal instruction; against overreliance on technology in lieu of an examined educational ideology; against the illusion of "computer literacy" as an educational cure-all; against the separation of writing from thinking; against rigid schemes of problem-setting and -solving in mathematics and science education; and, above all, against the twin hazards of reason without imagination and imagination without reason.

On the positive side, one finds arguments for carefully integrated philosophical and psychological inquiries into human symbolic competence; for a more coherent balance between observational and theoretical approaches to science education; for a supporting use of computer models and simulations in science and mathematics education; for a new generation of learner-centered software; for a reunion of the tools of reasoning and proper expression in writing instruction; for the couching of new instructional technologies within the larger dynamic of educational means, ends, and ideals; for more sensitive and flexible methods of instruction in the design professions; and, in the round, for a broader perspective on the teaching of reasoning and problem-solving skills than is now fashionable.

While the essays comprising this volume keep to a philosophical tone and approach, not all the contributors are philosophers by trade, and each essay shows the influence of other disciplinary viewpoints or practical concerns. Collectively, they might best be described as exercises in "applied philosophy," where by that phrase is meant an examination of the thought and practice characteristic of a given field or trained capacity in terms of avowed aims and principles, explanations and justifications, basic concepts, hidden presumptions, and implications. For purposes of this volume, the idea has been to put philosophy to work collaboratively with other theoretical and practical disciplines to examine the nature and nurture of thinking at different levels in several fields exhibiting diverse thinking activities.

By the same token, read from the standpoint of the authors' different interests and perspectives, each paper also represents a critical commentary on current trends in the philosophy of education, the psychology of learning, science education, design education, computer studies, writing instruction, or curriculum studies as those fields approach the topic of thinking in all its variety.

References

Aristotle, *Nicomachean Ethics*, trans. Martin Ostwald (New York: Bobbs-Merrill, 1962).

Aune, Bruce, "On Thought and Feeling," *Philosophical Quarterly*, 13, no. 50 (January 1963), pp. 1–12.

Aune, Bruce, "Thinking," *Encyclopedia of Philosophy*, vols. 7 & 8, (New York: Collier-Macmillan, 1967).

Dewey, John, *How We Think: A Restatement of the Relation of Reflective Thinking to the Educative Process*, in *John Dewey: The Later Works, 1925–1953*, vol. 8 (1933), edited by Jo Ann Boydston (Carbondale: Southern Illinois University Press, 1986).

Dewey, John, *Art as Experience* (New York: Putnam, 1980), first published in 1934.

Hanson, N. R., *Patterns of Discovery* (Cambridge: Cambridge University Press, 1961).

Howard, V. A., *Artistry: the Work of Artists* (Indianapolis: Hackett, 1982).

Howard, V. A., and J. H. Barton, *Thinking on Paper* (New York: William Morrow, 1986).

Lipman, M., A. M. Sharp, and F. Oscanyan, *Philosophy in the Classroom* (Philadelphia: Temple University Press, 1980).

Matthews, G., *Philosophy and the Young Child* (Cambridge: Harvard University Press, 1980).

McPeck, John, *Critical Thinking and Education* (London: St. Martin's Press, 1981).

McPeck, John, "Critical Thinking and Trivial Pursuits," *Teaching Philosophy,* 8:4 (October 1985), pp. 295–308.

Nickerson, R. S., D. N. Perkins, and E. E. Smith, *The Teaching of Thinking* (Hillsdale, N.J.: Lawrence Erlbaum: 1985).

Passmore, John, *The Philosophy of Teaching* (Cambridge: Harvard University Press, 1980).

Perkins, David N., *The Mind's Best Work* (Cambridge: Harvard University Press, 1981).

Perkins, David N., *Knowledge as Design* (Hillsdale, N.J.: Lawrence Erlbaum, 1986).

Polanyi, Michael, *Personal Knowledge: Towards a Post-Critical Philosophy* (London: Routledge & Kegan Paul, 1958).

Ryle, Gilbert, *The Concept of Mind* (Chicago: University of Chicago Press, 1984), first published in 1949.

CHAPTER 1

Problem theory
David N. Perkins

How problems are problematic

Consider the variety of problems. Formal problems such as proving a mathematical theorem or deriving a formula in physics call for finding a path from givens to the target expression by means of strictly deductive steps. Practical dilemmas such as deciding for whom to vote pose difficulties of weighing incomplete evidence, assigning rough probabilities to uncertain future scenarios, and summing up the weight of evidence and conjecture to yield a decision. Sports such as football or tennis place a premium on the quick and precise execution of bodily movements. Games such as chess or *go* emphasize the players' abilities to foresee courses of play. A painter faces the problem of depositing pigment on a canvas in a way that will engage an audience aesthetically.

The amazing range of situations that might be called problems leads to some natural questions. First of all, how can problems in general be characterized? Newell and Simon (1972) offered a formulation that, extended slightly in the next section, will serve well here. Second, can the differences between various sorts of problems be systematized? A sound classification could lead to insights about the different ways in which problems are problematic and the distribution of kinds of problems in different environments—the laboratory, schools, home—and in different professions—poet, physicist, preacher. Third, what do the differences in problems suggest about the skills and abilities needed to deal with them? Is it the case, for example, that formal problems such as proving theorems in mathematics call for a fundamentally different repertoire of skills than do nonformal problems such as painting a picture?

Questions like these define the content of what might be called *problem theory*—theorizing about the nature of problems. This paper presents a

I would like to thank Jon Baron and Ray Nickerson for their very helpful comments on an earlier draft of this paper. The article was written at Bolt Beranek and Newman Inc., Cambridge, Massachusetts with support from the National Institute of Education, Contract Number 400–80–0031, and at Project Zero of the Graduate School of Education, Harvard University, with support from the Spencer Foundation. The views presented here do not necessarily reflect those of the host or supporting agencies. Reprinted by permission, *Social Research* 50, no. 4 (Winter 1984).

particular problem theory. The need for such a theory stems in large part from the confusions and gaps apparent in the haphazard distinctions that now provide a casual problem theory—sweeping divisions of problems into scientific and humanistic, formal and informal, convergent and divergent, for example.

At the very least, such categories seem too simplistic. Consider, for example, the classical distinction between convergent and divergent problems and associated styles of thinking. We usually think of convergent problems as logical or mathematical in character. However, a convergent problem is also supposed to have a single answer, an answer that the problem solver arrives at by converging upon it through a series of inferences. Then what about the problem of constructing a mathematical proof? Surely formal, it is nonetheless hardly convergent. The same theorem can often be demonstrated in many quite different ways, as the diverse proofs of the Pythagorean theorem testify. Or take the well-known puzzle of arranging six matches to form exactly four equilateral triangles. This problem has one answer, but a tricky one— arrange the matches to form the edges of a tetrahedron in space. As a single-answer problem, it could be said to require convergent thinking. But the spirit of such a classification seems wrong. Instead, the problem solver needs to diverge—diverge from the initial assumption nearly everyone makes that the matchsticks are to be arranged in a plane.

If anything is clear here, it is that the casual vocabulary of convergent and divergent, formal and nonformal, scientific and humanistic problems is muddled. This article proposes a classification of problem types that tries to do better.

The nature of problems

Newell and Simon (1972) proposed a general characterization of problems that can be adapted to present purposes. They pointed out that many, perhaps all, problems involve 1) a set of states, 2) a set of operations each of which transforms the current state into some other state, 3) an initial state, and 4) a goal—an efficient test for whether the current state is a goal state. Solving the problem consists in transforming the initial state into a goal state by applying some sequence of operations.

Consider how this account fits a formal problem such as proving a theorem in logic. The states can be taken as lists of logical sentences. The initial state is the list of axioms and theorems already proved. The operations are the rules of inference, which when applied to the current state add theorems to it. The goal is any state containing a sentence that expresses the theorem to be proved. Another rather similar problem is a derivation, where the aim is to derive a formula for one variable in terms of others from a given set of equations relating the variables. The states are lists of algebraic equations. The initial state consists of the given algebraic equations. The operators are any legal algebraic manipulations—substitution, transposition, and so on—each of which adds a new equation to the list. A goal state is any list including an equation with the variable of concern isolated on one side and the desired independent variables on the other side.

Newell and Simon (1972) pointed out that what counts as the solution to a problem varies from situation to situation, an observation that applies here. The solution to the problem of proving the theorem is the path of operations—the proof. The solution to the derivation problem is the derived formula, the last expression in the final state. But such differences should not obscure the common framework provided by a characterization in terms of states, operators, and goal.

Newell and Simon also pointed out that nonformal problems allow such a characterization too. Consider, for instance, the very nonformal problem of painting a watercolor. The states could be taken as deposits of the watercolor pigments on the paper. The operations are acts of depositing pigment. The initial state is the blank piece of paper. Goal states are defined by the test of the artist's judgment: does the painting look finished?

The general framework offered by Newell and Simon provides a basis for designing a system to classify problems. However, some clarifications and liberalizations are necessary to make room for the immense variety of problems the present problem theory means to accommodate.

Non-problematic problems. The general framework of states, operations, and goals applies not only to problematic tasks, but to nonproblematic ones, such as fetching the dictionary from its usual place on the bookshelf. Should such tasks be called problems at all? This is an issue of usage. Here we will depart from normal practice and consider nonproblematic tasks as well as problematic ones problems. This will lead to a simpler use of vocabulary.

Liberalizing goals, states, and operations. Goals, states, and operations call for liberal interpretations in the present problem theory. For instance, if painting a watercolor is to be considered a problem, certainly it is an "open" or "ill-defined" one (Reitman, 1965; Hayes, 1981). Much of the artist's effort may consist in "problem finding," (Getzels and Csikszentmihalyi, 1976), that is, in narrowing down just what the problem is. In terms of Newell and Simon's model, this means that the goal may change in the course of solving the problem. Also, the goal test is not necessarily neat and efficient. The artist, for example, may stand in front of a work for a long time, trying to decide whether it is done.

As to states, in Newell and Simon's model as usually conceived, states change only through the application of operations. But the present analysis needs to accommodate cases where the current state changes for other reasons. For example, watercolors run and change color upon drying, and, in the problem of winning a game of chess as opposed to the problem of choosing an individual move, the state of the game changes with the opponent's moves as well as one's own.

Finally, operations cannot necessarily be carried out reliably. For instance, in sports, operations like hitting the ball or throwing a pass come with no guarantee of success.

Unreliable operations, states that change by themselves, and goals that change in the course of performing a task might be taken as grounds for considering the task not a proper problem at all. But the present strategy is different. Here, such tasks will count as problems. Distinctions about the reliability of operations and the changeability of states or operations will help to differentiate various types of problems.

Structured and unstructured problems. A problem as given might leave ambiguous what the states and operations are. For example, if your chosen goal is to make a million before you are thirty, what are the boundary conditions on operations? Must you proceed legally? Must you proceed morally? What states will you see yourself as moving through—states of investment, of employment, of marriage to widowed millionaires? Any and all?

The way of classifying problems to be discussed requires knowing what the states and operations are. When this is clear, either because the problem statement or the context makes it plain, the problem will be called a "structured problem." Otherwise it will be called an "unstructured problem." Note that a problem with a vague goal may be structured. For instance, the problem of painting a watercolor is structured because it is clear what the states and operations are—arrangements of pigment on the canvas and acts of depositing pigment.

Subproblems. The structure of even a relatively well-defined problem might seem confusing because many perspectives could be taken on it. For example, in the case of chess, are the operations the actual moves the player might make, or the mental moves the player might consider in selecting an actual move, or both? However, such ambiguities disappear when we distinguish between problems and subproblems. In the case of chess, it is natural to consider legal arrangements of pieces on the board as the states and legal moves as the operations. But this does not mean that the decision making of the chess player must be slighted. Selecting a move is best considered a subproblem. For that subproblem, the states are imagined arrangements of pieces and the moves imagined moves, as in Newell and Simon's analysis.

Furthermore, notice that problem and subproblem may present quite different characteristics. For example, in the main problem of winning a game of chess, operations are irreversible—once a move has been made, the player cannot retract it. On the other hand, the player pondering possible chains of moves mentally makes no commitment. Accordingly, distinguishing between problems and subproblems not only allows resolving confusion about problem structures, but permits acknowledging the different ways problems are problematic at different levels.

Some features of formal problems

Why do we think of some problems as formal problems—for example, proving a mathematical theorem or deriving a given formula in physics? Perhaps there are features possessed by such problems that set them apart systematically from painting a picture, making a career decision, or even playing chess.

This question makes a good starting point for an effort to classify different types of problems. Below, a number of important characteristics of formal problems are suggested. As it turns out, the characteristics also provide a useful set of dimensions for distinguishing among different kinds of nonformal problems.

Stability

Stability refers in general to the absence of changes in state, operations, and goal. Consider first *stable states*. Experience teaches that for formal problems, as well as many others, the current state only changes through the action of an operator applied by the problem solver. However, in competitive games or in watercolor painting this is not the case. Accordingly, a *stable state* is one distinguishing feature of formal problems.

As also noted earlier, problems such as painting a picture may find the problem solver refining the goal in the course of solving the problem. In strictly formal problems, that does not happen. To express this characteristic of formal problems, we will say that a formal problem has a *stable goal test*.

It also makes sense to speak of operations as stable. Just as stable states and the stable goal test refer to aspects of the problem that do not change, so an operation that is stable means an operation that, if carefully executed, does not change into something else in the process of applying it. Operations where care suffices will be called *tractable operations* ("tractable" seems a better reminder of the point than "stable").

For example, applying a rule of inference in logic as well as moving a pawn forward in chess are tractable operations, operations that the problem solver proceeding with care can count on carrying out. In contrast, many other problems involve intractable operations, operations that even the careful problem solver cannot expect to execute reliably every time. The bowler may mean to roll a strike or pick off the remaining ten pin, but may very well fail to do so. The watercolorist may mean to render a leaf with a single stroke of the brush, but may botch it.

Transparency

The person attempting to prove a theorem benefits from full knowledge of the current state, the goal, and the effects of any operation on the current state. This benefit of full knowledge will be called, in general, *transparency*. As with stability, transparency can be assigned distinctive meanings with reference to states, goal, and operations.

Transparent states means that no information about the current state is concealed. For example, in theorem proving and in chess, the problem solver has full access to the current problem state. In contrast, in most card games, such as bridge, poker, or solitaire, some cards are concealed from the player, even though the distribution of those cards is part of the current state.

A theorem prover or a chess player can in principle anticipate the effects of any operation performed. But not all problems offer this convenience. For instance, the result of a draw in poker or a roll of the dice is concealed from the player. When the problem solver can always in principle discern the effects of operations on the state, the problem will be said to have *known-effect operations*. One could say "transparent operations" instead, but "known-effect" makes the point more clearly.

Note that this definition does not require that the states be transparent. For example, the game of bridge has nontransparent states but known-effect operations: the player can discern the effect of laying down a particular card within the limits of his knowledge of the state of the game. In contrast, draw poker has both nontransparent states and operations that are not known-effect, for the player certainly cannot anticipate the effects of the draw on the state of the game as far as the player knows it.

Finally, how does transparency apply to goals? A problem will be said to have a *transparent goal test* providing the test is explicit and objective. For instance, the standards for whether a theorem has been proved, or a game of chess or bridge won, are explicit and objective. In contrast, whether a poem or a painting is complete requires a subjective judgment based upon largely tacit standards.

A technical point: intractable operations, such as trying to bowl a strike, have unpredictable consequences, so one might conclude that known-effect operations must necessarily be tractable, else the effect would not be certain. But it is desirable to preserve the logical independence of the two criteria, known-effect operations and tractable operations. To do that, in deciding whether the effect is known or not, we assume a *successfully executed operation*. For example, consider the archer executing an operation called "hitting the bullseye." The operation is intractable, but, if executed successfully, the operation has a known effect on the score and the state of the game.

Simplicity

Simplicity means that the structure of the "problem space" determined by the states, operations, and goal is very simple. As usual, different interpretations of simplicity will be assigned to states, operations, and goal.

A problem will be said to have a *simple goal test* when the goal test involves no difficulties of subtlety or complexity. Recall that, in Newell and Simon's original characterization of problems, the goal test was supposed to be quick and easy. However, the present treatment allows for problems where the goal test is subtle or complex, for instance as in judging whether a painting is complete, or in an Apollo countdown. Formal problems characteristically have quick and easy goal tests. For example, it is not difficult to check whether the last statement generated is the formula to be derived.

Structural simplicity applies to operations as follows. A problem will be said to have *surveyable operations* when the available operations are few enough so that the problem solver can consider them one by one. This typically is the case in games, for instance chess. Also, many formal problems have surveyable operations. For example, in proving theorems in the propositional calculus, there are very few available operations, and the problem solver can consider them all.

However, not all formal problems have surveyable operations. For instance, in trying to prove a theorem in plane geometry, one faces a multitude of operations, especially considering the variety of constructions that might be performed. Because not all formal problems have surveyable operations, the notion extends the concept of formality. To single them out, formal problems that also have surveyable operations will be called "very formal problems."

Yet another extension of the concept of formality finds an ideal example in the algorithm. Intuitively speaking, the task of executing an algorithm is a kind of limiting case of a formal problem—the problem solver does not even have to make choices about what to do next. Consider, for example, executing the long-division algorithm on a given pair of numbers. From each state, there is only a single legitimate next state. To be sure, the problem solver can back up a step, crossing out work, but this is pointless unless an error has been made. Indeed, the problem solver may make an error, moving into an "improper state." However, basically there is only one clear path from initial state to goal state, a path determined by the division algorithm plus the pair of numbers. In general, a problem with this characteristic will be said to have a *simple-state path*.

Not all problems with simple-state paths are formal. Consider, for example, the problem of playing a piano composition. As the pianist proceeds through the piece, the score defines the next state—the next notes to be struck. But the problem is not formal because, among other reasons, the operations of striking various combinations of notes are not tractable. The example also shows that problems with simple-state paths need not have surveyable operations. There may be a number of ways of playing the next chord—too many to survey in the time available!

As the examples suggest, problems with simple-state paths might just as well be called procedures or programs. To solve such a problem simply means to execute the procedure. Some procedures, for instance mathematical algorithms, satisfy the other requirements for formality. These *formal procedures* are limiting cases of formality as discussed here, the most formal of formal problems.

Deliberation

One more characteristic of formal problems deserves note: the problem solver typically has plenty of time to think about them and never makes a move that constitutes an absolute commitment. For example, theorem provers who take a step they regret can take it back. Such flexibility marks one extreme of a dimension that might be called "deliberation." The values along this dimension are defined as follows.

Reversible operations. The problem solver can always restore a problem to a previous state by some sequence of operations, "undoing" the effects of intervening operations or, let it be added, any other intervening transformations. (Transformations that are not operations include operations that go awry, as in missing the nail you are hammering, and natural transformations such as the running of paints.) In formal problems, operations are reversible. In oil painting the same is so, because, for example, scraping or overpainting can rectify mistakes. In contrast, games like chess and activities like watercolor painting do not offer reversible operations. One cannot always back up.

Ponderable operations. The problem solver can think as long as necessary, but operations cannot be retracted, as in playing chess (with no time limit).

Urgent operations. The problem solver has little time to think, and operations cannot be retracted. Football, in which the players have just a few seconds to play the next operation, is an example.

Continual operations. There is no real distinction between phases of planning and acting. The problem solver acts continually and the problem state changes continually, as in wrestling.

How and how well do the foregoing criteria single out what we mean intuitively by formal problems? The attributes of stability (stable states, stable goal test, tractable operations), transparency (transparent states, transparent goal test, known-effect operations), simple goal test, and reversible operations define a class of problems that includes proofs and derivations and excludes most other problems.

Is anything excluded that ought not to be? One interesting test case is the problem of discovering a new theorem in mathematics. Perhaps this should be considered a formal problem. However, the criteria exclude it because, among other considerations, the problem does not involve a stable or transparent goal test—what makes for a worthwhile theorem is about an imponderable as what makes for a worthwhile poem. Maybe this is a flaw in the criteria, but it is at least arguable that theorem hunting ought to be excluded from the realm of formal problems exactly because it is a relatively ill-defined quest, even though carried out in a formal domain.

What about nonmathematical problems that the criteria admit as formal? A good example is the popular Rubik's Cube. The puzzle meets all the requirements of formality and also has surveyable operations, since there are only a few ways to turn the cube out of any given state. Does this point up a flaw in the criteria? Well, Rubik's Cube is a problem with quite a formal flavor. It would not do too much violence to the intuitive concept of formality to consider Rubik's Cube a formal problem.

In summary, let me suggest that the criteria of formality discussed here capture and sharpen the intuitive concept of formality. In addition, certain of the criteria extend the concept, surveyable operations allowing for "very formal problems" and simple-state paths allowing for "formal procedures," the most formal of formal problems.

Problematics

Formality is interesting in itself, but there is a larger aim. The dimensions of formality provide the foundation for an analysis of what might be called "problematics"—of what makes problems problematical. Each dimension of formality defines a way in which a problem might be problematic or not. To see this, and by way of review, consider the dimensions again along with some examples.

Stability: stable states. When this condition is met, the states only change through the intervention of the problem solver, as in theorem proving, solitaire, or poetry writing. The changes of state outside the intervention of the problem solver in chess, football, or watercolor painting make these problems problematic in that respect.

Stability: tractable operations. The problem solver can count on executing operations reliably by being careful, as in theorem proving, chess, poetry writing (where an operation is taken as adding or deleting a word or phrase). But difficulties of execution make football and water-color painting problematic in this respect.

Stability: stable goal test. The test for goal states does not change in the course of problem solving, as in theorem proving, card games and football. However, some problems are more problematic in calling for the problem solver to clarify the problem while resolving it, for example, in discovering theorems, writing poetry, or painting.

Transparency: transparent states. The problem solver has access to complete information about the current state, as in theorem proving, chess, tennis, painting. But in card games, playing the stock market, or fighting a war, the lack of complete-state information is part of what makes the problem problematic.

Transparency: known-effect operations. The problem solver has sufficient information to predict the effect of operations on the state so far as it is known, assuming the operations are carried out successfully, as in theorem proving, chess, bowling, and painting. However, the effects of successfully executed operations are problematic in draw poker or dice.

Transparency: transparent goal test. The test for a goal state is objective, as in theorem proving, football, or chess. However, in painting, writing a poem, or discovering a theorem, the problem solver may feel uncertainty and loss of direction due to the problematic subjectivity of the goal.

Simplicity: simple-state path. There is only one sequence of states leading to a goal state, as in executing the standard arithmetic algorithms or dialing a phone number. But the options for different routes make proving a theorem or even looking up a phone number more problematic.

Simplicity: surveyable operations. The operations are few enough and/or clearly enough organized so that all can be considered, as in proving theorems in the propositional calculus or playing chess. On the other hand, proving geometry theorems, painting, or playing football are more problematic in that the problem solver cannot straightforwardly scan all operations that might be performed, but must discover or select likely candidates for consideration.

Simplicity: simple goal test. The test for a goal state does not involve subtle judgments nor a complex sequence of activities, as in proving theorems or playing chess. In contrast, subtleties and complexities may make evaluation of goal states problematic in painting or writing a poem or approving the launch of a moon rocket.

Deliberation: reversible operations. Operations can be retracted at no cost, as in theorem proving, writing a poem, or painting in oils, so there is room for as much deliberation as might be needed. However, problems with the following characteristics become successively more problematic in terms of deliberation.

Deliberation: ponderable operations. Although operations cannot be retracted, there is ample time for deliberation, as in playing chess without a time limit, competition diving, painting in watercolors, playing the stock market.

Deliberation: urgent operations. Operations cannot be retracted and there is little time for planning, as in rapid-pass chess, football with its brief huddles, debating contests.

Deliberation: continual operations. The problem solver is executing operations more or less continually with no time specifically set aside for thinking, as in wrestling, hockey, playing a musical instrument.

How well do the dimensions defined capture the ways in which problems are problematic? Not perfectly, to be sure. Several qualifications have to be made.

First of all, failing a condition of formality is only a necessary but not a sufficient condition for being problematic with respect to the condition. That is, if a problem satisfies a condition of formality, it cannot be problematic in that way. But if a problem fails the condition, it still might not be problematic anyway. For instance, a problem with intractable operations is not thereby problematic if the problem also happens to be reversible. In that case, the problem solver can undo any operations that go awry and keep trying again and again until successful.

For a second qualification, some problems as given are not yet structured. The criteria apply to structured problems, where the problem solver is already working within a framework of states, operations, and goals. Accordingly, there is another way in which problems can be problematic: in being unstructured. This sort of problematicity has the same logic as those discussed above—an already structured problem is *not* problematic in that respect, but an unstructured problem may or may not be. Some unstructured problems are easy to structure, and some difficult.

Finally, there is one more way in which problems can be problematic, even though they satisfy all the criteria listed. For example, executing the addition algorithm (assuming accurate knowledge of it) is a problem that satisfies every condition of formality. Yet we all know that mistakes can and do occur. Such mistakes are mere slips, to be sure, but even slips are problematic. In short, some problems that otherwise pose no difficulties are problematic simply in demanding precision.

Where do these qualifications leave the theory of problematics proposed here? With the following conjecture: the ways of being problematic listed exhaust the ways a problem *can* be problematic. Any problem is problematic only in being unstructured, demanding precision, or failing one of the conditions of formality. Any description of the way a problem is problematic can be analyzed into one or more of those ways of being problematic.

Some cases in point

How to classify a problem

Throughout the foregoing, one crucial question has been deferred: can a problem be classified reliably? This is no small matter. After all, the theory presented here purports to offer a classification system illuminating the ways in which problems are problematic. Unless problems can be categorized reasonably reliably, the principal objective is forfeit.

One point should be confessed right away: no algorithm for classifying problems is offered here. On the contrary, categorizing problems is an art somewhat dependent on the judgment of the classifier. Nonetheless, the case can be argued that fairly reliable classifications are possible. Let us begin by considering some rules of thumb about defining the structure of a problem and then pass on to some particular difficulties.

What are the states? Given a description of a problem, what are the states? They are considered to be equivalence classes of states of the world. Two states of the world in the same equivalence class are the same so far as the problem is concerned. For instance, in chess, it makes no difference whether the queen's rook is placed a little further to the left or right, so long as it rests in its proper square. But in a hockey game, the position of a player slightly to the left or right may prove important. Whereas the states of a chess game vary intermittently, as one or another player moves, the states of a hockey game vary continuously, because the position and motions of the players from second to second may make a difference in who wins.

Note that sometimes certain situations arise that might be called "illegal" or "improper" states. For example, a novice chess player might set up the board with knight and bishop reversed. A person doing an addition problem might enter the wrong digit under one of the columns of digits. By definition, operations always transform states into other proper states. Improper states arise through operations gone awry or in other accidental ways (see the remarks on operations below.)

What is the goal test? Problems as given necessarily specify the goal, even if in terms as vague as "write a poem." Such ambiguity poses no difficulty, given the present classification system, since the system explicitly allows for ill-defined goals through accommodating unstable, nontransparent, and nonsimple goal tests.

What are the operations? Broadly speaking, operations are actions carried out in order to transform one state into another. Operations are defined in terms of possibilities for intentional action. They are specified in terms of the state change expected or hoped for, and, sometimes, in terms of the means to be used. For instance, a pool player might plan in terms of an operation like "eight ball in the corner pocket," or, adding a constraint on the means, "eight ball in the corner pocket by banking the cue ball."

In general, operations certainly do not include all acts one might execute. For example, peeking at one's hole card in blackjack does not effect the state of the game in any meaningful way. Hence, it should not count as an operation. However, an issue arises about strategies adopted while effecting an operation. For instance, suppose a pool player finds help in advising himself, "Think of something else while shooting." Should this count as part of the operation? To call it so seems counterintuitive, because the advice has nothing strictly to do with the action of the game. This intuition can be stated more precisely as follows: *operations should be restricted to actions described as carried out upon objects or features of the states*. What the player thinks about while shooting does not meet this criterion.

It should also be noted that transformations of state may occur by means other than operations. For one point, "acts of nature" sometimes transform the problem states of problems without stable states, as in, for example, the running of watercolor pigments. For another point, when operations are intractable, they often go awry. For instance, the player receiving the football may fumble.

Ambiguity in structuring. The foregoing rules of thumb may help in categorizing problems, but what if the same problem as given leads to different structured problems? This means that the problem as given would not have a unique classification.

Although in principle a threat, this difficulty does not seem to be so serious in practice. First of all, many problems as given define their structures. For example, the rules of chess specify the operations to be used. Moreover, for many physical activities, the operations correspond naturally to the physical acts that can be executed upon the states. For an example mentioned earlier, in watercolor painting it seems more or less inevitable that the operations are acts of depositing pigment.

It was suggested earlier than other seeming ambiguities disappear when care is taken to separate problems from subproblems. For instance, does the problem of playing chess involve reversible operations? No for the game as a whole, where the operations are actual moves of pieces. But in the subproblem of choosing a move, operations such as trying out a move mentally can, of course, be retracted.

In general, experience in classifying problems suggests that most problems have a single "natural" structuring, perhaps with minor variations. As to the exceptions, they simply call for multiple classifications acknowledging their ambiguity. So long as such cases are infrequent, no great confusion arises.

Variation of problem structure with progress through a problem. The classification of a problem may change as the problem solver progresses. For example, at the beginning of solving an algebra word-problem, the problem solver typically will have many options. But close to the end, the problem solver may merely be executing arithmetic algorithms, and the problem will then have a simple-state path.

This is a point to recognize, but it poses no real difficulty for our problem theory. Clearly, a problem should be classified according to its characteristics as the problem solver begins. If there is a special interest in the subproblem posed by some later stage in the solution process, then it can be classified independently.

Variation with expertise. An expert and a novice may work with very different problem structures. For example, contrast a person who faces a maze for the first time with someone who has solved the same maze several times. For the novice, each branch is a choice point. But the expert is simply executing an algorithm: he knows where to turn at each branch. In terms of the classification system, the problem has a simple-state path for the expert but not for the novice.

Again, this sort of variation poses no real difficulty for a problem theory. The problem certainly should be classified with the novice in mind, because that best captures what is problematic about the problem as given. If there is a special interest in the problem as the expert sees it, that can be classified too.

Moreover, we should not assume that what is problematic about a problem usually varies a great deal with expertise. For example, so many are the options for play in chess that even a grand master does not find the game presenting a simple-state path. The options for depositing pigment on canvas are surveyable neither by a hack nor a Rembrandt. The champion bowler can bowl a strike much more reliably than the Saturday sportsman, but still the fundamental problem for the champion is the intractability of the operation—the champion cannot count on bowling a strike.

In short, for many problems, perhaps for most problems, an expert gets better at dealing with the various respects in which a problem is problematic without ever making them nonproblematic. This is a point as much about the way we talk about problems as the nature of problems themselves. When expertise truly transforms a problem, so that it is problematic in quite a different way, we tend to think of it as a different problem. For instance, consider navigating up a familiar river "the same problem" as exploring a new one. We do not consider reproducing a proof for a theorem to be "the same problem" as finding a proof in the first place.

Games

Now let us apply this machinery. Life is so full of problems that it seems paradoxical to find people making up more of them. But, in fact, the handiest supply of problems to analyze is the many games people have invented with which to puzzle themselves. It is interesting to examine increasingly informal categories of games, categories generated by reversing several of the conditions for formality one by one.

As discussed earlier, Rubik's Cube is a very formal problem. It shares all the characteristics of a mathematical proof or derivation, and in addition has surveyable operations.

While Rubik's cube also has reversible operations, some other games of similar flavor do not. For instance, there are those puzzles that ask the player to jump pegs over others, removing each peg that is jumped. The objective is to end with one peg in a given position, often the center. Lack of a reversibility makes a substantial difference, since the problem solver now cannot explore states by physical manipulation but must think ahead in order to avoid culs-de-sac.

If the game not only has irreversible operations but also unstable states, one comes to competitive games like chess or *go*. Transparent-state problems, these games give the players full information. Winning becomes solely a matter of sound foresight and strategy.

Considering games without transparent states yields games that withhold information from the players, for instance bridge. Such games can still have known-effect operations, however—so far as a player knows the state, the player knows the effect of any available operation on the state. Games without known-effect operations include draw poker, where the player executes actions with chance effects on the state of the game as the player knows it.

Relaxing the requirement of surveyable operations leads to games with a large number of operations, such as Scrabble, which calls upon the players' skills in drawing upon their vocabularies. Perhaps it is worth adding at this point that many games have been left unaccounted for in this chain of negated conditions for formality. For instance, solitaire is an irreversible stable-state game which, however, does not have transparent states or known-effect operations.

The conditions not yet negated are stable, transparent, and simple goal tests, and tractable operations. Can any of these attributes be changed to yield another category of games? Probably not stable, transparent, and simple goals, because it is good design in a game to define clearly what constitutes success. What about tractable operations? In general, intractable operations are a characteristic of sports rather than games. However, there are some activities called games that have intractable operations—for instance, tiddlywinks and many computer games.

There are two approaches to dealing with this. One is to say that the requirement of tractable operations only distinguishes roughly between sports and games. However, the position preferred here is to say that tractable operations mark the fundamental difference between sports and games. Activities like tiddlywinks are simply miscalled, due to false analogy and persistent convention. They should be considered sports.

This position recognizes that sometimes a systematization finds arbitrariness in common usage and should take the opportunity to purify the language.

Finally, a few games have not only nonreversible, but nonponderable operations—rapid-pass chess, for example. These are rare, so, in the present article, all nonreversible games will be lumped together.

The universe of games

We have seen that the criteria for formality provide a way of characterizing varieties of games. All games have stable, transparent, and simple goals, and, as argued above, tractable operations. No games have simple state paths, because what is the point of a game that allows the player no choices? Games very according to whether they have stable states, transparent states, known-effect operations, surveyable operations, and reversible operations. As just noted, no distinction will be made between the varieties of nonreversible operations, since urgent and continual operations are rare among games. Therefore, the five attributes and their opposites make room for thirty-two classes in the universe of games. Are all these classes occupied?

In fact, certain combinations of attributes can be excluded on logical grounds.

Virtually all games with reversible operations have stable states. This is a consequence of the fact that games are designed. Imagine a game with reversible operations but unstable states, unstable either because of an opponent's moves or because of some other source of perturbation. Because of reversibility, the player can restore the previous state, cancelling the effects of the change. Thus, the player could stall endlessly. Games are virtually always designed to prevent this, since there is no point in having instability that the player can cancel.

All stable-state problems with known-effect operations have transparent states. This is a general conclusion about problems, not just games. The argument is as follows. If states are not transparent, either the undisclosed information affects the course of problem solving or not. If it does not, then the information may as well be omitted from the description of the problem, since it is irrelevant. If it does, this must mean that the information bears on what state changes the operations effect and/or which states are goal states. This in turn means that some of the operations must be, at least implicitly, information disclosing operations. That is, the problem solver's actions inevitably reveal something about the initially hidden information. But an operation that exposes previously hidden information cannot be a transparent operation, since its action cannot, by definition, be predictable.

The remaining combinations of attributes all have a place on table 1.2 below. Games satisfying the constraints have been filled in where I could think of them, but six slots remain empty. I have no reason to believe that they must be empty, and invite the reader to try to think of examples to fill them. For instance, the first pair of blank slots, opposite T T T F, could be filled by a game where the player must discover what the operations do by trial and error. Perhaps such a game exists and, if not, surely it could.

Sports

What makes a sport a sport? The case of competitive sports will be taken up first, since noncompetitive sports turn out to have quite a different nature, not at all analogous to noncompetitive games. Some characteristics emerge immediately from the restriction to competitive sports. They cannot be stable-state, since the competitor changes the

Table 1.1. Possible and Actual Games

Reversible operations	Stable states	Transparent states	Known-effect operations	Surveyable operations	Nonsurveyable operations
T	T	T	T	Rubik's cube	Crossword puzzles
T	T	T	F	?	?
T	T	F	F	Real physical mazes	Decoding letter ciphers
F	T	T	T	Peg jump games	?
F	T	T	F	?	?
F	T	F	F	Solitaire	Hangman
F	F	T	T	Chess	Password
F	F	T	F	Spinner games	?
F	F	F	T	Bridge	Quiz games
F	F	F	F	Poker	Scrabble

"Letter ciphers" means letter-substitution ciphers.

"Peg jump games" are those where one jumps a peg over another, removing the jumped peg from the board. The goal is to end up with one peg in a given location.

"Spinner games" refers to the many common children's games where the player spins a spinner to determine how many spaces may be moved.

"Quiz games" refers to any competitive quiz game where the players have no choice of categories of question. The latter feature would result in operations without known effects; such games fall in the last category with Scrabble.

state, and cannot be reversible, since if the player could restore the state autonomously there would be no point to the competition. Competitive sports are like competitive games in these respects.

It was argued earlier that tractability of operations distinguishes sports from games. All sports have intractable operations, but very few games, and these might be considered misnamed. That is, in all sports, part of the problem is executing the selected operation—bowling a strike, kicking a goal, putting the eight ball into the corner pocket, leading the other runners over the finish line. In games, one can, with care, execute the move one wants to make, although the consequences of the move may be unpredictable, as in rolling dice.

This does not mean that games involve no performance problems in a sense. For instance, tournament chess imposes a time limit and efficient thinking can be very important. Such efficient thinking even has an athletic flavor to it, analogous to the efficient use of one's body. However, the present theory treats such difficulties as difficulties of deliberation rather than operation execution, classifying problems where there is time pressure on operation selection as having "urgent operations."

Sports tend toward transparency, with certain qualifications. Many sports have transparent goal tests—the objective matter of who gets over the finish line first or who scores the most goals. Although referees judge such matters, they are considered to be making objective judgments. There is a right answer, even if sometimes a misperception may give a wrong one. Some sports have nontransparent goal tests, for example competitive diving or skating, where judges must make subjective assessments of several aspects of the athlete's performance. However, even in that case there is a considerable effort to define the dimensions to be assessed, and multiple judges are always used in an effort to average out subjective differences.

Sports also tend to have transparent states and known-effect operations. Whereas many games involve extensive concealment of state information and the effects of operations, this is so only to a minor extent in sports. Typically, the player of a sport can see where the other players are, knows who has the ball, and so on. Of course, fake moves and concealment are important elements in such sports as football. However, there is no massive and impenetrable concealment, as in card games for example. As to operations, in games operations can have unknown effects in two ways—because they reveal concealed state information or through designedly random factors, as in rolling dice. The former is not germane when states are transparent, and designedly random factors occur in sports only in a few minor ways, as in the flip of a coin at the beginning of a football game.

How are we to understand this trend toward transparency? Probably it is part and parcel of the commitment to intractable operations. Intractable operations are quite chancy enough without adding chance in the form of operations with unknown effects even if rightly executed. Likewise, nontransparent states would divert some of the player's mental and physical resources from the difficulties of operation execution to those of disclosing hidden information. It is the style of competitive sports to highlight difficulties of execution and minimize other problems.

Competitive sports usually have nonsurveyable operations simply because they call for physical actions that might be executed with many different nuances. For instance, a football player passing the ball might throw it a little further or a little nearer, a little more to the left or to the right. In addition, the ball can have various degrees of spin and tumble. In general, that is, the "space" of possible operations is continuous and multidimensional, forbidding any exhaustive survey of the operations. There are a very few sports with simpler circumstances. For instance, in pinball, all that counts is the timing of the button presses, time being a single dimension.

Finally, competitive sports virtually always have complex-state paths, and for a reason similar to that advanced above: sports are played in a physical continuum. Thus, a player always has such options as being a little more to the right or a little more to the left. There is no single path toward the goal state.

The universe of competitive sports

With all this in mind, it is interesting to try to chart the range of competitive sports, as was done for games. We decided that all competitive sports have unstable states, a stable goal test, intractable operations, a complex-state path and irreversible operations. Nearly all have nonsurveyable operations. Since sports tend toward relatively transparent states and known-effect operations, it seems best not to sort them on the basis of nuances in this respects. However, the transparent goal test, which serves to single out sports where judges make subjective assessments, is worth keeping. In summary, we can sort sports along the deliberation dimension as ponderable, urgent, or continual, and besides that as having simple-goal tests or not, and transparent goal tests or not.

As in the discussion of games, a general conclusion reduces the number of combinations.

In competitive sports, a simple goal test implies a transparent goal test. Consider the contrapositive. If a goal test is not transparent, this means it involves subjective factors, as in competitive diving or skating. But if subjective factors are involved and one performance is weighed against another, as is inevitable in competitive sports, there will be some close cases that are hard to call. Therefore, not just subjective but subtle judgments must be involved. But, by definition, subtle judgments effecting the outcome mean that the goal test is not simple.

The result is a three-by-three sorting of competitive sports. Along each dimension, an aspect of the sport becomes increasingly problematic. One dimension is deliberation, where "time to think" may be problematic. Some sports like competitive diving are ponderable—a performer has ample time to set himself or herself for executing an operation; some sports like football have urgent operations—there is only limited time for planning in the huddle; and some like hockey involve continuous operations. The other dimension concerns goal tests, which may be problematic in their simplicity and objectivity. Some sports, like pool, involve a simple goal test—no subtle judgments are involved because physical events such as a ball falling into a pocket decide whether a score has occurred; some, like races, involve nonsimple but objective goal tests—which runner crosses the finish line first may be a subtle matter, but is an objective one; and some, like competitive diving, involve subjective judgments and hence a nontransparent goal test.

The combinations with examples are tabulated in table 1.2 below. The variation along the dimensions can be appreciated by reading across the rows or down the columns. One slot is unfilled; I could think of no competitive sport with urgent operations and nontransparent goal test. Perhaps the reader can.

Noncompetitive sports

One might expect that noncompetitive sports would be somewhat analogous to noncompetitive games—stable-state but otherwise ranging much as do competitive sports. Nothing could be further from the truth. Consider such noncompetitive sports as hiking or sailing. States are *not* stable—a storm may hit the hiker, a gust of wind the sailboat. Neither are they transparent—who knows what the hiker will find around the next bend? Moreover, goals are not even stable. Broadly speaking, the activity is its own reward. But, in particular, what the hiker aims to get

Table 1.2. The Universe of Competitive Sports

Goal test	Deliberation		
	Ponderable	Urgent	Continual
Simple	pole vault bowling pool	pinball many computer games	hockey
Nonsimple, transparent	broad jump hammer throw	football baseball	races
Nontransparent	bodybuilding diving	?	gymnastics boxing skating

out of a hike may change considerably from hike to hike or in the course of a hike. Indeed, hikers may not even know afterwards just what they have gotten out of a particular hike. More or less the same story can be told for skiing or sailing.

Perhaps the most striking symptom of this is the vagueness concerning when one should be done hiking, skiing, or sailing. Well-defined for competitive sports and for competitive and noncompetitive games, being done is a very ill-defined matter for noncompetitive sports. However, noncompetitive and competitive sports do have something in common. Like competitive sports, noncompetitive sports highlight problems and skills of execution—intractable operations. The hiker needs to know how to use bodily energy efficiently, and may well run out of energy. The sailor may fail to control the boat and it may capsize. The skier may fall. Other than that, noncompetitive sports seem remote from games and competitive sports alike.

Real problems

So far, the dimensions of formality have been used to illuminate the boundaries and varieties of sports and games. In case this seems too frivolous, let us apply the dimensions to some "real problems." Table 1.3 below classifies five very broad sorts of problems with reference to each of the dimensions. A discussion follows the table.

Perhaps there is a need to explain how problem states and operations are understood for such vaguely circumscribed problems. First of all, exactly because the problems are vague, some of the classifications might be debated. But that aside, consider for example the case of running a business. The problem states are taken to be business situations at a certain point in time, including current advertising, employee traits and wages, inventories, and so on. Also part of the state is the current economic environment. The available operations consist of the decisions a manager can make: to price differently, advertise more, diversify products or services, seek new markets.

For another example, in writing an essay the states are taken to be the drafts of the essay from moment to moment. The operations are additions and deletions of text. Accordingly, the states are transparent and the operations are nonsurveyable but of known effect, since the writer can in principle anticipate how they will affect the text (although in practice seeing a change "in print" may be revealing).

It should come as no surprise that the chart holds mostly F's rather than T's for such broad, open-ended problems. Naturally, they tend to be problematic in many ways. However, an interesting pattern of exceptions appears in the tabulation. T's are frequent opposite stable states and, even more so, tractable operations, and the operations in most cases are at least ponderable. These traits signify that the problems

Table 1.3. Some "Real Problems" Classified

	Running a business	Fighting a war	Making a career decision	Diagnosing a disease	Writing an essay
Stable states	F	F	T	T	T
Transparent states	F	F	F	F	F
Simple state path	F	F	F	F	T
Stable goal test	T	F	F	F	F
Transparent goal test	T	F	F	F	F
Simple goal test	F	F	F	F	F
Tractable operations	T	F	T	T	T
Known-effect ops	F	F	F	F	T
Surveyable ops	F	F	F	F	F
Deliberation: Reversible/Ponderable/Urgent	P	U	P	P	R

are deliberative and detached. The problem solver need make no immediate commitment, but can accumulate evidence, think things over, and change tentative decisions, all the time expecting that the problem situation will not change and that operations the problem solver would like to perform—operations such as launching an advertising campaign, requesting a laboratory test, or putting a sentence down on paper—can be executed reliably, although their more remote consequences may be uncertain.

As a generalization, perhaps stable states and tractable and ponderable operations are the maximum luxuries that one can routinely expect in broad, messy real-life problems. However, this does not mean that such problems should be understood as extremely nonformal through and through. A point mentioned earlier should be recalled: the attributes of subproblems may diverge from those of the parent problem. Accordingly, problems like fighting a war or running a business can be broken down into component problems, and those classified in turn to gain insight into the kinds of difficulties posed by different components.

A theory of challenge

The concept of challenge

According to problem theory, there is a simplest sort of problem, one that not only has all the attributes of formality but even a simple state path and surveyable operations. This is a formal procedure. It is not problematic at all, except in calling for precision of execution. What, then, if all the attributes of formality were negated? Does this yield a most problematic problem symmetric to the least problematic one?

No, not really. Although the way a problem is problematic can be understood in terms of the dimensions of formality, it is not the case that informality on more dimensions necessarily means "more problematic." Rather, it often means problematic in a different way. Consider, for example, chess. One factor that makes chess difficult is the need for a long "look ahead" that takes into account the strategic possibilities. Suppose we change just two attributes of chess, seeking a problem with intractable rather than tractable and nonsurveyable rather than surveyable operations. Football fits this pattern. The effect of introducing intractable, nonsurveyable operations has not been to make the activity harder overall but to alter radically the nature of the difficulty. A long "look ahead" is much less relevant to football exactly because unstable operations make it impossible to predict very far ahead.

Generalizing from this example, we should ask not only what is problematic about a problem, but what is challenging about it. For chess, the strategy is the special challenge. For football, strategy may be important but, as with other sports, operation execution is the special challenge. What is challenging is not just a matter of problematics, because often something can be too problematic to be challenging. What is challenging is a matter of what is just problematic enough to pose difficulties but leave opportunities to surmount them.

This point suggests a need for an extended account of problematics, one that considers varieties of challenge. Perhaps certain combinations of values on the dimensions of formality lead to distinctive sorts of challenges. It also seems likely that different sorts of challenge call for different cognitive abilities, styles, and strategies of thinking. However, even given a certain type of challenge, truly skillful problem solving may well depend on familiarity with a particular problem domain within that type. Perkins (in press) and others have argued that many supposedly general cognitive skills do not have as much power and reach as one might hope. The following subsections examine this and other matters, pursuing a theory of challenge linked to cognitive skills.

3.2 Six types of challenge

Performance problems (intractable, irreversible operations)—the challenge to execute operations successfully

When operations are intractable and irreversible, this makes their accurate first-time execution important. Irreversibility is crucial here. Were operations reversible, the problem solver could simply undo mishaps and attempt to execute an operation again and again until successful. Problems where the principal challenge lies in executing intractable operations can be called "performance problems." As noted earlier, unstable irreversible operations make strategic considerations less prominent, because a long look ahead becomes difficult.

Performance problems in their purest form should have transparent states and known-effect operations, as well as stable, transparent, and simple goal tests, so that the challenge stays focused on execution. When these other factors do figure, the problem seems less purely a performance problem, although one might say that it has a performance aspect.

Performance problems predominate in all sports. However, such problems also arise in intellectual and artistic contexts. Painting in watercolors, one of the first examples offered, has a strong performance aspect in the form of many performance subproblems because certain mistakes cannot readily be corrected and the behavior of the brush and the liquid paint calls for adroit handling. Such crafts as acting and musical performance constitute performance problems because the word or note, once out, cannot be recovered, nor can reliable execution be counted upon.

Concerning cognitive skills, evidently performance problems benefit from extensive experience with the task of concern, which builds a repertoire of automatized skills that can be used in combinations to meet varying circumstances. A classic example is the improvisational singing of epic songs in an oral tradition, an art dependent on a repertoire of standard scenes, half-lines, and other components (Lord, 1974). However, high levels of skill in activities that are not, strictly speaking, performance problems sometimes depend on large schematic repertoires too, as Simon and Chase (1973) have argued for master-level chess play.

A fundamental question arises here. Is there such a thing as an ability for performance problems in general, an ability to coordinate and execute with precision physical or mental performances in real time? No immediate answer suggests itself, but the issue is an intriguing one.

Strategic problems (tractable, known-effect, irreversible operations and transparent states)—the challenge to plan far ahead

The look-ahead characteristic of chess can be taken as the hallmark of "strategic problems." A long look-ahead is only feasible and meaningful when a problem has particular attributes. There must not be much uncertainty concerning the effects of attempting a given operation—hence, tractable operations and known-effect ones. On the other hand, if the problem solver could try any course of action and back up should it not succeed, there would be much less advantage to looking ahead. Consequently, irreversible operation is a requirement too.

Strategic problems may be stable- or unstable-state problems. If the latter, it is also necessary that the state changes that occur other than through the problem solver's operations follow some rather predictable pattern. This condition is met in chess because the problem solver can assume rational play on the part of the opponent and anticipate the opponent's actions accordingly. As with performance problems, problems where one thinks of the principal difficulties as strategic are likely to have stable, transparent, and simple goal tests, just because otherwise the goals would pose difficulties in themselves.

Concerning cognitive skills, strategic problems demand that the problem solver explore alternative courses of action a number of steps ahead, an activity that requires very selective searching to avoid a combinatorial explosion and, when memory aids are not allowed, to remain within the cognitive load capacity of the problem solver. Much depends on being able to judge whether a possible scenario is worth examining closely or can safely be pruned from the search tree. Such assessments are likely to depend heavily on experience with particular sorts of problems—chess, *go*, or whatever (Simon and Chase, 1973).

Since strategic problems tend to impose a heavy cognitive load, persons with the capacity to handle such loads, with habits of using external memory aids where possible, and with general strategies for efficient search are likely to do better on such problems, experience being equal. But experience and the chunking that accompanies it do more than anything else to reduce cognitive load and enhance pruning decisions, a point that must always be kept in mind before vesting too much credence in the possibility of powerful skills of strategic thinking that cut across tasks. If there is a general ability of strategic thinking, it might more likely take the form of a learning ability, one for efficient chunk-formation and rapid accumulation of a repertoire of schemata.

Probabilistic problems (tractable, unknown-effect and irreversible operations)—the challenge to reason well in terms of probabilities

When operations are tractable but not known-effect, this usually means that chance partly determines their effects. Again as in strategic problems, if operations are reversible this poses no difficulty. If operations are irreversible, the element of chance puts a premium on short-term prediction of particular events, and perhaps long-term prediction of statistical trends, in contrast with the long-term prediction of particular events characteristic of strategic problems. Probabilistic problems make the latter unfeasible because each operation is so chancy.

The resources of probabilistic prediction are well-known. They are the elementary laws of probability, Bayes's theorem, knowledge of odds for particular situations as in playing Blackjack, and so on. Skill in dealing with probabilistic problems involves considerable know-how, and ample research demonstrates that this requires formal learning, since the rules are often counterintuitive (Tversky and Kahneman, 1971, 1973, 1974; Nisbett and Ross, 1980).

Creative problems (unstable, nontransparent, and nonsimple goal test)—the challenge to find the goal as well as the solution

The kinds of problems considered so far tend toward stable, transparent, and simple goal tests, because unstable, nontransparent, and complex goal tests would pose difficulties in themselves and dilute the emphasis on difficulties of performance, strategic look-ahead, or probabilistic prediction. What happens when such difficulties with goals come to the fore?

A plausible answer is that the problem solver faces a task especially calling for human inventiveness. Rather than striving for a goal well-defined in advance, the problem solver must shape the goal along the way, a characteristic of open or ill-defined problems that calls on the problem solver's inventive resourcefulness (Reitman, 1965; Hayes, 1981). Of course, there is ample room for inventiveness in more formal activities such as playing chess or proving theorems. But a matter of degree is involved. When someone instead of playing chess or proving theorems, is bent on inventing a game or discovering a theorem, creativity comes that much more to the fore.

There is some experimental evidence for the importance of goal-shaping activities in creative pursuits. Getzels and Csikszentmihalyi (1976) investigated the abilities, attitudes, and working methods of student artists, concluding that those judged most creative engaged in the most "problem finding." Roughly speaking, problem finding means exploring directions extensively at the outset before settling on one, and remaining ready to change directions later when alternative courses of action come to light. Getzels and Csikszentmihalyi also discovered in follow-up research that the students who were vigorous problem finders had achieved, seven years later, more success in the highly competitive world of galleries and exhibitions than had other students. Moreover, various measures of skill and academic competence did not predict their success.

This and other arguments on the nature of creative activity (for a survey, see Perkins, 1981) suggest that creative problem solving calls for a particular cognitive style and strategies suited to it. Certainly the problem solver must have the habit of accepting the problem as, in part, one *of* problem finding. This could be a general trait of the problem solver that cuts across domains. However, especially insightful problem finding involves more than just giving time to that activity, since the problem solver needs to engage in a kind of forecasting. The problem solver must foresee the potentials in bits and scraps, for instance the potential of a poem in a phrase or of a general theory in a seemingly isolated phenomenon. Such forecasting seems to be largely intuitive, and very likely depends on pattern-recognition abilities built up through domain-specific experience.

Formal problems (all the attributes except for simple-state path and surveyable operations)—the challenge to find a path

Here we come full circle, back to formal problems. What can be said about the sorts of cognitive skills and strategies formal problems call upon? Formal problems pose difficulties quite different from the sorts reviewed above. There are no performance problems because operations are stable. There are no strategic problems in the sense defined because operations are reversible. Probabilities are not involved and goals are precisely defined. What challenge is left?

One might say that the principal challenge is "path finding." The combinatorial explosion of possible paths, which occurs in most problems, is particularly challenging since there is no uncertainty about an opponent's move, as there is in chess, to render extremely deep searches futile, and since the path needs to end up in a fairly constricted "place." To make that point more clearly, in poetry writing it hardly matters *what* poem one writes so long as the poem is good. But in producing a proof, one is supposed to prove the theorem in question. Hence, the premium is on following paths that might end up in the right place. The cognitive skills involved include strategies like planning and working backwards, as characterized by Newell and Simon (1972).

Path finding poses an additional challenge when a formal problem does not have surveyable operations. Then the problem solver cannot simply review all the possible operations, but has to generate likely candidates from the outset.

The importance of experience with a particular problem domain varies. If a formal problem has surveyable operations and a short solution-path, a problem solver unfamiliar with the domain may do well simply by pushing around the possibilities systematically. The problem is merely combinatorial, so to speak. However, if the problem does not have surveyable operations, or if the solution path is long, insightful high-level planning is needed, and that would seem to require familiarity with the ins and outs of the problem domain.

Routine problems (formal procedures)—the challenge of precision

Recall that the discussion of the ways in which problems are problematic identified one way not represented among the dimensions of formality: even a formal procedure that presented no choice of paths could be problematic in demanding precision. Precision, then, becomes the last of the six challenges treated here.

In a sense, this challenge is trivial compared to the others. After all, by definition meeting the challenge of precision only requires careful attention. Yet experience teaches that this is not so easy to provide. We all make errors from time to time in such routine tasks as calculating income taxes, dialing a phone number, typing a letter, or following the recipe in a cookbook.

The challenge of precision does have one peculiarity in comparison with the other challenges reviewed here: it is ubiquitous. While formal procedures pose challenges of precision without rivalry from other sorts of challenge, challenges of precision also occur frequently in creative, probabilistic, formal, performance, and strategic problems. There is no escape from the challenge of precision, wherever the problem solver sets up shop.

As a psychological trait, precision can be thought of as a cognitive style. It appears to involve care in executing operations and, at the same time, the habit of and a repertoire of strategies for checking results. Thus, many of the errors made despite vigilance are later caught and corrected. Jon Baron (in press), using the term "accuracy," identifies precision as one of three especially important dimensions of cognitive style, the other two being efficiency and originality.

Questions of scope

Through this account of challenges, problem theory offers another way to understand the nature of problems and their difficulties. Now there is no claim that the six types of challenge discussed exhaust the possibilities. There may well be other distinctive types. On the other hand, the challenges defined here appear to cover quite a range of circumstances.

For example, one seemingly different type of challenge in fact is not so different. Recall that many a problem as given needs translation into a structured problem. One might think that such a task presents a challenge not discussed above. However, the class of creative problems accommodates it. In general the problem of structuring a problem provides no clear standards for a good structuring. In particular, the problem of structuring a problem involves an unstable, nontransparent, and nonsimple goal test, a lack that is the hallmark of creative problems as defined above.

The present analysis gains more generality by allowing for mixed as well as pure types of challenges. Consider, for example, the problem of constructing an informal argument, and argument concerning an everyday issue such as for whom to vote or whether to buy this or that car. Such a task poses a challenge of path finding, much as with the formal problem of constructing a mathematical proof: the problem solver must construct lines of argument defending one or another choice. But, at the same time, it poses a challenge characteristic of creative problems, because, in the informal domain of votes and purchases, the goal test for a sufficient argument is somewhat subtle, subjective, and changeable. (For a discussion of some important differences between formal and informal argument, see Perkins, Allen, and Hafner, in press.)

There is also a question of generality concerning the cognitive skills and styles that assist with various types of challenge. As mentioned earlier, Perkins (in press) and others have urged that general cognitive skills and styles often do not wield as much power as one might hope. The discussion of challenges bears this out. Although there was no effort to treat thoroughly the skills and styles a given challenge might need, even in terms of those considered, a distinctly mixed picture emerged. There were some cognitive skills and styles that seemed relevant to a type of challenge regardless of the particular problem. For instance, a problem-finding approach is a trait that a person might be likely to carry from problem to problem, and a trait that would assist generally in meeting creative challenges. A precise cognitive style would pay off in nearly any problem domain. A basic understanding of probabilities is important for all probabilistic challenges.

On the other hand, identifying fertile problems in problem finding surely depends on familiarity with the particular problem domain. So also does selecting likely operations when the operations are not surveyable. So also does pruning the search tree wisely in dealing with strategic problems. And so on.

This mixed picture presents both an opportunity and a caution. It shows that there do seem to be general cognitive skills and styles worth inculcating. On the other hand, it warns that general skills and styles are not enough. There is no substitute for experience with particular kinds of problems. Accordingly, a problem-solving approach to education would require an attack both from the top down, in terms of general skills and styles, and from the bottom up, in terms of attention to the particular sorts of problems most important in various disciplines.

Formalizing

The compartmentalization of problems into types of challenges leaves no home for one very important cognitive skill, a skill that actually changes the type of problem addressed. That skill is formalizing itself.

Most straightforwardly taken, formalizing means making a formal problem out of a nonformal one. This, of course, changes the structure of the problem. As a challenge, the task of formalizing is a creative one, since there are no simple objective standards for a good formalization. But if the standards are uncertain, the history of success is plain. For example, past achievements can be found in the building of mathematical models of physical phenomena, in game theory, which represents competitive situations in terms of matrices and minimax strategies, and probability theory, which assimilates uncertainty into a strictly deductive system.

What may be less obvious is that formalizing ranges far beyond just those cases where the result is a fully formal problem. Any transforming of a situation so that it has more formal features than the parent situation amounts to a partial formalization. Consider these examples. Writing is formalized speech; two of the important gains are stable states and reversible operations—stable states because the writing stays put upon the page whereas the oral utterance is transient, and reversible operations because writing can be edited. For another example, law can be considered in part a formalization of ethics and custom brought about by making goals transparent—written down with explicit standards—and stable—not changed to suit the special interests of the occasion.

Competitive sports such a football or boxing are rather obviously formalized physical combat. Competitive sports like diving or skating, on the other hand, are formalizations of noncompetitive sports more usually practiced for their aesthetic payoffs, formalizations where the criteria for judging are designed to capture important aesthetic elements as transparently as possible. (Although competitive diving and skating do not have transparent goal tests, the written principles of judging and the multiple judges push the goal tests in the direction of transparency, as discussed earlier.)

Even the ability to explore alternative possibilities mentally rather than physically is a kind of formalizing accomplished by evolution. Where physical action often involves irreversible and intractable operations on unstable states, the imaginary exploration of possibilities involves stable states and reversible and often tractable operations. To be sure, the thinker eventually will have to select a course of physical action. But by exploring possibilities mentally, the problem solver both defers commitment and takes commitment into account, by considering the risks of the various commitments that might ultimately be made.

It seems clear that formalizing is one of the most fundamental and powerful strategies in the human repertoire. Many problems are solved not within their problem types, but through transforming them into more formal problems amenable to a different approach. Accordingly, besides the cognitive skills and styles suited to particular kinds of problems, there is the all-important skill and style of formalizing itself. Besides the potentials of teaching better problem solving with particular kinds of problems, there is the potential of teaching the art and craft of formalizing, and not in some vague sense, but in the senses defined by the dimensions of formality. In many respects much of education has always been about formalizing. Perhaps more of it should be so, in a more explicit way.

With all that said, there is an important caveat. Formalizing is double-edged. Although the net advantages averaged over many cases are plain, unfortunate individual cases are not hard to find. It is clear that the law does not always encode justice adequately, that scientific models sometimes ignore interesting and, in the end, crucial subtleties of the natural phenomenon, or simply that sometimes formalizing makes mountains out of molehills. There are surely many occasions when the best way through is to muddle through.

Moreover, there is one kind of problem solving that is often a matter of "de-formalizing"—creative problem solving. As discussed earlier, a creative problem involves unstable, nontransparent, and complex goal tests, which become more defined as the problem solver proceeds. Well, such goals do not always start so ill-defined. They may have to be made that way during the process of problem solving, as the thinker escapes from too narrow a concept of the problem. That is, creative problem solving not only involves problem finding, but, sometimes, problem losing—losing the original problem in favor of a quest for a better version of it. For all these reasons, the art and craft of de-formalizing needs attention too.

References

Baron, J. "What kinds of intelligence components are fundamental?" In S. Chipman, J. Siegel, and R. Glaser (eds.), *Thinking and Learning Skills, Volume 2: Current Research and Open Questions*. Hillsdale, NJ: Erlbaum, in press.

Getzels, J. and Csikszentmihalyi, M. *The Creative Vision: A Longitudinal Study of Problem Finding in Art*. New York: Wiley, 1976.

Hayes, J. *The Complete Problem Solver*. Philadelphia: The Franklin Institute Press, 1981.

Lord, A. *The Singer of Tales*. New York: Atheneum, 1974.

Newell, A. and Simon, H. *Human Problem Solving*. Englewood Cliffs, NJ: Prentice-Hall, 1972.

Nisbett, R. and Ross, L. *Human Inference: Strategies and Shortcomings of Social Judgment*. Englewood Cliffs, NJ: Prentice-Hall, 1980.

Perkins, D. *The Mind's Best Work*. Cambridge: Harvard University Press, 1981.

Perkins, D. General "Cognitive Skills: Why Not?" In S. Chipman, J. Siegel, and R. Glaser (eds.), *Thinking and Learning Skills, Volume 2: Current Research and Open Questions*. Hillsdale, NJ: Erlbaum, in press.

Perkins, D. N., Allen, R., and Hafner, J., "Difficulties in Everyday Reasoning."

In W. Maxwell (ed.), *Thinking: The Frontier Expands*. Philadelphia: The Franklin Institute Press, in press.

Reitman, W. *Cognition and Thought*. New York: Wiley, 1965.

Simon, H., and Chase, W. "Skill in chess." *American Scientist*, 61 (1973), 394–403.

Tversky, A. and Kahneman, D. The belief in the "law of small numbers." *Psychology Bulletin*, 1971, *76*, 105–110.

Tversky, A., and Kahneman, D. "Availability: A Heuristic for Judging Frequency and Probability. *Cognitive Psychology*, 5 (1973), 207–32.

Tversky, A., and Kahneman, D. "Judgment under Uncertainty: Heuristics and Biases." *Science*, 185 (1974), 1124–31.

CHAPTER 2

Understanding critical thinking

Kenneth Hawes

If we are interested in learning how critical thinking can or ought to be a part of education, we should realize that the phrase "critical thinking" has many different meanings. How can we connect and comprehend these various meanings? One way to approach this question is simply to recall briefly the meanings of "critic," "critical," and "criticism." An overly narrow definition of "critical" is that it means fault-finding. A critic then would be someone who finds fault, and criticism the activity of fault-finding or the written or spoken expression of that activity. But there are meanings more important for education than these.

Much more important is the idea that a critic is someone who gives a reasoned evaluation of, for example, a movie, a work of art or literature, or a course of moral or political conduct. We might expect such an evaluation to include the highlighting or exploration of various virtues and defects, and the tracing of their sources and causes. It might well also include comparison to other works, performances, or historical events. In short, one meaning of "critic" is someone who renders evaluation or judgment along with some explanation. The evaluation need not be a negative one. It can be an effort of appreciation, of helping oneself or others to see the charms, strengths, or inner logic of a work of an action.

"Criticism" and "critical" can be understood by reference to this idea of "critic." "Criticism" would be understood to be reasoned or reasonable evaluation of something—a book, a policy, a curriculum, etc. It could refer either to the activity or process of evaluation, or to the product of evaluation.

Similarly, "critical" would mean "characterized by reasoned or reasonable evaluation." Thus "critical discussion" is discussion consisting of or exhibiting the qualities of reasoned or reasonable evaluation. And "critical reading" is reading in which what is read is subjected to some kind of evaluation or test.

Critical thinking

What then is critical thinking? Following these ideas it is thinking which is characterized by some kind of reasoned or reasonable evaluation. Since there are many different kinds of evaluation—depending on the type of thing being evaluated, the purposes for evaluation, and the method used—there will be many kinds of critical thinking.

What is the purpose of trying to join all these kinds or instances of thinking together under one heading? The great hope is, of course, that there will be found some generality of method or skill, so that in learning to think critically in one way or one area, a person will be more able to do the same, or to learn to do the same, in another area. If generality of method or skill is not possible, at least generality of theory or understanding or appreciation or attitude might be. Mostly the possibilities for generality are an open question. In trying to talk about and understand critical thinking in a comprehensive way, we are here testing some of these possibilities for generality.

Thinking and thinking-related activities

One peculiar thing about the phrase "critical thinking" is that thinking is part of all other human activities or performances that might be described as "critical." Thus in "critical discussion" and "critical reading" there is thinking going on, and presumably some of it is critical thinking. So in understanding critical thinking we are faced with the following question. When we say "critical thinking," are we trying to pick out some particular phase of thinking *within* reading, problem-solving, decision-making, creative activity, etc.? Or are we grouping together all the above activities *under* the heading of critical thinking? Again, do we mean by critical thinking the particular phases of thinking that are specifically evaluative, or do we use "critical thinking" as a handy descriptive tag when we wish to talk about the larger activities which we know have important phases of reasoned or reasonable evaluation or judgment within them?

In the current discussion about critical thinking and education, I think that "critical thinking" is mostly used in the second way, as a label for activities requiring careful judgment and, often, sustained reflection. But these activities require more than just good judgment. In problem-solving, decision-making, reading, writing, interpretation, and expression, we require also the forming of problems and purposes, invention of possibilities and tests, the making of new connections, and other creative acts. John Passmore uses the phrase "critico-creative thinking" to express this fact.[1]

The broad activities treated under the heading of "critical thinking" require both the production of things (anything a person can produce: ideas, sentences, drawings, arguments, alternatives, reasons, plans, experiments, actions, movements) and the evaluation (choice, judgment, selection, etc.) of these according to the purposes and constraints of the situation.

But why label these activities (or the abilities and attitudes that go along with them) as "critical thinking" as many people do? One motive for using this label is that there are aspects of evaluation which have a long history of being taught, especially the evaluation of arguments and fallacies in reasoning. This tradition stretches back for example to the ancient Greeks, and is expressed elaborately in the logical treatises of Aristotle. That there is such a tradition gives hope that the evaluative, critical aspects of activities requiring judgment can be taught.

The problem however is that the kinds of critical abilities needed in the many activities in question are far broader than the evaluation of arguments and logical form. And, as we have said, the activities require abilities that are not strictly evaluative at all, but are productive or creative. But the explicit teaching of creative thinking is a much newer enterprise than the teaching of critical thinking, and as yet inspires no deep confidence. "Critical thinking" as a label sounds more hard-headed, more testable and teachable, and so is often the label preferred.

An illustration

Illustrations of the above points can be found in the writings of Robert Ennis, who has long been concerned with critical thinking. In 1962 Ennis published a long article treating critical thinking as "the correct assessing of statements."[2] The main body of the article is the elaboration of criteria for making twelve basic kinds of assessments of statements. The twelve kinds of assessment include "grasping the meaning of a statement," and judging ambiguity, contradiction, and whether conclusions are warranted.

Ennis implies that his broader concern is for "evaluation of the products of thought," not just evaluation of statements.[3] He mentions in his introduction not only "making judgments about the worth of statements," but also judging "answers to problems," and also, "the acquisition of the knowledge and mental skills needed for judging solutions to complex problems."[4] Now since judging the solutions to complex problems involves judgments far beyond the twelve aspects of judging statements that Ennis lists, I take this early approach of his to be an example of the tendency to rely on the tradition of logical analysis, even when the overall concern is with evaluation more generally.

In his more recent writings on critical thinking, Ennis broadens his field of consideration in two ways. First, he is no longer concerned only with *statements*. His new working definition is that "Critical thinking is reflective and reasonable thinking that is focused on deciding what to believe or do."[5] The concern is now with *decision*. Decision about beliefs is broader than assessment of statements, and decision about actions is again different in many ways. Second, he is no longer concerned only with *assessment*. He says, "Note that there are creative activities covered by this definition, including formulating hypotheses, questions, alternatives, and plans for experiments."[6] This later view of Ennis's is then an example of taking critical thinking to label activities which require a wide range of thinking abilities, both critical and creative. There remains however in Ennis's treatment a strong emphasis on the tradition of logic, under the headings of "clarification," "inference," "advanced clarification," and (a lesser heading) "employing and reacting to 'fallacy' labels," and much less emphasis on the language of design, performance, expression, and craft.[7]

Evidence for thinking being reasoned or reasonable

Let us take up another question about the meaning and implied connections of "critical thinking." We noticed before that if we extend our familiar ideas of critics and criticism of things like books, movies, and moral actions, then we would expect critical thinking to be thinking characterized by reasoned or reasonable evaluation. We expect not just judgments themselves, but some way of knowing where these judgments come from, what their credentials are, or what they are worth. How do we assess the worth of the judgments or evaluations made by thinking?

There are, I believe, two main ways to assess the worth or validity of evaluative thinking. One is to examine its methods, the other is to examine its results. (Often the two are used in combination.) Thus, if the method exhibited by thinking (insofar as this is known) is a method which we regard as a reliable one for the problem at hand, then knowledge of the method used is one evidence of the worth of a judgment.

Or, if the evaluative result is seen to solve or advance the problem or project at hand, then that knowledge of usefulness of result is evidence of worth. If we use the phrase "reasoned or reasonable evaluation," then we can regard "reasoned" as reminding us that we can test the worth of an evaluation by looking at its method, and "reasonable" as reminding us that we can test the worth of an evaluation by assessing its result.

There is a tendency in talking about critical thinking to characterize it in terms of its method, but it is also necessary to understand it in terms of its purpose. Understanding these two aspects of how we describe critical thinking is helpful in many ways. We can illustrate this by examining descriptions of critical thinking by several writers.

John Dewey

We begin with John Dewey. Dewey analyzes what he called "reflective thinking" or "deliberation," devoted to any kind of problem. He used the term "critical" to describe judgments made within the whole problem-solving process.[8] These judgments act upon the spontaneous productions of thought.

In *How We Think,* Dewey actually gives two separate accounts of reflective thinking, one which emphasizes purpose and one that describes a method. The account which emphasizes purpose is the more general account, applying to any instance of sustained reflection. Dewey says that,*"reflective* thinking . . . involves (1) a state of doubt, hesitation, perplexity, mental difficulty, in which thinking originates, and (2) an act of searching, hunting, inquiring, to find material that will resolve the doubt, settle and dispose of the perplexity."[9] The method by which the inquiring is done is not specified in this account. All that is said is that thinking is regulated by its purpose and that "the end controls the process of thinking."[10]

This account has sometimes been interpreted as being a purely psychological description of thought, and having the implication that a "problem is solved when the solver thinks it is solved."[11] But it is also an analytical account: a problem is solved when it is solved. That is, the test of an instance of thinking is to compare the result to the problem at hand. To evaluate an instance of thinking, one must have an exact problem that one takes as the criterion. Now of course we may never be able to decide what the exact problem is. Surely the thinker himself may be mistaken about what his purpose was or ought to have been. But the advantage of this purpose-oriented account is that it emphasizes the specificity of thought, adapted to particular problems and situations. In contrast, method-oriented accounts emphasize generality of method.

Dewey's method-oriented account is consistent with the purpose-oriented account, but it specifies particular features of method to be used in getting from problem situation to solution. His description includes ideas like problem definition, elaboration of suggestions into hypotheses, reasoning using observations and available knowledge, and testing of hypotheses.[12] This account of method tries to be general. We want advice about method to apply to as many cases as possible (while still remaining effective). But no account of method can be both completely general (applying to all problems) and completely helpful (the exact advice we need to solve the problem).

When we think of or teach about critical thinking in terms of purpose, we can be open-minded as to the method, willing to use whatever works or whatever we or our students come up with. This may allow better control of thinking by the specific purpose or problem at hand. When we think of or teach about critical thinking in terms of method, we attempt to share with others accumulated, tested experience of what has worked in other situations. But in many cases our advice about method will not be particularly illuminating.

Attention to the relation of the viewpoints of method and purpose leads to an interesting view of other theories of critical thinking besides Dewey's.

Richard Paul

Richard Paul contrasts "the logic of technical problems and those of a dialectical nature."[13] Technical problems, he says, are those that can be solved within one frame of reference, within one discipline or system of ideas. But, in contrast, "The most vexing and significant real life problems are logically messy. They span multiple categories and disciplines."[14] What is called for by these nontechnical problems, says Paul, is dialogical reasoning, "argument for and argument against," moving "back and forth between opposing points of view," or considering "how this or that situation might be handled if we looked at it this way, or how if we looked at it that way."[15] This dialogical reasoning is recommended as the method of critical thinking in the strong sense. "Dialectical thought is the master-principle of all rational experience and human emancipation. It cultivates the mind and orients the person as technical training cannot."[16]

There is much of value in Paul's treatment, but there is an important ambiguity. Paul says rightly that many important problems fall outside established disciplines or systems of ideas. No clear method then exists for solving them. The only method we have is "dialogical reasoning," trying out various approaches and points of view. But is this a method, or an admission that we have no method, that we are just searching for an answer, guided mainly by the purpose or question at hand? Is "dialogical reasoning" a method that can be usefully specified, or is it more a willingness to search when we do not quite know how to proceed, except to keep trying? How we answer this question will make a great difference in how we teach or plan for the teaching of critical thinking.

Paul's definition of critical thinking is given in terms of its purpose and its place in the nature of the person. Critical thinking skills "in the strong sense" are "intrinsic to the character of the person," "essential to the free, rational, and autonomous mind," and "generate not only fundamental insight into but also some command of one's own cognitive and affective processes."[17] More explanation is needed to understand why we can move from this definition to the claim that dialogical reasoning is *the* method of thinking to be used for all nontechnical problems. Just to understand the claim, we have to know more specifically what dialogical reasoning is.

John McPeck

Another writer, John McPeck, author of *Critical Thinking and Education,* defines critical thinking in terms of a method. He says that critical thinking is "the appropriate use of reflective scepticism within the problem area under consideration."[18] This reflective scepticism is "suspension of assent, towards a given statement, established norm, or mode of doing things."[19] The purpose of suspension of assent is to allow construction of alternatives which might advance progress toward the resolution of the problem.[20] The question is, why identify "critical thinking" with the method, or method-description, "reflective scepticism"? This may be a leading method of critical thought, but it is not the only method. Or, if it is a *necessary* aspect of all critical thinking, surely it is not the only important aspect.

One motive McPeck had for using this description is that he wished to emphasize the area-specific nature of critical thought, in contrast to general, logical methods. His description says that the application of reflective scepticism must be "judicious" or "appropriate." These are the words that, it seems to me, mark the purpose- or problem-controlled nature of critical thought. McPeck does say that the purpose of the thought is to make progress on the problem. But he obscures the importance of the problem idea by saying that "the criteria for the judicious use of scepticism are supplied by the norms and standards of the *field* under consideration" (emphasis added).[21] For, while of course much guidance does come from the field, the criterion of what specifically turns out to be judicious is found in the *specific problem* under consideration, whether progress on it is made or not. The importance of this point is increased by Richard Paul's observation that many important problems fall in between fields.

Robert Ennis

The interplay of the viewpoints on purpose and method is also interesting in the work of Robert Ennis. As mentioned before, Ennis defines critical thinking as "reflective and reasonable thinking that is focused on deciding what to believe or do."[22] This is a purpose-oriented definition. But the main task of Ennis's work is to prove a list of skills and attitudes that he believes are central to the purpose of deciding what to believe or do. Upon examining his list we find that the skills are described either in terms of method or in terms of purpose. For example, under "Abilities," item 4 is "Judging the credibility of a source," which is a description by purpose.[23] But, under this heading, eight criteria are given, use of which would constitute a method, although not the only available method for making such judgments.

There are several questions a user ought to ask before using Ennis's list of skills. He might ask: do I accept the goal of learning or teaching "thinking that is focused on deciding what to believe or do," as an adequate description of my purpose? If I do, is the list of skills a valuable enough or extensive enough account of the skills that achieve that purpose? What important is left out, either in terms of skills that achieve specific subsidiary purposes, or methods known to be useful for making such decisions for helping others learn to make such decisions?

Varieties of meaning

We have seen that there are many variations and complexities in the meanings attached to "critical thinking." These arise in part because it is possible to describe thinking and thinking skills in terms of purpose or in terms of method. Thus Dewey gives one account of thinking in terms of specific purposes or problems, and another, separate account of method. Ennis defines critical thinking in terms of its purpose, but takes as his main task a thorough listing of skills, some of which are defined by methods and some by purposes. McPeck defines critical thinking ostensibly in terms of a particular method, but includes reference to the problem at hand.

Other variations in the meaning of "critical thinking" occur because all purposeful thinking of any kind requires judgments, and effective thinking requires good judgments. So there are small critical acts in any effective purposeful thinking. We may hardly be aware of these judgments, but they may be assumed to be there as selective acts of attention, assumption, and direction. We could, in the name of critical thinking, examine these small critical acts within any kind of thinking that seemed important to us. Or, in the name of critical thinking, we could give attention to the overall activities themselves: problem-solving, decision-making, writing, academic inquiry, and various other kinds of productive and performing activities, even though we know that these activities require productive, creative thinking as well as evaluative thinking.

Having "critical thinking" as a goal does not make these choices of meaning for us. We have to examine our own needs as learners, or the needs of our students, classes, schools, or other groups. Having an understanding of the meanings and possibilities of critical thinking may give us some new points of view from which to examine these needs.

Purpose, method, result and thing evaluated

We can organize our understanding of critical thinking further by noting the four aspects of thinking that have consistently stood out in the whole preceding discussion. Besides purpose and method, there are the thing evaluated and the result of thinking. These four aspects of thinking are four points of view for considering critical thinking, either as individual instances or in terms of general ideas. These aspects are also four ways in which, or dimensions along which instances of critical thinking can vary.

The four aspects seem to apply not only to evaluative thinking but to any thinking which has a purpose, whether evaluative or not. As mentioned before, any purposeful thinking requires critical judgment, and so any variety of purposeful thinking may be an object of concern under the heading of "critical thinking." But for simplicity I will speak here as if the *overall* purposes are critical, in the sense of being evaluative.

The four aspects of thinking are things picked out of a whole situation or context in which thinking occurs. The very idea of an *instance* of thinking is itself already a selective idea, since thinking is continuous and what we pick out as an instance is determined by some purpose or method of analysis that we have. In any case, it is clear that instances of thinking occur as part of a situation or context. The situation is made up first of all by the person thinking (including his abilities, experience, knowledge, languages, purposes, and habits) and everything around him (including things, people, and events).

In an instance of critical thinking something is being evaluated: a book, a situation, a method. There is a purpose for evaluating, something is wanted or intended: e.g., to know the value of a book for a course or as a literary achievement, to know the limitations of a method or how it can be improved. Some method or approach is used, perhaps the exercise of an unanalyzed ability we possess, or the following of a few familiar hints, or the following of a detailed, even standardized, procedure. And there is some result: a spoken or written opinion, an action taken, a new line of inquiry, a changed attitude. We will now proceed with a more detailed examination of each of these four aspects of critical thinking, along with some implications for education.

Thing evaluated

It is important to realize that there are many intersecting categories of things we might evaluate. We might categorize things evaluated by subject of interest: e.g., as a topic within mathematics, politics, business, ethics, family life, health. We might also categorize things evaluated by kinds of thought or knowledge: theories, policies, arguments, advice, feelings, claims, methods, and evaluations. The choice of categories serves various purposes, but these purposes are not given a priori to us as educators. We might very well choose to emphasize evaluation of arguments, since this is an important skill and since some good general advice is available to give about it. But how big an emphasis to give it and when to give it are matters open to deliberation.

A large part of education is simply showing that many things are open to evaluation that the student might never have tried to consider on his own. For example, it is useful to learn that someone's arguments can be evaluated separately from the policy he advocates (the policy could be good and the arguments bad, or vice versa). It is useful to learn how to evaluate one's feelings while writing.

Purpose

Whatever kind of thing we are evaluating, our purpose is our reason for doing the thinking: it is what we are trying to do. Evaluation generally is a broad family of purposes. When we evaluate a particular thing in a particular situation there is some particular set of values or needs that we have reference to. Thus, a movie could be evaluated by a critic in order to decide what rating to give it, or to describe the kind of tastes it will especially appeal to, or why it has the appeal (or lack of appeal) he believes that it does. Similar variations of purpose apply to evaluation of other kinds of things: books, policies, theories. There is not just one purpose for each kind of thing. The novel *Pride and Prejudice* and the Pythagorean theorem each exist in multiple connections to our values and to other things. The same is true of aspects of individual experience which might be objects of critical thought, for example of a person's own specific feelings or beliefs.

The distinction between a consciously articulated purpose—an end-in-view to use Dewey's term—and a background purpose or activating tendency is a useful one. An end-in-view can often serve as an idea guiding thought (and as such be a part of method), yet it may not be the actual thing that we want or are tending toward. An end-in-view may be provisional and be replaced later by a new vision of what we want. Or, we may have purposes motivating our thinking of which we remain only dimly aware. But in describing thinking from the point of view of an observer (another person or oneself in a different frame of mind) it is often useful to refer to the purpose or purposes we believe the thinking is serving.

Our purposes and our understanding of our purposes directs much of our activity. Once we start giving attention to thinking, questions of purpose and choices about purposes can easily arise. This opportunity can be embraced or not. Students need to discover what purposes it is possible to have and to consider how they will deal with the growth or choice of new purposes to guide their thought and activity.

Method

Method refers to how we do some piece of thinking. A method is supposed to further some purpose or need that we have, but it may turn out to serve that purpose well or badly. In teaching critical thinking we can advocate purposes even when we are unsure about methods. Even when we know a lot about a method, we seldom or never know that it is the *only* method that will serve a given purpose.

One problem in discussing method is that it is ambiguous whether we mean by "method" an actual process of thinking or a description of the process. And even if we do mean a description, there are many different kinds of description we could be interested in. We could be thinking of a publicly known, orderly procedure, or a description that a person himself might give of how he specifically did some thinking, etc.

One thing seems clear. Descriptions of thinking methods will always be partial and selective. For example, to do long division requires doing multiplication and subtraction, but a typical description of long division would not specify in detail how to multiply and subtract. Human learners need to be told only some things, depending on what they already know and can do. Generally, we do not want too much detail in method, or else that detail actually slows us down. We want to know just the thing we need to know to get our mind to do what it needs to do. This is why in complicated activities like tennis or writing we can use the help of a coach who can try to discern just *which* piece of advice will be helpful. Thinking instruction will probably often be like this.

Also, we may distinguish between a generally shared method and an individual method. There is much publicly available advice on how to think, and teachers may pass this on as well as share their own experience. Whatever advice learners receive, it is their task to make it work for them. They meet this advice from the standpoint of their own present abilities, knowledge, habits, attitudes, and purposes. That advice has to fit into their framework. Learners in other words have to develop their own abilities or methods, using whatever descriptions or ideas of method or pieces of advice prove useful to them. Descriptions of method and advice are meant to be general, but they are only tools to be adapted and used according to the particular needs and characteristics of each person.

Another aspect of individual method is that the individual can take his own method as an object of observation and evaluation. With help from teachers and colleagues, he can try to find out what works for him and what does not.

This problem of developing individual method is particularly pertinent when comparing school and non-school settings. In school, problems are set in a familiar and well-structured way. Even if a student finds a problem hard, he usually knows what he is being asked to do and he is usually given a method. In out-of-school settings however (e.g., in work and personal life), the demands on us are usually much less structured intellectually. We have to decide which purposes and problems to take as our own, and we have to select from among conflicting advice on how to proceed.

Method is multi-media

Further, method is "multi-media." It is important to consider the full range of modes of thinking. It takes place not only in the language of statement, evidence, logic, alternatives, and decision, but also in the language of performance, design, and craft, and using story and metaphor. And critical thinking can take place in modes other than language. It will normally use feelings and images, or those language-feeling and image-feeling combinations that are typical of inner life.

Also, critical thinking need not be confined to the reflective, in the sense of being entirely in the head. It can take place in interaction with putting words on paper, drawing, or speaking out loud. And it can take place in interaction with materials, pictures, devices, people, computers, or books, which interactions greatly extend its possibilities.

The mode of thinking and the out-of-the-head interactions that accompany thinking do not settle the question of whether thinking is performed critically or not. That is determined by whether the method used is proven reliable or whether the results obtained meet the purpose or problem at hand.

Most broadly, we can say that virtually any activity can be carried out critically or not, because in every activity we are trying something out. Often we may be perfectly confident how things will turn out. But if they do not turn out as expected, then there is something new to be learned. Or if we find that we do not want what we thought we wanted, then there is something new to learn about what we value.

Result of thinking

The result of thinking has already been discussed in several connections. If thinking is successful then we get a result which meets the purpose or problem for whose sake the thinking is done. Or, if we are assessing thinking by assessing its method, then "result" means in this case the correct completion of a performance according to the method.

One point to add is that there is no reason to think of critical thinking as always yielding verbal or numerical results. An episode of critical thinking might issue directly in an action, a shift of attention, or a change in feeling, if that is what is needed. Of course, it is often easier to know whether a verbally formulated result is a reasoned or reasonable one. But retrospectively we can make judgments about whether, for example, dropping a line of inquiry was a reasonable thing to do.

It may often be an important part of method to take the trouble to formulate explicitly problems, conclusions, decisions about directions of work, etc. But experience shows that it is not a necessary condition of all reasonable evaluative thought to do so. Think of all the learning a young child does, or an adult in a foreign country.

Episodes of thought interleave with one another, and somehow purposes are taken up intermittently across long periods of time, but thoughts do not seem always to connect via remembered verbal statements.

Also, experience is stored up within a person, in his judgment, sensibilities, convictions, and tendencies. That these are modified by thought is a main reason for paying attention to critical thinking. But we see here no mere shifting of verbal results.

Critical perspective

When we consider the cumulative effects of experience and critical thinking, we come upon the idea of critical perspective. If we have had some range of experience in an area or manner of thinking, including perhaps encounter with common problems, main ideas, key knowledge, and useful methods and points of view, and if this encounter has had the necessary kind of effect on us, then we may have an acquired range of reference that we employ in critical thinking. This we may call having a critical perspective, having a variety of states of mind and reference points that we use in dealing with problems or projects in an area.

One aim of education ought to be to get students to acquire an adequate range of experience, by getting them to try ways and areas of thinking and activity that they would not otherwise have tried. (What kinds of thing a school should attempt to get its students to try is a perennial question.) But it is not only range of experience that is important, but how that experience is understood and integrated, how new experience is considered in the light of old experience, or old in the light of new.

The tradition of liberal education (the idea of which has varied considerably throughout the centuries) is concerned in part with giving critical experience in important areas. The Yale Report of 1828 expressed the aims of liberal education in this way: "The great object of a collegiate education . . . is to give that expansion and balance of mental powers, those liberal and comprehensive views, and those fine proportions of character, which are not to be found in him whose ideas are always confined to one particular channel."[24] Part of the reason for trying out new ideas and points of view is to affect the student's mind in an integrated way.

The critical attitude

We have spoken only in passing of attitudes. Let us turn to the question of the attitudes appropriate to critical thinking. If we take "critical" narrowly, as "fault-finding," a critical attitude would be the tendency to find fault. But if we take "critical thinking" to be evaluative thinking that is reasoned or reasonable, then the critical attitude is the tendency to do this kind of thinking when it is appropriate, and to assume the frame of mind necessary for doing it. In general, critical attitude is the attitude appropriate to critical thinking, however we understand it.[25]

With respect to the beliefs and practices by which one works and lives, the critical attitude is the attitude that what I now believe, or what tradition teaches, may not be the final word, and that it is open to me and to others to make revisions and improvements in beliefs and practices, and that these revisions can be demonstrated to be reasonable. This critical attitude can apply in any area: science, art, personal or political life, learning and teaching. It can apply to purposes and methods themselves.

A clear expression of the critical spirit in reference to science has been given by Karl Popper in an essay on Pre-Socratic Greek philosophy:

I'd like to think that Thales was the first teacher who said to his pupil: "This is how I see things—how I believe that things are. Try to improve upon my teaching."

It was a momentous innovation. It meant a break with the dogmatic tradition which permits only *one* school doctrine, and the introduction in its place of a tradition that admits *plurality* of doctrines which all try to approach the truth by means of critical discussion.[16]

We need not worry over Popper's claim that Thales was the *first* teacher who encouraged a critical attitude on the part of his pupils. The important thing here is the attitude itself: the expectation within a school of thought or other group that there are revisions or innovations that will make the group's beliefs, practices, or attitudes more satisfactory than they now are, and that each member of the group has a responsibility to make a contribution.

If we seek to foster the critical attitude, several points are worth noting. A person may have the critical attitude or spirit in one area but not in another. To become critical in a new area, a person needs to acquire not only some skill, but also some confidence in his new skill and some confidence and understanding that it serves his overall purposes to think critically in the new area or manner.

Critical thinking in a new area or in a new manner can seem not only hard and unfamiliar, but also risky. Some of our beliefs and attitudes are very closely held. They seem like part of us and we are strongly inclined not to consider them even as candidates for revision.

Wisdom is needed in what we choose to push students (of any age) to be critical about. One guide is to help them to think critically about their own questions and problems. One of the great tasks of each person's education is to find convictions and methods that he does have confidence in and that do serve him well. A process of testing is required to gain sound convictions and confidence in them. Starting from the impersonal materials of school subjects, a student may broaden the areas in which he is able and willing to be critical. He may then acquire the conviction that the critical attitude itself is a source of stability and value, because, for one thing, it helps maintain a dynamic equilibrium in his thought and activity.

Notes

1   John Passmore, "On Teaching to be Critical," in R. S. Peters, ed., *The Concept of Education* (London: Routledge & Kegan Paul, 1967), pp. 200–201.

2   Robert Ennis, "A Concept of Critical Thinking," *Harvard Educational Review*, 32:1 (Winter 1962), p. 81.

3   Ibid., p. 81.

4   Ibid., p. 82.
5   Robert Ennis, "A Logical Basis for Measuring Critical Thinking Skills," *Educational Leadership* (October 1985), p. 45.
6   Ibid., p. 45.
7   Ibid., p. 46.
8   John Dewey, *How We Think* (D. C. Heath and Company, 1933), p. 16.
9   Ibid., p. 12.
10 Ibid., pp. 14–15.
11 Ennis, "A Concept of Critical Thinking," p. 82.
12 Dewey, *How We Think,* pp. 106–18.
13 Richard Paul, "Critical Thinking: Fundamental to Education for a Free Society," *Educational Leadership* (September 1984), p. 10.
14 Ibid., p. 11.
15 Ibid., p. 11.
16 Ibid., p. 14.
16 Ibid., p. 5.
18 John McPeck, *Critical Thinking and Education* (New York: St. Martin's Press, 1981), p. 7.
19 Ibid., p. 6.
20 Ibid., p. 9.
21 Ibid., pp. 7–8.
22 Ennis, "A Logical Basis," p. 45.
23 Ibid., p. 46.
24 Quoted in Merle Borrowman, *The Liberal and Technical in Teacher Education* (New York: Teacher's College, Columbia University, 1956), p. 38.
25 Thus, for example, since Harvey Siegel defines the critical thinker as "one who is appropriately moved by reasons," then, for him, the critical attitude or critical spirit is the willingness, desire, and disposition "to *do* reason assessment and to be guided by the results of such assessment." See his "McPeck, Informal Logic and the Nature of Critical Thinking," in *Philosophy of Education: 1985* p. 65.
26 Karl Popper, "Back to the Pre-Socratics," in his *Conjectures and Refutations: The Growth of Scientific Knowledge* (New York: Harper and Row, 1963), p. 150.

CHAPTER 3

Representation, comprehension, and competence
Catherine Z. Elgin

Although many philosophical dualisms have been debunked, the dualism of nature and convention continues to haunt discussions of representation. Pictorial representation is thought to be natural—a matter of resemblance between image and object. This resemblance, moreover, is taken to be an objective matter, visible to the human eye and evident to all who look. Linguistic representation, on the other hand, is considered conventional—working by rules and stipulations that secure the connection between words and the world. The bifurcation of symbols into the natural and the conventional is not without difficulties. A number of symbols, including star charts, hieroglyphics, and Chinese pictographs, seem intermediate cases. It is not clear whether they should be considered natural or conventional signs. Indeed, the criteria for classifying signs as natural or conventional are themselves obscure. The distinction is more easily formulated than applied. It is not my purpose here to mount a frontal assault on the dichotomy. In fact it is widely accepted. And once it is accepted, theorists have reason to limit their inquiries. Since the conventional is patently different from the natural, theorists concerned with the one can safely ignore representations belonging to the other. As a result, affinities between the two realms are often overlooked, and differences—because anticipated—unheeded. If, however, we abandon the presumption that theories of linguistic and pictoral representation are mutually irrelevant, the results of each can be taken to bear on the other. Then neglected affinities can be recognized and acknowledged differences rendered salient. This, I hope, will enhance our understanding of representations of all sorts.

I want to concentrate on a single problem that is shared by linguistics and the theory of depiction: the problem of explaining our ability to understand representations we have not previously encountered. We regularly comprehend sentences we've never before heard and pictures we've never before seen. Our competence, of course, has its limits. Sentences that are mumbled, garbled, or in an alien tongue, like pictures that are out of focus, poorly executed, or in an unfamiliar style, are apt to elude us. Still, our findings may be less troublesome than our successes. If the ability to interpret symbols depends on experience, then lack of experience with a particular symbol seems readily to account for

Reprinted by permission, *Social Research*, Vol. 51, No. 4 (Winter 1984)

failure to understand it. Not so readily explained, however, is the wide range of symbols which are understood without difficulty despite lack of experience with them. Whether or not our capacity to interpret symbols depends on experience, it plainly extends beyond experience. The problem is to say how.

Although the problem is common to linguistics and art theory, the solution is thought not to be. Central to each discipline is an account of competence that cannot plausibly apply to the representations of the other. Linguistic representation is taken to depend on rules. These rules, being general, settle the interpretation of novel as well as familiar expressions. Pictorial representation is taken to depend on likeness. Since likeness can be seen directly, no prior acquaintance with the pictorial symbols is required to understand a picture. Words, manifestly, do not resemble their objects. So the theory of pictorial competence cannot be true of linguistic competence. And we have neither grammars nor lexicons of pictorial forms, so the linguistic theory cannot account for pictorial competence. Still, the problem deserves more attention, for the mutual indifference of linguistics and art theory is such that the relation between the two competences is not taken to be in the province of either. Moreover, the mutual indifference of the disciplines is not argued for; it is simply given in the demarcation of the subjects. So any relevance of theories in one discipline to problems in the other is apt to be unnoticed.

Linguistic competence

Contemporary theorists contend that linguistic competence consists in the mind's having and being able to use a lexicon and a grammar.[1] The mental lexicon determines the meanings of individual words; the mental grammar determines how the meanings of significant strings of words derive from the meanings of their constituents. The mind is thought to be, or to be closely analogous to, a digital computer; the lexicon and the grammar, part of the program; and interpretation, a type of data processing. We understand a sentence we have never before heard because its words are contained in our lexicon and its form in our grammar. We thus already know the meanings of the individual words and the rule of obtaining the meaning of the whole from the meanings of the parts. To interpret the sentence, we simply apply the rule to the words. We do exactly the same in interpreting familiar sentences.

This account has a certain appeal, for it models inaccessible internal processes on familiar public activities. When confronted with an English sentence we don't understand, we consult grammar books and dictionaries. Often the information they contain settles the interpretation straightaway. Moreover, consulting such works may be the only general method we have for interpreting problematic sentences. Why not assume that the same sort of process occurs naturally in the interpretation of unproblematic sentences? Only in these cases, the process is effortless, instantaneous, and unconscious. For the requisite grammatical and lexical information is already stored in the mind.

In learning a foreign language we may memorize vocabulary lists and grammatical rules. This seems extraordinarily like attempting to supply ourselves with an internal lexicon and grammar for the language.[2] Moreover, in the early states, we may explicitly appeal to the rules and lists to generate interpretations of sentences. As we gain fluency, conscious appeals to the rules and lists we have learned occur less often. Perhaps, however, the process of interpretation does not fundamentally change. We simply internalize the vocabulary lists and grammatical rules and so come to apply them without thinking.

One final attraction of this picture of linguistic competence is this: we know how computers work. So if the human mind is, or is analogous to, a computer, we can use our knowledge of computers to learn about ourselves. A good deal of research in the cognitive sciences is grounded in the conviction that the computer is a model of the mind. Indeed, according to Jerry Fodor, it's the only model of the mind we've got.[3]

The appeal of this account stems from analogies to overt linguistic or quasi-linguistic activities. But they are only analogies. Interpreting unproblematic sentences in our native tongue involves no conscious consultation of an internal grammar or lexicon. Nor does introspection reveal any such activity. Proponents of the view under consideration admit that accessing the internal code is a deeply unconscious process. The reason to believe that it occurs is the power of the linguistic theory in which it is embedded. We should believe that speakers access an internal syntactic and semantic code for the same reason that we believe that distant bodies are drawn together by gravitational attraction—because the theses are supported by powerful, comprehensive, explanatory theories. Still, it is important to notice that the linguistic theory receives no direct support from a speaker's own sense of how he understands what is said.

Moreover, the competences we are said to have at the unconscious level are not competences we have at the conscious level. We typically cannot state the grammatical rules for our own language, or give the meanings of our terms. Nevertheless, we speak grammatically and meaningfully. Perhaps, as the linguists suggest, we do so because deep down we know the requisite grammatical and lexical rules. Or perhaps we do so because neither deep nor superficial knowledge of such rules is needed for meaningful, grammatical speech.

The case of meaning is particularly telling. Sameness of meaning seemingly involves more than coextensiveness of terms, but satisfiable, intuitively adequate standards of synonymy have not been found.[4] Since the internal lexicon is said to contain the meanings of our terms, the unclarity surrounding the notion of meaning results in an unclarity about what information the lexicon is supposed to contain. Minimally, it seems, this much is required: the lexical entry for a term should constitute a criterion for the term's application. Criteria for the applicability of terms are as difficult to articulate as meanings. On the broadest construal, such a criterion is adequate if it allows for the application of a term to all and only the items in the term's extension. Even if we require no more than this, the internal lexicon does not measure up.

Often nothing in the mind of the speaker determines the extensions of his terms. I may know that "Feynman" and "Gell-Mann" name eminent physicists but know nothing that distinguishes one from the other. And I may know that "beech" and "elm" designate separate classes of deciduous trees, but have no idea how to tell them apart. My linguistic competence is not imperiled by my ignorance, for I normally use the terms in contexts in which the differences do not matter, and I know enough, when the situation warrants, to defer to members of the linguistic community who possess the knowledge that I lack.[5] Moreover, the knowledge in question is not primarily linguistic. In the one case it is biographical; in the other, botanical.

Fodor concedes this point and concludes that the lexicon is referentially opaque.[6] Its entries determine the concepts we think in, but not what we think about. The lexical entry for "elm" then yields an elm-concept. And this concept is involved in our elm-thoughts. But since the concept is opaque, there is no reason to think that it determines the extension of "elm."

The analogy between minds and computers is illuminating here. For computer simulations are strictly ambiguous, having a referential and a computational interpretation. Under the former, a computer simulation represents, say, a complex molecular interaction. Under the latter, it defines a sequence of states of the computer. The former enables the scientist to interpret it as a representation of physical reality; the latter enables the machine to perform its calculations. The computer, of course, knows nothing of the referential interpretation. Moreover, its capacity to compile and execute its program would not be enhanced if the referential interpretation could somehow be imparted to it. To perform its calculations, the computer requires only the computational interpretation: the specification of its original state and of the changes it undergoes in response to various commands. The fact that the program has another interpretation that maps the operations and results onto physical reality is computationally irrelevant.

Correspondingly, if all we knew about the computer simulation was the interpretation available to the computer, we would not know that it represents a molecular interaction. (Indeed, we would not know that it represents at all.) But, according to Fodor, this is precisely our situation with respect to the sentences we comprehend. The internal lexicon is the machine language of the human computer. It yields computational interpretations which enable us to use sentences in our reasoning. But it does not yield referential interpretations, for lexical entries are opaque. Thus the information about the sentence that the lexicon provides does not determine what the sentence represents. Questions concerning the truth value of the sentences or the referents of its terms are inappropriate on a computational reading. Fodor's theory can explain neither how we know what novel sentences represent nor how we know what familiar sentences represent.[7] (Indeed, if his account is correct, it is surprising that we know such things.) The role of the lexicon has evolved to serve other purposes.

There is another limitation on the linguists' account: it cannot explain our understanding of figurative language or of locutions in which grammatical rules are deliberately violated. Understanding a stream-of-consciousness work, for example, is not a matter of forcing on its claims an interpretation that accords with our ordinary grammatical conventions or their "deep-structure" counterparts. For the work achieves its effects not in spite of but because of its odd, ungrammatical constructions. To force a grammatical reading on the work is to miss the point.

Typically the objects to which a term applies metaphorically are not in the term's literal extension. Nor does the metaphorical usage play the same computational role as the literal usage. In calling Wilber a workhorse, we liken the man to literal workhorses. The metaphor suggests that like literal workhorses he is plodding, diligent, but perhaps a bit uninspired. And understanding the metaphor involves picking up on some of these (or related) suggestions. It also involves recognizing that Wilber is not said to be in the literal extension of the term "workhorse." So some of the predicates of literal workhorses—"quadruped," "herbivore," etc.—are not being ascribed to Wilber. Since the lexicon is the repository of literal meanings exclusively, it follows that the lexical counterpart of the term "workhorse" enters into computations or inferences that are invalid when the term is used metaphorically. For example, the literal reading permits and the metaphorical reading prohibits the inference: if x is a workhorse, x is a quadruped.

It cannot plausibly be maintained that the metaphorical meaning of a term is contained along with its literal meaning in the lexicon. For there are potentially an indefinite number of metaphorical applications of a given term. The term "workhorse," for example, might be applied to automobiles—picking out jeeps and other such vehicles. Not only does its reference change as the term is applied metaphorically to sort different realms, so does its computational role. Inferences like "if x is a workhorse, x is dull" or "If x is a workhorse, x is uninspired" might be allowed when the term "workhorse" is applied metaphorically to people, but not (at least not under their literal interpretations) when it is applied to cars. In that application, however, "If x is a workhorse, x is capable of pulling heavy loads" is allowable, although we would not accept such an inference (literally construed) about human workhorses.

It will not do for linguists to dismiss such cases as deviant—to contend that metaphorical sentences are strictly false, and stream-of-consciousness locutions strictly ill-formed. For even if this were true, it would be irrelevant. Whether we characterize them as true or false, as well-formed or ill-formed, we do understand such sequences of words. And linguistics claims to explain our comprehension of and competence with words. Although sustained, systematic violations of grammatical rules are relatively rare, they are often not hard to understand. This being so, it is reasonable to expect the theory of linguistic comprehension to explain how we understand them. An account that applies only to cases in which our standards of grammaticality are met seems seriously incomplete. Moreover, metaphors are ubiquitous. So the failure of linguistic theory to explain our understanding of sentences containing metaphors is a failure to explain a considerable proportion of its subject matter.

What remains is an impoverished notion of linguistic competence. Knowledge of word-world connections, and understanding of nonliteral and nongrammatical uses of words are excluded from linguistic comprehension. (Conceivably they are cases of, or are involved in, comprehension of some other sort.) Surely they are involved in understanding sentences we have never heard before. For example, to understand the sentence "Descartes is the Robinson Crusoe of the mind" I need to know something about who Descartes is and what he accomplished, about who the fictional character Robinson Crusoe is and the story in which he appears, about how fictive terms can be applied metaphorically to characterize actual individuals, and about how a proper name prefaced by an article functions metaphorically as a general term. Since I have the requisite knowledge, I have no difficulty understanding the sentence the first time I hear it. It seems somewhat eccentric to maintain that my understanding is not linguistic, for it is surely grounded in an appreciation of how the words in the sentence function.

Pictorial competence

The linguists' model plainly cannot be extended to pictorial comprehension. Lexicons and grammars are possible only for systems whose symbols are determinate and discriminable. For lexicons and grammars consist of generalizations that apply to symbols because they are tokens of specific syntactic types. Where it is impossible to determine the type to which a symbol belongs, it is impossible to take it to be subject to lexical and grammatical rules. And where it is impossible to tell whether two symbols belong to the same type, it is impossible to treat them as syntactically interchangeable.

But this is precisely the situation with regard to pictorial symbols.

For such symbols belong to systems that are syntactically dense and nondisjoint. There is no way to differentiate pictorial symbols sharply from one another, hence no way to determine which symbol a particular mark belongs to or whether two marks belong to the same symbol. Any difference among pictorial marks might be syntactically significant. And for pictorial systems there is no principled basis for ruling that certain differences among marks are irrelevant.[8] Understanding a picture then is not a matter of bringing to bear universal rules that determine the identification and manipulation of its competent symbols.

That the linguists' solution is inapplicable to pictorial representations may be unimportant. For perhaps pictures belong to a realm in which the linguists' problem does not arise. It might be argued that determinate, satisfiable rules are required for the interpretation of linguistic representations because the connection between word and object is not naturally secured. Then if there is a natural connection between pictures and their subjects, this obviates the need for grammatical and lexical rules of pictorial representation.[9] Resemblance is often held to be that connection.[10]

The argument goes roughly as follows: we know what a picture represents because we recognize its resemblance to its subject. This resemblance, moreover, is discernible to the uneducated eye. If it were not, we could not tell what a picture represents just by looking. But we do that all the time; we regularly understand pictures we've never seen before.

Manifestly, resemblance is not sufficient for representation. For representation is asymmetric; resemblance, symmetric. A picture represents its subject; that subject does not represent the picture. But the subject resembles the picture as much and in the same ways as the picture resembles the subject. Moreover, items that resemble one another often do not represent one another. Identical twins are typically not each other's stand-ins.[11] Still, where we know on other grounds that something is a representation, perhaps it is on the basis of resemblance that we determine what it represents.

Resemblance may be as difficult a notion as meaning, but for a different reason. Whereas meanings are elusive, resemblances are common. Any two objects resemble each other in some respect. The problem is to specify the sort of resemblance that is required for pictorial representation.

The obvious answer is: visual resemblance. Although obvious, this answer is not obviously correct. We often know what a picture represents without knowing (or caring) whether it resembles its subject. Crucifixion being an outmoded method of public execution, we do not know whether pictures of Christ's crucifixion look like the real thing. Nevertheless, we can typically tell straightaway what those pictures represent.

Moreover, pictures with fictional subjects do not resemble their referents. Unicorn pictures do not resemble unicorns, there being none to resemble. Still, we have little difficulty recognizing unicorn pictures for what they are. Whatever enables us to comprehend such pictures, it cannot be resemblance of a representation to its denotation. The denotation of a unicorn picture is null, and so is identical to the denotation of a satyr picture. But we are unlikely to mistake the subject of the one for the subject of the other.

To be sure, many pictures resemble their subjects. If resemblance can be shown to explain how we understand these pictures, perhaps a way can be found to extend the explanation to more problematic cases. But even the seemingly clear cases raise difficulties. For pictures can resemble their subjects in any number of ways. For example, successful impressionist works capture fleeting, ephemeral properties of changing visible surfaces—shimmering juxtapositions of sunlight and shadow that are taken in at a glance and are gone in a flash. Pictures on the walls of Egyptian tombs are schematic representations of the ineluctable cycle of the seasons. In their changelessness and generality, the pictures represent and resemble the eternal and unalterable order of nature.[12] The evanescent moment that the impressionist captures is an instant in the eternal cycle that the Egyptian records.

Any thing looks many ways. So to contend that a picture looks like its subject is not to specify a particular relation between the two. Pictures that resemble the same thing may look very different from one another. And pictures that look very much alike may represent quite different things.

Indeed, pictures that resemble their subjects do not always resemble the ways their subjects look. In medieval paintings, for example, the images of the madonna and child are often significantly bigger than the images of the saints that surround them. According to the religious tradition within which these works were produced, the infant Jesus and his mother are far more significant than other people. And size in such pictures is a measure of religious significance. To represent the Christ child as no greater than an ordinary baby would be incorrect. For in this system, pictorial magnitude is a measure of real (theological or metaphysical) magnitude, not of apparent (physical) magnitude.

This phenomenon is not peculiar to religious pictures. Scientific photographs—for example, X-rays and cloud-chamber photographs—likewise do not resemble the visible aspects of their subjects. They function, rather, to render visible what is normally invisible. Their images resemble features of their objects which are not directly seen.[13]

The thesis that pictorial competence is a matter of resemblance shares a weakness of the thesis that linguistic competence is a matter of rules—namely, the inability to account for our comprehension of figurative symbols. Understanding a picture often involves knowing what its symbols represent figuratively as well as knowing what they represent literally. For example, when a knight is depicted with a dog at his side, the dog typically symbolizes loyalty. To understand the picture fully, we have to know both that the configuration on the canvas literally represents a dog and that, because it does, it metaphorically symbolizes loyalty. The dog image thus contributes to the pictorial representation of the knight as loyal. Many pictorial metaphors are more subtle. But whether the metaphor is subtle or stereotypical, knowing what the image resembles does not suffice for knowing how and what it represents.

Even where a picture bears a decided resemblance to its subject, we are not always able to discern it. Unless we know what to look for, what to focus on, and what to overlook, we may fail to see a likeness that is right before our eyes. And such knowledge is not a native endowment. It is a complex constellation of acquired abilities. Humans do not automatically see variegated pastel patches as mottled light and shadow. We learn to see that way as we learn to understand impressionist painting. Nor is it intuitively obvious that figures in Egyptian paintings represent generally. The difference between the general and the particular, and the way that difference is captured pictorially, are things that have to be learned. And in different pictorial systems, different devices are used. These are not special cases. Learning is required even to recognize what photographs represent. As E. H. Gombrich notes, until relatively recently, unposed snapshots were incomprehensible.[14] And manifestly, a good deal of learning is required to be able to read X-rays.

Recognition of what a picture resembles is sometimes a consequence of knowledge of what it represents. The experience of looking at photographs of other people's babies bears this out. In general, baby pictures look like babies. But it is not always obvious which picture resembles which baby. When we learn whose picture we're looking at, certain features may acquire salience. We see the wide-open eyes and skeptical tilt of the chin as characteristic of Emily. The resemblance, we admit, is remarkable, even though it was not in fact remarked until we learned the identity of the picture's subject.

Similarly, it is often easier to discern the subject of a cubist painting after reading the caption. I have no trouble finding an image of a woman with a guitar, once I know what to look for. And I recognize that, in its way, the image resembles a woman with a guitar. But I might never have seen it had I not known it was there.

Sometimes the identification of the subject of a picture occasions a reinterpretation of the work. What once looked to be a beatific smile on the face of an apostle becomes a malevolent sneer when the apostle is identified as Judas. This can occur for figurative symbols as well. The dog that was taken to be a symbol of loyalty is reconstrued as an ironic symbol of treachery when the knight beside him is recognized as King Arthur's faithless knight, Mordred.[15]

Resemblance turns out to be a red herring. Its apprehension does not assure, nor its absence preclude, understanding what a picture represents. Moreover, resemblance does not designate a single relation between pictures and their subjects; it designates the members of a fairly comprehensive class of relations—a class whose boundaries are not clear. And relations of resemblance are not always immediately evident to the uneducated eye. Knowing how to look at a picture is required to discern the ways it resembles its subject, just as it is required to discern other pictorial properties. Knowledge of other matters may be required as well—pictorial conventions, referential connections, historical, scientific, or mythical lore that sets the context of the work. Such matters are not taken in in a glance.

To deny that resemblance is the basis for pictorial representation is not to say that anything can be a picture of anything else. There may well be limits on the structure and complexity of systems we can master. And some systems may be more easily mastered than others. But ease of mastery may have little to do with our estimations of pictorial likeness. Illustrations in picture books and Saturday morning cartoons are among the earliest pictures children master. They are not, however, thought to be particularly accurate likenesses of their objects.

Pictures are ubiquitous. A child in our culture is likely to encounter them on billboards, posters, and packages, on the walls of the buildings he frequents, in books, comic strips, and cartoons. He is likely to begin to learn to identify pictures at the same time and in the same ways as he learns to identify other things. He is taught to recognize dog pictures and house pictures, just as he is taught to recognize dogs and houses.

Learning to comprehend pictures often occurs in the context of learning about other things. The child who learns to differentiate horses from zebras by looking at their pictures learns simultaneously to differentiate horse pictures from zebra pictures. The student who learns to recognize diseased organs by studying a medical text is also learning to interpret medical illustrations. In such cases, the occurrence of pictorial learning and the consequent development of pictorial competence are apt to be overlooked, since learning to interpret the pictures is a means to some other end.

That end can, of course, be achieved in other ways. Some children learn to recognize zebras by looking directly at zebras. And an observant operating-room technician might learn to recognize liver disease by looking directly at diseased livers. But these people do not thereby acquire the correlated pictorial competence. Medical illustrations may remain unintelligible to the technician and animal pictures to the children. To use a picture to identify its subject, or the subject to comprehend the picture, requires understanding how the picture represents its subject. So even when its subject is familiar, a picture remains enigmatic to those who are ignorant of the relevant pictorial practices.

Pictorial learning involves acquiring a wide range of perceptual and conceptual skills, and developing a sensitivity regarding their exercise. Pictures represent in many different ways. And different skills are needed to understand pictures of different kinds. But each system need not be learned from scratch. For pictorial learning also involves developing second-order skills. These enable us to modify and extend our interpretive abilities and so comprehend pictures in systems related to those we know. The viewer who is already adept at interpreting traditional realistic paintings is likely to have little difficulty learning to understand realistic works with multiple vanishing points.

Having mastered a pictorial system, we simply see what its pictures represent. The process is so nearly automatic that we are apt to forget that interpretation occurs. Deliberation is not normally required to understand what is represented in newspaper photographs or realistic drawings. So the failure of such pictures to conform to our expectations is disconcerting. A paradoxical drawing by Escher forcefully reminds us that pictures are two-dimensional surfaces on which we try to impose three-dimensional interpretations. And a photograph of the surface of Mars reminds us that the medium does not supply its own scale of size and distance. The frustration of our expectations thus highlights our cognitive contribution to pictorial interpretation. It brings to consciousness factors that are frequently overlooked.

Holism

Despite serious failings, the theory that linguistic competence depends on rules and the theory that pictorial competence depends on resemblances endure. Why? Primarily, I think, because of a dearth of plausible alternatives. And this in turn is explained by the conception of competence that the theories share. Both take the competence in question to be a general ability to comprehend symbols of a given kind, and to do so on the basis of the syntax and semantics of the symbols exclusively. Given this conception of competence, it is hard to see how anything except universal rules or particular resemblances could serve.

But this conception of representational competence is itself questionable. Although we plainly have the ability to understand some representations we have never before encountered, we do not understand every English sentence we hear or every pictorial representation we see. A sentence from Henry James's *The Golden Bowl* or a picture like Manet's *Le Déjeuner sur l'Herbe* may elude understanding, despite the comprehensibility of the individual syntactic and semantic elements. We just do not know what to make of it.

Moreover, our understanding of representations often depends on knowledge that is not specifically syntactical or semantical. Such knowledge, we have seen, may be required to differentiate Feynman from Gell-Mann, a beech from an elm, a smile from a sneer. These matters may need to be settled to determine just what a particular symbol represents. And such knowledge may be required to decide whether the representation of a dog in a picture or story is a symbol of loyalty, a symbol of treachery, or simply a symbol of a dog.

The alternative to a piecemeal approach to interpretation is representational holism. Interpretation of a symbol depends on its place in the various symbol systems to which it belongs. And it depends on the systems available and appropriate for classifying the symbol itself.

A symbol system is a system of implicit alternatives that collectively sort the objects in a realm.[16] And the same symbol can belong to several systems and so participate in a variety of sortings. The extension of "fish," for example, sometimes includes, sometimes excludes, shellfish. And the truth values of many sentences about fish vary depending on which system is in play. "All fish are vertebrates" is true under the narrow interpretation, false under the broad interpretation of the term. But many other sentences are indifferent as between the two readings. "Fish are aquatic" and "Fish are a good source of protein" remain true under both interpretations. So the sentence itself need not favor either one.

Similar things occur in pictorial representations. A single drawing might represent a trout, a rainbow trout, a steelhead. Differences in markings that exclude a fish from one of the classes that the drawing represents do not exclude it from another. To understand the picture in its various functions, we have to realize that in one system it excludes fish that are not trout; in another it also excludes trout that are not rainbow trout; and in another it also excludes rainbow trout that are not steelheads.

Manifestly, the issue becomes even more complicated when the symbols have fictive or figurative applications in addition to, or instead of, literal, factual ones. Often a symbol belongs to several systems, and we need to know which and how many of them it is functioning in to understand what and how it represents.

Symbols are themselves subject to classification. And understanding a representation involves knowing some of the ways it is classified. We classify representations by subject, as crucifixion pictures or medical bulletins; by style, as impressionist paintings or symbolist poems; by genre, as still lifes or short stories. And we classify them by medium, as water colors or news reports; by author, as Monets or Flauberts; by historical and cultural milieu, as Renaissance or Victorian works. There is no obvious limit to the knowledge of a representation and its context that could, in principle, enhance our understanding of it.

These points do not pertain exclusively to works of art. To understand a newspaper article, for example, we need to classify it as a news report, a feature, a column, or an editorial. We do well to know whether it was subject to military censorship or to editorial policies that restrict what is said or the way it is said. And we need to know the systems of alternatives to which its terms belong. In calling a country a friendly power, do we exclude only such regimes as are actually belligerent to us, or all those that do not actively support our interests? Although we do not ordinarily deliberate about them, appreciation of such matters forms the background against which our reading of the news makes sense.

Holism threatens to make our original problem intractable. It takes so much to be relevant to the interpretation of a symbol that understanding a representation seems a remarkable achievement, not an everyday occurrence. The richness and complexity that the holist attributes to symbols is hard to square with our ordinary unsophisticated comprehension of pictures and sentences.

The objection rests on a pair of related misconceptions: the first is the conviction that understanding a symbol is an all-or-nothing affair; the second, that a symbol has a single, uniquely correct interpretation. Ascertaining that interpretation is then necessary and sufficient for understanding the symbol. Nothing less will do, and nothing more is needed to understand what a symbol represents.

But understanding admits of degrees. A little knowledge of a symbol and its context can yield some small understanding of what the symbol represents. For example, we recognize that the pronoun "he" and a conventional stick figure represent a male even though we cannot identify him further. And the greater our store of relevant knowledge, the greater our resources for (and hence prospects of) understanding what the symbol represents. Moreover, the growth of understanding may involve the recognition of several admissible alternative interpretations and may occasion the reconsideration of some we have already accepted. A symbol that had been construed literally is reconstrued metaphorically, sometimes by revoking the literal reading, sometimes by augmenting it. Or several separate literal readings are identified.

To be sure, some modes of representation are so simple and familiar that understanding is easily achieved. But even here the understanding may be illusory or incomplete. An apparent compliment contains a hidden slight; a passing remark, a manifestation of deep-seated resentment. Psychoanalysts and critics have shown that even seemingly simple representations contain significantly more than a superficial reading reveals.

Understanding a representation is like understanding anything else. We use the cognitive resources we have, realizing that they may be inadequate. We bring to the task of interpreting an unfamiliar picture or sentence the background of related representations we already understand, along with any additional knowledge and skill we can press into service. Often these suffice. If not, then by modifying and extending our previous understanding we can sometimes arrive at an adequate interpretation. But not always. No rules or relations guarantee that a correct interpretation will be achieved. There are no recipes.

Notes

1   Cf. Noam Chomsky, *Aspects of the Theory of Syntax* (Cambridge: MIT Press, 1965), and Jerry Fodor, *The Language of Thought* (New York: Crowell, 1975).
2   Contemporary linguists do not believe that this is how fundamental grammatical and lexical information is acquired. My point here is that the appeal of the account to nonlinguists may stem from such analogies.
3   Jerry Fodor, "Methodological Solipsism Considered as a Research Strategy in Cognitive Psychology," *Representations* (Cambridge: MIT Press, 1983), pp. 225–53.
4   W. V. Quine, "Two Dogmas of Empiricism," *From a Logical Point of View* (Cambridge: Harvard University Press, 1961), pp. 20–46.
5   Saul Kirpke, "Naming and Necessity," in Donald Davidson and Gilbert Harman, eds., *Semantics of Natural Language* (Dordrecht: D. Reidel, 1972), p. 292; Hilary Putnam, "The Meaning of 'Meaning'," *Mind, Language and Reality* (Cambridge: Cambridge University Press, 1975), pp. 245–46.
6   Jerry Fodor, "Tom Swift and His Procedural Grandmother," *Representations,* pp. 204–24.
7   Fodor uses the term "representation" somewhat differently. He takes the computational interpretation to be a representation. As I use the term, only when functioning referentially do symbols represent.
8   Nelson Goodman, *Languages of Art* (Indianapolis: Hackett, 1976), pp. 130–41.
9   C. S. Pierce, *Selected Papers,* ed. Philip Weiner (New York: Dover, 1958), pp. 368, 391.
10 Alan Tormey, "Seeing Things: Pictures, Paradox and Perspective," in John Fisher, ed., *Perceiving Artworks* (Philadelphia: Temple University Press, 1980), pp. 59–75.
11 Goodman, *Languages of Art,* pp. 3–5.
12 E. H. Gombrich, *Art and Illusion* (Princeton: Princeton University Press, 1969), pp. 122–25.
13 E. H. Gombrich, "Standards of Truth: The Arrested Image and the Moving Eye," *The Image and the Eye* (Ithaca: Cornell University Press, 1982), pp. 245–47.
14 *Ibid.,* p. 273.
15 Goodman, *Languages of Art,* p. 83.
16 *Ibid.,* p. 72.

CHAPTER 4

The power and the peril of the particular: thoughts on a role for microcomputers in science and mathematics education

Judah L. Schwartz

The cognitive odyssey from percept to concept and back

Science is generally understood to be the study of the phenomena of nature and the building of models to describe and explain those phenomena. Within that framework there seem to be fashions that develop among educators and that, at any given moment, seem to form the basis of much of what is done in schools. In the past we have swung from one pole of fashion to another, each time grasping our newly found insights with vigor and zeal.

Although in some measure we are not as fickle educationally as we once were, it is still the case that there are many science educators who see one part of the spectrum that ranges from phenomenon to model/ explanation and back as more important than the other. For example, there are those who place primary importance on the observation of the natural phenomena. They tend to emphasize open education and the importance of the discovery method. In the elementary schools one typically finds the classrooms of such teachers filled with leaves and furry animals. At the secondary level many of the courses that fit under the general rubric of science (e.g., physics) for the unlikely student of said science (e.g., poet) are the product of this approach.

There are several obvious advantages to this approach to science education. To begin with, it puts the student into direct interaction, and occasionally even confrontation, with nature in all its elegance, quirkiness, and mystery. Students who are taught science in this way are likely to develop a respect for both the aesthetics and the complexity of nature.

On the other hand, there are disadvantages to this approach to science teaching. Absent careful attention to the defining of appropriate abstractions and the exploration of the relationships that hold among these constructs, students are robbed of the power of making predictions and extending the domain of their understanding by the exercise of their rational faculties.

Reprinted by permission, *Machine-Mediated Learning* 1, no. 4. 0732–6718/86/ 010345–00$2.00/0. Copyright © 1986 Crane, Russak & Company, Inc., and Mentor Systems, Inc.

At the other end of the spectrum of fashion in science education are those who place primary importance on the explanation of nature, often without direct empirical observation of the phenomena. The advantages and disadvantages of this pedagogical approach are clear. On the plus side, students who are taught this way often learn to analyze formal models with great skill, and if they have a reasonable sense of the referents in nature of the constructs they are manipulating, they can derive insight and understanding from their manipulations. On the negative side, we find such barbarisms as fifth-grade students, who haven't a clue in the world about why it should be so, learning to parrot the words of science, like "atom" and "molecule," "DNA" and "protein." At more advanced levels the effects of this approach can be even more insidious. We find students enchanted with their models and unwilling to give them up even in the face of being contradicted by nature.

Obviously, says the thoughtful reader, there is no inherent contradiction between the two approaches. Why have we not incorporated the best of both into what we have done? I do not understand why fashions in science education have tended to oscillate from strong devotion to one of these approaches to strong devotion of the other, with educators taking stands that have tended to accentuate the positive characteristics of their approach and to de-emphasize its limitations. To be sure, we need to understand better the origins of our pedagogical instability. But that understanding is likely to be a long time in coming. While we try to develop that understanding, let me suggest that we have a new tool available to us that may help narrow the distance between the approaches. Simulations of natural phenomena, in particular, microcomputer-based simulations, are just such a tool. *However, the possibility of using microcomputers in this way is not in any way intended to suggest that there should be any lessening of attention paid to the direct observation of phenomena on the one hand, or to the study of formal and analytic models, on the other.*

What properties should a simulation have in order to play this bridging role? In my view there are two primary ones:

1. There ought to be screen displays that are, from a *perceptual* perspective, reasonably evocative of the phenomena being simulated.[1]
2. The primitive constructs of the simulation that can be manipulated by the student ought to be reasonably evocative of the *conceptual* structure of the model we hope the student will come to understand.

---

[1] It is never obvious which of several possible visual representations is "close" to a percept. Often, we regard visual representations that we have become accustomed to as evident and clear, forgetting that our students have not had the opportunity to make the connections that we have.

Two primary examples of these properties are given in the following discussion.

Suppose one were interested in helping youngsters think about and understand something about the way in which bodies move under the action of the forces that are exerted on them. There has been a great deal of research in recent years to confirm the all-too-easy-to-make observation that people, in the main, are persuaded that objects move in the direction of the net force that is exerted on them. This sort of a theory is very Aristotelian in character and quite inadequate to explain the motions of the heavens, or, for that matter, motion on an ice-skating rink.

How is it that we develop such theories and why are they so robust in the face of the efforts of many physics teachers to persuade students of their shortcomings? I believe that these theories are as robust as they are because they are quite consistent with a wide range of motion phenomena in our lives on a planet in which damping and dissipative forces of all sorts (e.g., friction, viscosity, electrical resistance) are commonplace.

Imagine now, if you will, a "microworld," a microcomputer simulation of a wide range of motion phenomena in which it were possible for the student to control the strength of the dissipative forces that are present in the microworld. At one end of the range of variation would be dissipative forces strong enough to be consistent with the building of Aristotelian dynamical theories. At the other end of this range the dissipative forces would be totally absent and mechanical energy strictly conserved. At this end of the range it would be possible to make clear the special roles that can be played by such quantities as linear and angular momentum as well as the importance of symmetry and invariance properties of the system.

This microworld is to be found in a program entitled *Sir Isaac's Games* [1], intended on its face for youngsters from mid-elementary level through high school. It has the property that at one end of the range of variation of dissipative forces, the screen displays are indeed evocative of the motions one sees around oneself in a frictionful world. At the other end of the range, students find themselves considering the problem of the vector addition of velocity and change in velocity. That this program might be of interest and utility to the physics student will probably not surprise the reader. On the other hand, the reader may be surprised to learn that this program once led a seven-year-old to give a remarkably cogent explanation for the fact that the acceleration a body undergoes in making a turn is directed toward the center of curvature of the turn.

Simulations that allow students to make the journey from percept to concept and back need not be limited to what is normally regarded as introductory science curricular materials. Let us imagine a second example of this kind of simulation. Consider a simulation of a mechanical oscillating system with linear viscous damping, a system that provides a powerful metaphor for the analysis of oscillatory phenomena across wide ranges of biology, chemistry, physics, and many branches of engineering. Let us assume that the simulation offers the student the capability of varying the parameters of the oscillating system as well as the initial conditions.

At the perceptual end of the spectrum of the simulation's capabilities, it ought to be possible to see a display of a visual representation of the natural system oscillating in time, with the student having the ability to measure positions (and consequently velocities and accelerations) at any instant of time. Activities of this sort can challenge the student to try to model the nature of the driving force as well as the restoring and damping force in the system.

At the conceptual end of the spectrum of the simulation's capabilities, it ought to be possible for the student to plot position, velocity, and acceleration against time or against one another. It also ought to be possible for the student to discover under what conditions there are any conserved quantities and how the fact of their conservation is reflected in the representations they are using as well as in the visual appearance of the system being simulated. The simulation ought to allow for the teasing apart of the specific effects of the initial conditions from those due to the natural motions of the system.

There are two caveats that need to be stated clearly before the enthusiasm for computer-based simulations gathers too much momentum. First, nature is always subtler than our models are. Indeed, it is necessary that this be the case if we are to learn anything from our models. Students must learn that when a discrepancy between nature and a model of nature is discovered, it is overwhelmingly likely that the model is inadequate. Second, any "run" of a simulation is always a particular instantiation of a model, and thus it is only with the greatest of caution that we may make general inferences about the properties of a model or about the behavior of that aspect of nature that the model deals with.

The power and peril of the particular

Percepts are of necessity particular. Concepts, if they are to be useful, must be general and apply more broadly than simply the particular cases that provoked them into existence. The problem of helping students go beyond the particular and induce generalities whose validity must be explored is central to the entire educational endeavor. In the following two examples, which are drawn from the mathematics curriculum of the upper elementary and early secondary levels, I will try to illustrate this idea in a domain other than science.

Let us start with an observation. The primary reason for mathematics in the curriculum of the culture is its use as a set of tools for modelling those aspects of the surround that are quantitative in nature. This immediately implies the use of quantity with particular referents, something rarely done in mathematics classes, although it is, in fact, more common in high school science classes. This is often a serious problem at the lower grades, where quantities such as "3 apples and 6 oranges," "3 feet and 6 yards," and "3 cats and 6 animals" regularly appear in the problems children are asked to do. While it is not necessary to use the computer to help to solve these problems, it seems that the microcomputer-based environment called *The Semantic Calculator* is a help [2]. Its ability to help is not limited to simple addition problems but extends to such problems as

> If a car that gets 33 miles to the gallon travels at 55 miles per hour, how long does it take to consume 1 gallon of gasoline?

People who use the *Semantic Calculator* to multiply 33 mi/gal by 55 mi/hr will be told that the result of their efforts is

33 mi/gal × 55 mi/hr = 1815 mi × mi/gal ;ts hr

People who use the *Semantic Calculator* to divide 33 mi/gal by 55 mi/hr will be told that the result of their efforts is

33 mi/gal ÷ 55 mi/hr = 0.6 hr/gal

People who use the *Semantic Calculator* to divide 55 mi/hr by 33 mi/gal will be told that the result of their efforts is

55 mi/hr ÷ 33 mi/gal = 1.666667 gal/hr

Each of these computations is correctly executed, but only one of them correctly answers the question posed! The correctness of one of them and the incorrectness of the other two does not lie in the numbers and the computations performed with them but rather in the referents of the numbers and the computations performed with the referents. The *Semantic Calculator* is a computer-based environment that extends dimensional analysis beyond continuous quantity, to which it is usually applied, to discrete quantity and makes this powerful tool ordinarily taught at university level available to students from about fourth grade up.[2]

The quantities that have been discussed here employ numbers in an adjectival fashion, that is, they are numbers with referents. While attention to the referents of the numbers can aid materially in the fashioning of a model, the particularity of the referents can also hamper the extension of a concept. If we limit ourselves to numbers that can be derived from nature by counting, we do not get beyond the integers. If we include numbers that can be derived from nature by measuring, we do not get beyond the rationals. It is only after we allow ourselves to abstract from a variety of adjectival uses of the number *3*, such as 3 apples, 3 shoes, 3 mm, 3 lb, and 3 km/sec, that we can begin to build structures like real numbers, complex numbers, rings, and fields. Here, too, we see the need for our students to develop a nimble ability to move between the particularity of the "threeness" of shoes and millimeters to abstract "threeness."

The second computer-based environment for mathematics education that I want to discuss is one that helps to address the problem of invention in the mathematical domain. Moreover, it provides a setting that is informed by our theme of induction from the particular and deduction from the general. Before exploring this example, two points must be made: (1) that geometry is peculiarly burdened by the dialectic between the particular and the general, and (2) that we normally do not teach nor do we normally ask students to carry out the mental activity that constitutes the key act in the making of mathematics.

Let me expand on the first point. Geometry as an area of study in mathematics is peculiarly burdened by the perils of the particular. We have all had the experience of being fooled by a construction in geometry into believing that something was generally true, when, in point of fact, it was true only in the particular case we were considering. The suggestion that we avoid this sort of stumbling block by avoiding the use of diagrams and constructions is unacceptable because our learning depends very heavily on the power of the diagram to exemplify and instantiate. The difficulty, of course, lies in the fact that we do not have a way of drawing a picture of an "arbitrary" triangle in the way we can write down an expression for an "arbitrary" term in a mathematical sequence or series.

As to the second point, there is a problem with the way we teach

---

[2]The computer is in no way logically necessary for the use of this sort of generalized dimensional analysis in the mathematics curriculum. Indeed, many of the youngsters who have used the program have discovered, as one of them put it, "I don't need this program. If I pay attention to the units, I can use my own calculator!" It does, however, serve to attract the attention of both children and teachers to a strategy that, while otherwise available to them, does not seem to be used.

people mathematics. We ask students to learn only the mathematics that others have made. If we were to teach language the way we teach mathematics, we would continually be asking students to learn a short story by Poe, an essay by Emerson, or a sonnet by Donne. At no point would we ask students to compose language of their own.

In order to make new mathematics, a student must be in a position to make, explore, and inspect the validity of conjectures. To bring about this state of affairs, it seems to me that at least two things must happen:

1. Students must be given tools that make the making, exploring, and verifying of conjectures easy and engaging to do.
2. Student must be told, both explicitly and implicitly, that such activity is meritorious and exemplary, rather than disruptive.

There is some reason to believe that appropriately crafted microcomputer-based tools can help to answer the first of these needs. For example, *The Geometric Supposer* [3, 4, 5] is a microcomputer-based environment that allows students to make arbitrarily complex Euclidean constructions on a primitive shape such as a triangle, quadrilateral, or circle. The *Supposer* remembers the construction as a procedure that can be executed on any other exemplar of the primitive on which it was made. In this environment, students have a ready way to break away from the particularity of specific constructions and to explore, detect regularities in particular instances, and immediately inspect any conjectures they might make based on those regularities. In two years of pilot testing, we have begun to be less startled when a student formulates a new theorem, or when students argue that demonstration, while encouraging, is not equivalent to formal proof[6].

What about the need to tell the student that the making of conjectures is meritorious rather than disruptive? This is a need that permeates the problem of the improvement of science and mathematics education. Addressing it will almost certainly not involve the computer or any other of our tools. It will involve us and our convictions. Ultimately, answering this need will require resolve, knowledge, and very hard work.

Afterword

The need to educate youngsters to attend to the particular and to infer generality from it permeats every field and every level of educational endeavor. Traditionally, we have thought of this ability as one that is associated with intellectual maturation, a process that we might recognize but not be able to influence in important ways.

I have tried to show that, at least in the domains of mathematics and science, the new information technologies offer a peculiar opportunity for helping this process along. The thoughtfully designed microcomputer environment can provide a unique way of multiplying the variety of students' experiences and intensifying their impact. If we seize the opportunity, perhaps we can begin to educate our citizens of all ages in richer and more fulfilling ways.

References

1   J. L. Schwartz. *Sir Isaac's Games*. Pleasantville, N.Y.: Sunburst Communications, 1985.
2   J. L. Schwartz. *The Semantic Calculator*. Pleasantville, N.Y.: Sunburst Communications for Education Development Center, Newton, Mass., 1983.
3   J. L. Schwartz and M. Yerushalmy. *The Geometric Supposer: Triangles*. Pleasantville, N.Y.: Sunburst Communications for Education Development Center, Newton, Mass., 1985a.
4   J. L. Schwartz and M. Yerushalmy. *The Geometric Supposer: Quadrilaterals*. Pleasantville, N.Y.: Sunburst Communications for Education Development Center, Newton, Mass., 1985b.
5   J. L. Schwartz and M. Yerushalmy. *The Geometric preSupposer*. Pleasantville, N.Y.: Sunburst Communications for Education Development Center, Newton, Mass., 1985c.
6   R. M. Kidder. "How high-schooler discovered new math theorem." *Christian Science Monitor,* April 19, 1985, p. 19.

CHAPTER 5

Thinking on paper:
a philosopher's look at writing

V. A. Howard

1. The communication fetish

I first perused the literature on writing improvement not as a philosopher or symbol theorist but as a teacher looking for practical advice for my students, particularly those who complained that they "had all the ideas but simply could not find the right words to express them." What I found was good advice and bad theory; that is, the suggested procedures for overcoming "writer's blocks," for collecting and editing ideas on paper, and the like, did not square with the prevalent opinion that writing is first and foremost communication. That view of the nature of writing struck me as being at odds with the advice given but at the core of many of my students' problems.

Especially harmful, in my view, is the way preoccupation with communication reinforces the tendency to dwell on either the final results or the psychological origins of writing, to the exclusion of the activity of writing. As teachers and students we are understandably concerned with results, with writing that communicates well. But when the preoccupation combines with the popular notion that writing ability is a "gift" or inborn talent, the effect is to cloak the activity of writing in false mystery. Add to the pot the mistaken belief that good writers find "just the right words right away," and the mystery is complete. Little wonder that writing takes on the proportions of a Quixotic quest.

Communication is surely an important objective of writing, but not the only one, nor the first. I shall take a differing view that the primary goal of writing, like reading, is to *understand* and then to make that understanding *available* to others in writing. In other words, the first use of writing is to think *with*—to articulate ideas—and by reshaping those thoughts on paper, to communicate them. In elaborating this view, my objective is to revise our understanding of writing instruction so as to bring theory and practice into closer proximity.

2. Bringing words and ideas together

Oscar Wilde said, "To be intelligible is to be found out." Wilde's remark captures the essence of what I shall call an articulation (to contrast

This article is adapted from *Thinking on Paper*, co-authored with James H. Barton (New York: William Norrow, 1986.)

with a communication) theory of what writing is. Writing both articulates and communicates if it is intelligible, but it is precisely the *dual* nature of writing that is obscured by subsuming so much of it under the label 'communication.'

From the practical side, my explanation to students of articulation, or thinking on paper, runs like this.

> The idea is to learn to write primarily for your own edification and only then for the eyes of others. The aim is to use writing to become more intelligible to yourself—to find your meaning—as well as to communicate with others—to be found out.
>
> In simplest terms, thinking on paper is the practice of writing things down as you go, as you think things through. That includes note-taking, marginalia, shopping lists, private reflections (as in a diary or journal), calculations and diagrams, queries and ideas jotted down in haste on scraps or envelopes, and so forth. Feelings and attitudes, values and wishes, figure prominently in such scribblings. Indeed, thinking on paper is anything set down to help you to remember, organize, relate, deduce, explain, evoke, express; in other words, anything that aids your understanding of the topic at hand.

This is fairly standard advice whether it is called "thinking on paper," "free writing" (Elbow, 1981), "generative writing," or "unconscious writing" (Trimble, 1975). Why is this paper thinking so important to writing? Obviously, such jottings as referred to above constitute the raw materials of a finished piece of writing after editing, when it is intended not merely to record one's thoughts but to communicate them to an audience. It is a question of becoming accustomed to thinking concretely, be it with pencil and paper or on a word processor. The writing manuals are full of clever strategies for getting ideas down on paper. However, in the interest of better explaining such practice, I will focus on the parallel question, why is this paper thinking so important to understanding?

3. Three propositions

What I am calling for convenience an articulation theory of writing rests upon three propositions that help to explain the complex relations among writing, thinking, and communicating. They are:

1. Writing is a symbolic process of mean-making;
2. Writing for others is a performance, rather like a well-rehearsed stage presentation; and
3. Writing serves understanding first and communication second in the broad senses inclusive of thinking, feeling, and perceiving.

From these three propositions it follows that writing is thinking on paper in which both writer and reader are witnesses to meaning-in-the-making, a meaning that the writer creates and the reader attempts to recreate. Each of these propositions clarifies different aspects of writing actively.

Proposition 1: Writing is a symbolic process of meaning-making

Symbols are essential to any process of meaning-making, including writing. The fact bears mention, for many people seem unaccustomed to think of letters, words, or language as such as consisting of symbols, perhaps because speech itself appears so "second nature." To others, the word 'symbol' connotes the idea of obscure meaning, meaning that is esoteric or hidden, requiring special training or sensitivity to understand. Examples of the latter would include poetic imagery, religious icons, the hidden meanings of dreams, or the "body language" of gestures.

Symbols can be either special, like the aforementioned, or quite commonplace. In fact, the word 'symbol' applies to anything that carries meaning, usually by standing for something else: like the word 'cat,' or *gato* in Spanish. So the realm of symbolism in the prosaic sense of the term encompasses words, languages generally, and a host of other kinds of symbols: maps, road signs, gestures, numerals, diagrams, pictures, and the like (cf. Goodman, 1972).

Symbols mediate not only communication but thought itself, and language is our most common symbolic tool to think with: silently to ourselves, or aloud or in writing to ourselves or to others. Everywhere symbols are used, the purpose is the same: to make meaning, to shape the world in some way, to fix, as on a photo plate, our view of things. If symbols are confused or one fails to grasp *how* they mean—as with abstract paintings, abstruse codes, or unknown languages—communication fails. Certainly we do not create the world with our symbols, but whatever the world comes to *mean* to us is literally a symbolic achievement. And the meanings we attach to things and events outside ourselves shape us in turn, including how we think, feel, act, and react. We grasp what our grasp of symbols enables us to grasp.

Practically what this means is that communication in writing is never perfect and seldom complete. Perfect communication, in the sense of direct transmission of meaning from one mind to another (telepathy), never occurs in writing. Writing is always *mediated thought*, thought that is embodied in an intervening structure of language. Communication is seldom complete except in very simple statements like, "Go left!" or, "It's raining"; and even those can misfire if the context is unclear. "Go left!"—at the next intersection or politically? "It's raining"—outdoors or in my heart?

The best a writer can do is to create a tapestry of meaning that enables the reader to unravel that meaning as best he or she can. Of course there are no guarantees that one will fully articulate the intended meaning or that one's reader will fully grasp it. Success or failure can occur on either or both sides.

Attending to these simple facts lays to rest two inhibiting preconceptions about writing already mentioned: namely, that it aims solely at communication (ignoring articulation), and that such communication should be perfect and complete. Both engender the self-defeating quest to get it right the first time, perhaps the single greatest "block" to writing at all.

Proposition 2: Writing for others is a performance, rather like a well-rehearsed stage presentation.

Writing is a performance in two ways. First, the text continues to perform in meaning long after it is written. One has only to read over an old newspaper, essay, or letter to realize how much the written word has a life of its own. The prospect of reinterpretation, of acquiring new meaning, lies in wait for all surviving texts however humble.

Writing becomes a personal performance, however, the moment the writer becomes conscious of a possible audience (including one's later self). Up to that moment, writing is a private activity of thinking on paper, a relatively unselfconscious effort to shape one's thoughts without any intention to share them as such. No sooner does one ask how the words look or sound, or step back to criticize their gist, then one is performing for others' eyes. That marks the difference between mere articulation and *revision,* a critical second phase of writing directed at communication.

Psychologically, we shift constantly from the one state of mind to the other, from the struggle to articulate to the struggle to communicate, and often the two are combined in fluent speech and writing. To put it another way, a moment comes in the writer's odyssey when discovery and criticism recombine in a single effort. When that happens, like a stage performance, writing becomes performing. Virtually all the instructional manuals agree, however, that it is crucial for efficiency to separate writing for discovery from writing critically for presentation, particularly in the early stages of writing (see Elbow, 1981; Trimble, 1975; Jacobi, 1976; et al.).

This is because discovery and criticism are often mutually disruptive, originating in different mental attitudes and having different objectives. Discovery connotes exploration, speculation, intuition, imagination, risk-taking, a suspension of doubt, a headlong plunge down corridors of new thought and experience. Criticism, on the other hand, connotes cool detachment, doubt, skepticism, testing, rigorous assessments of logic and evidence. Above all, criticism differs from discovery in its ruthless penchant for rejection. Together, they represent the True Believer and the Doubting Thomas within us—two mighty antagonists not easily appeased at the same time. Neither will it do in theory to cloak them indiscriminately under the label of "communication."

Proposition 3: Writing serves understanding first and communication second in the broad senses inclusive of thinking, feeling, and perceiving.

The act of writing is father to thought itself. The fact that our private scribblings may be unintelligible to others as they stand, or even to ourselves later on, should not obscure their use as *thoughtful* scribblings. This is not to underrate the importance of writing that communicates well, but, rather, to underscore the fact that writing—the act of writing itself—can span the painful gap so many writers feel between first thoughts and their final expression. Putting articulation before communication also reminds us that whether thinking silently, aloud, or in writing, our thoughts are not so much in pursuit of words as we use words to pursue our thoughts. Later, by revising the words that first snared our thoughts, we may succeed in capturing the understanding of others.

The main difficulty with the writing as communication idea is that it is a half truth parading as a whole truth. It overlooks writing's first meaning-making or articulation phase that is so crucial to getting started. Writing as communication also carries two further inhibiting suggestions: first, that thinking always precedes writing in two stages, of thinking now and finding the "right" words later; and second, that "genuine" or "real" writing is the public, final expression rather than the personal instrument of thought (cf. Trimble, p. 15). No better recipe for so-called "writer's block" could be devised, for it aggravates the worst of perfectionist tendencies; namely, the irrational drive to get everything right the first time. Half truths die hard, however, and do a lot of damage before they do; so let us briefly examine how premature stress on communication can frustrate the very effort to write.

4. Waiting for the muse

We have already observed how writing as communication tends to drive a false wedge between thinking and writing. An especially paralyzing version of that separation is the notion that the Muse resides somewhere within the "unconscious" and that one must wait for *it* to act rather than oneself prodding, probing, and producing. The Muse is supposed to work behind the scenes, secretly manipulating conscious awareness and suddenly dispensing gifts of gab.

On this widely accepted view, writing is usually seen to be the outcome of "incubation"—passive unconscious thinking—or "inspiration" in the form of sudden flashes of insight. No doubt such things happen, but it is debilitating to reply upon them. Writing is an activity, something one does, not something that "happens." Waiting for the Muse to act *for* one easily becomes an excuse for not writing and is a natural ally of procrastination—the writer's blood enemy.

From a practical point of view, both incubation and inspiration are better seen as the rewards for making an effort, not the secret puppeteers of hand and mind. Anyway, incubation occurs, if at all, when one is *not* working, in periods of rest or reverie (see Perkins, 1981, pp. 50–53). By and large, we invoke ideas like inspiration and incubation when we don't know what pushed us this way or that, or, having done well, we wish to cloak our achievements in mysterious origins. It is not that we are deliberately deceitful; rather, these are the "throw-away" explanations that most readily come to hand.

This is not to say that concepts of the unconscious, of inspiration, of incubation, or of imagination are vacuous. Rather, they are so full of different meanings as to be useless and misleading when casually invoked to explain "creative" or merely thoughtful activities: useless because they explain nothing; and misleading because they nudge us towards false conceptions of what we are doing.

Nor is this to belabor a point, for the communication fetish and its attendant distortions afflict not only popular thinking about writing but the instructional literature as well. For example, in his otherwise excellent book, *Writing with Style,* J. R. Trimble speaks of "unconscious writing"—the kind that amounts to "simply putting thoughts on paper" (p. 15). Trimble contrasts that sort of writing with "genuine writing," where the writer is attempting to communicate with an audience. When writing unconsciously, the writer, he says, is "not writing at all; he's merely communing privately with himself" (ibid.).

First off, such writing is not at all "unconscious." Rather, it is deliberately *writing one's mind* as the thoughts occur. Or, to reverse the point, such writing is no more unconscious than any other thinking to oneself. Nor is it any less "genuine" than writing for others. But being of the opinion that "All writing is communication" (p. 16), Trimble is led to explain writing for oneself as somehow less genuine, less real, less conscious, than writing for others. Better no explanation than one that describes those all-important first thoughts on paper as "not writing at all." Trimble is not alone in his opinions. The majority of writing manuals offer similarly one-sided accounts of writing that fail to square with their often useful advice on how to do it.

5. The question of creativity

Because most writing manuals pass too quickly over meaning-making in their preoccupation with meaning-communicating, they overlook the role of writing as thinking in their explanations of the process. The net result is to make the generation of ideas and creative thought even more mysterious than they are.

To be fair, most manuals recommend jotting things down as a way to get started under such labels as "pre-writing," "free writing," "directed writing," or "unconscious writing." The labels vary somewhat, as do the specifics of the advice. By any name, this amounts to the wise counsel that new ideas more often come from writing than waiting. But why? What is the connection between writing and "creativity"? Are one's humblest jottings all somehow "creative"? Surely not. It helps to defuse the paradox to recall that the very act of writing itself is a way of thinking anew—of generating ideas—but that generativity and creativity are overlapping, not synonymous, concepts.

This in no way diminishes the ultimate mystery of "creativity"—of *original* thinking—but it does diminish the false mysteries of the relations between writing and thinking, on the one hand, and between generating and creating on the other. To be thinking *is* to be generating ideas: from which it follows that writing is also generating ideas. Is that to be creative too? That depends. One might only be creating nonsense. But in the minimal sense of being the cause of some result, it is indeed "creating."

Still, that is not what is usually meant by being creative. The stronger use of creativity means producing something original, new, of exceptional quality, insight, power, or incisiveness. In other words, judgments of creativity are judgments of merit over the results achieved. From which it does *not* follow that to be thinking, generating ideas, is necessarily to be creating anything worthwhile. It makes perfect sense for someone to assert, "I am writing," "I am thinking," "I am generating ideas." But the moment someone says, "I am creating," we are tempted to ask, how can you be sure? Let's wait and see.

Creativity mostly concerns the value of results achieved. *Creating,* the active verb, refers to whatever we do to get those valuable results, and that could be just about anything. We judge our activities to be creative only if their results are creative in comparison to other, similar efforts. One is a creative writer, thinking, planner, artist, only if one's prose, theories, forecasts, or compositions are better than or equal in quality to the best known or available (Howard, 1982, pp. 117–29).

Such judgments are highly variable, of course, and often mistaken. Moreover, they vary with the nature of the task. But the point is this: the question of creativity in writing as elsewhere is a question of how *well* we think, perform, and produce. It is not a question of mysterious origins so much as of meritorious achievements in any given domain. However "inspired" or enthusiastic one feels, results tell the tale, and there are no guarantees. Having little control over creativity as such, we nonetheless can control our thinking, writing, and shaping of ideas; for these can be brought together in the single activity of thinking on paper.

6. Summary thoughts on writing and thinking

I want to survey the ground just covered with an eye to what writing is, what it is not, and what it involves. The objective is certainly no definition, but instead, a clearer conception of writing instruction that clears away certain inhibiting preconceptions and half truths.

To the claim that all writing is communication, I reply that the first function of any symbolism, including language in any form, is to shape our experience and understanding of things. Hence, writing is a dual activity of meaning-making *plus* communication. One may do both at once as in speaking or familiar writing tasks, but not all articulation is communication or intended to be, nor is it any less "genuine" for never escaping beyond the first-person solitary singular.

To the question, "Where do the ideas come from that we seek words to express?" I reply that the question itself is wrongheaded. It is wrongheaded in suggesting that ideas come from some source other than the use of language (or other symbols), and wrongheaded also in suggesting that two tandem processes are involved: first the thinking "behind" the writing, followed by the writing itself.

To the persistent notion that writing is a matter of Creative Process or waiting for the Muse to goad one into it, I reply that thinking to oneself can be silent, or talking aloud to oneself, or writing to oneself. While all three are equally *thinking*, the most useful and accessible form is that which leaves a record on tape, disk, or paper. This way of putting the matter makes clearer *why* such a record enables one to take control of the writing process by activating further thought (symbolic activity) and thus avoiding an anguished wait for the gift of perfect words.

What these challenges to prevalent opinion illustrate is the practical utility of coming to grips with the nature of writing and the very different reasons for doing it. My emphasis upon writing as a symbolic activity is intended to unite thinking and writing in a conception of writing that avoids (1) the sheer terror that many people experience when confronted with the task of "finding words for their thoughts," (2) the paralysis and delays engendered by the perfectionist urge to get it all right from the start, and (3) the growing suspicions (usually false) when one waits too long to write *either* that one has nothing to say, *or* that one cannot find words to express one's ideas. All the practical strategies in the manuals for diminishing these obstacles could be summed up in a phrase such as, "Finding is doing." Giving proper weight to articulation as a necessary condition of communication in writing instruction corrects a serious imbalance in our understanding of what that means.

References

Berry, Thomas Eliott. *The Craft of Writing*. New York: McGraw-Hill, 1974.
Cassirer, Ernest. *Essay on Man*. New Haven: Yale University Press, 1945.

Elbow, Peter. *Writing With Power*. New York: Oxford University Press, 1981.
Goodman, Nelson. *Languages of Art*. Indianapolis: Hackett, 1972.
Hirsch, Jr., E. D. *The Philosophy of Composition*. Chicago: University of Chicago Press, 1977.
Howard, V. A. *Artistry: The Work of Artists*. Indianapolis: Hackett, 1982.
Jacobi, Ernst. *Writing at Work: Do's, Don't's, and How to's*. (Rochelle Park, NJ: Hayden, 1976.
Perkins, David N. *The Mind's Best Work*. Cambridge: Harvard University Press, 1981.
Trimble, John R. *Writing With Style*. Englewood Cliffs: Prentice-Hall, 1975.

CHAPTER 6

Computers at school?
Israel Scheffler

In an essay published a little over twenty years ago, I described American education as then in the throes of a return to formalism. What I referred to was the renewed emphasis of that period on academic values, and the rejection of earlier concerns with the child's growth as the center of the educational process. The return to formalism also involved what I described as a

> vast . . . emphasis on educational technology, the development of devices, programs, and new curricula for the more efficient packaging and distribution of knowledge. What [had been], in the days of progressivism, a broad concern for scientific inquiry into processes of growth, perception, and socialization [had], in the name of hardheaded research and development, become more and more a preoccupation with the hard facts comprising educational content, and their optimal ordering for transmission to the student.[1]

Having survived that return to formalism, and the wild swing to the opposite extreme succeeding it in the late 60s and early 70s, we are now heading back in the old formalistic direction, with the insouciant amnesia that has become a hallmark of our educational history. Then, the slogans were "excellence," "mastery," "structure," and "discipline"; and the devices were teaching machines, programmed instruction, and new school curricula prepared by experts in the disciplines. Now, the slogans are "excellence," "basics," "minimum competences," and "standards"; and the devices are television and, more particularly, the computer. Then as now, the rhetoric was couched in broad educational terms, but economic incentives were also at work, and educational motivations were powered by international rivalry. Sputnik was, to be sure, a Soviet achievement, whereas the feared plan for a fifth-generation computer is Japanese. Are we, nevertheless, simply experiencing a déjà vu, watching

Presented April 18, 1985 in the Schumann Distinguished Lecturer Series sponsored by the Interactive Technology in Education Program, at the Harvard Graduate School of Education, with the support of the Schumann Foundation. I also wish to call attention to Catherine Z. Elgin's critique of computer models of the mind in this volume, 51:4. Lastly, I am very grateful to my colleagues in the Philosophy of Education Research Seminar at Harvard, Catherine Elgin, Kenneth Hawes, V. A. Howard, D. N. Perkins, and Paul Smeyers, for critical discussion of a draft of my paper. Reprinted by permission, *Teachers' College Record* (Summer 1986) a rerun where only the names have been changed to protect the innocent of history?

I think not. There are certainly salient parallels of the sort just outlined—parallels of ideological direction and emphasis, of terminology and motivation. But two differences stand out. First, the progressivism against which the earlier formalism reacted was milder than the anti-establishmentarianism of the 60s and 70s, and plumbed shallower emotional depths in the nation at large. The anti-establishment trend of the recent period, tied as it was to the upheaval over the Vietnam war, the youth movement, and efforts to improve the status of minorities, had wider ramifications in society at large; it went far beyond the schools. The social, political, and educational reactions it has called forth have been correspondingly stronger and broader.

Second, the earlier formalism was independently narrower in its focus. It addressed the schools primarily, its vanguard composed of disciplinary scholars reforming school curricula, its technologies largely school-based. By contrast, the current technologies are broadly social in their impact; they are transforming society at large, and only secondarily the schools. Our children are living in a world already fundamentally altered by the television environment outside the school. They are growing into a world increasingly computerized in every sphere—industry, commerce, communications, transport, health care, science, government, and the military. Current technology is no mere affair of curriculum scholars. The school is now the tail, the whole world the computerized dog.

Indeed, the feeling that the computer revolution *must* be reflected in the school's basic offerings is widespread. Educators solemnly recommend computer literacy as a basic subject of study, advertisers frighten parents into buying computers so as to avert educational disaster for their children, salesmen present the computer as an instrument of achievement both in school and in life. Last year (1984), parents spent 110 million dollars on educational software alone, it was reported by Future Computing, Inc., according to the *New York Times*.[2] Swept by computer frenzy, the community is urged to express it at home and in the classroom no less than in other major institutions. If the general expansion of computerization is in fact here to stay, what are schools and educators to do? What *can* they do?

I suggest three things. First, they can take a critical attitude toward the pressures for computerization being brought to bear on education, recognizing that educational applications of the computer are not given or foreordained. There may indeed be good reasons of an educational sort for putting computers to use in the classroom. But I emphasize, "of an educational sort." Mere faddishness, or corporation hype, or status-seeking, or parental panic, or widespread social use are not enough. Second, taking an educational point of view respecting the computer, they can raise not only questions of effectiveness but also questions of value, alternatives, and side effects—ends as well as means. Third, they can be alert to the transfer of computer language to education and the consequent hazard that educational ends will be constricted to fit. In the remainder of my remarks, I shall elaborate on each of these three recommendations in turn.

These recommendations, it should be emphasized, are addressed primarily to educators rather than to the computer community. And I make bold to offer them despite my status as an outsider to this community because the use of the computer in education raises basic issues that are *general* rather than *technical,* and of serious concern to all of us.

The illusion of givenness

My recommendations, you will note, do not imply an anti-technology attitude. They do not urge educators to mount the barricades and fight the marauding technologists under the faded banner of humanism. There is, in fact, a know-nothingism about technology as there is a know-nothingism about pure science, arts, and humanities. Technology is no "evil empire" pitted in ultimate warfare against the realm of humane values. It is, after all, the transformation of the world through thought and, as such, essential and inescapable. Thought is ineffective without technique, technique impossible without thought. As John Passmore has put it,

> technology, the application of science, is itself an exercise of the human intelligence, the human imagination, the human gift for understanding. The pure mathematician who is reported to have rejoiced: "Well, thank God, no one will ever find a use for *that* piece of mathematics" is as ridiculous a figure as the Philistine depicted by Matthew Arnold, with his monotonous refrain, "What's in it for me?"[3]

The invention and development of the computer, specifically, are triumphs of the creative mind which all can applaud.

Yet it does not follow that the computer must therefore be regarded as a given for education. The illusion of givenness is largely an offshoot of strong independent pressures for computerization. There is, in fact, no necessity that compels an advancing technology to be mirrored in school offerings, nothing fated about it. We do well to note that the Japanese themselves, our primary competitors in the computing field, have not rushed to install computers in the classroom, relying instead on their traditional culture of schooling coupled with intensive academic work and school-family supports.[4] And Joseph Weizenbaum has reminded us of earlier technological enthusiasms, pointing to the example of home-movie cameras gathering dust in thousands of closets across the nation, by contrast with the rosy promise of home computers humming in a swelling crescendo from coast to coast.

I have described the illusion of givenness as largely an offshoot of the pressure for computerization. There is, I suggest, also a deeper source, i.e., the absolutizing of the computer as a means. Let me explain. The computer as a symbol-manipulating device for accomplishing various purposes in industry, management, research, and so forth is not *ipso facto* a means for achieving educational purposes. Its instrumental value does not automatically carry over from the former to the latter. To suppose it does is to absolutize its status as a means.

The point deserves some elaboration. To speak of an object as an instrument is to convey some implicit reference to a purpose. In abstraction from purpose, no object is an instrument or, what comes to the same thing, there are no all-purpose means. To describe a hammer as a tool is to imagine some purpose to which it is to be put, some context in which such a purpose is embedded. The concept of a means is a relational rather than a categorical one.

It follows that instrumentality for a designated purpose implies nothing about instrumentality for any other. A hammer's usefulness for driving nails says nothing about its suitability as a soup ladle. Nor, on the other hand, does it follow that driving nails is the only purpose to which it can be put. The stereotype of an object may indeed tend to constrict our thought of it to its standard or conventional use, but the stereotype is itself no more intrinsic to the object than its instrumentality. If a hammer *cannot* serve as a soup ladle, it *can* serve as a doorstop, or a bookend, or a paperweight. Its suitability for such non-conventional uses is neither guaranteed nor precluded by its stereotype but must be independently established for each case.

What holds for the hammer holds for any technology. That an object is described as a technological device bears implicit reference to a purpose; its usefulness for such purpose in itself neither implies nor excludes its fitness for any other. The property of being a piece of technology is not a physical but a teleological property. It is not given but acquired with purpose.

To question the educational usefulness of the computer is thus no denial of its usefulness in all sorts of other ways. Nor does its undoubted value in other of its roles imply anything about its value for education. To put the computer to educational use is in fact to transform it from one sort of instrument to another, to change its character as technology by throwing it into a new combination with human purpose. Its instrumental value for education is not a foregone fact, "out there," decreed by history. *What* our purposes are, *which* of these we choose to implement, *how* we apply our resources to the effort make all the difference—not merely to the application of technology but to its very constitution as such.

Educational ends and means

What educational purposes might then be served by computers? The answers that have been suggested are numerous and they will no doubt continue to proliferate. I will comment on four of these, not by any means to provide definitive appraisals, but only to illustrate the sorts of questions that should, I believe, be addressed to such proposals.

1. One answer that has been given is that training in computers would provide marketable skills to children growing up in an increasingly computerized world. The computer's role is that of a vocational educator, preparing the masses of our youth for jobs in the future. This answer has been disputed. It has been argued that while some of our youth will obtain employment as computer experts, the promise of such employment to the general student body is empty. Henry Levin and R. W. Rumberger, for example, hold that "the proliferation of high technology industries and their products is far more likely to reduce the skill requirements of jobs in the U.S economy than to upgrade them." And Seymour Papert has been quoted as saying that because computer technology is advancing so rapidly, "what children are learning today [about computers] is going to be irrelevant when they get out of school."[6]

All our youth will of course be affected by the computer in a myriad of ways. They will become familiar with it and its effects in banks, schools, businesses, supermarkets, hospitals, and libraries. But does it follow that, because these effects are widespread, the jobs will be as well? Should the masses of our youth be trained for Hollywood because of the prevalence of the movies, or for Detroit because of the widespread effects of the automobile? The question of future employment possibilities is of course an empirical one. There is, at any rate, no direct inference to be drawn from the social pervasiveness of the computer to the reliable promise of pervasive employment.

Even were such promise true, it would not follow that schools should provide the requisite training. Corporations and businesses have frequently argued, with respect to vocational education generally, that schools can best contribute to the general education of their students and to the development of students' social skills and character, leaving the rest to on-the-job experience. Whatever the truth may be on this issue, such alternatives must at least be explored. Again, it is worth noting the Japanese experience, in which schools have so far retained their traditional orientations, while the youth have acquired familiarity with the computer through informal means.

2. A second answer is more modest. It argues that schools should prepare students in a general way for the computerized world they will inhabit. This answer does not promise the youth employment in programming, for they will, in all likelihood, be consumers of programs rather than producers. However, so the argument runs, any child not

prepared to deal generally with computers in the future will be handicapped in a variety of ways, personal, social, and economic, no matter what occupation he or she may follow. For even as a consumer of programs, the child will require facility with computers and at least some understanding of the process of programming. Some such line of thought seems to underlie the notion of "computer literacy," merging as well with the "minimum competency" rhetoric and the "basic skills" idea. The role of the computer is here envisaged not as a species of vocational education but as perhaps akin to driver education in supplying our youth with abilities without which they would be handicapped in life.

Now let us concede that knowledge of the computer will indeed be essential for adequate functioning in the future and, as such, generally desirable. Does it follow that *schools* should invest a significant effort in this direction? Exactly what type and what level of knowledge are, in fact, thought to be required? Do the requisite abilities presuppose a theoretical understanding of computer science, or only one or another degree of operational facility? The way in which such questions are answered makes all the difference in the world in determining the school's proper role.

How many drivers understand the theory of the internal combustion engine? How many telephone or TV users have analogous theoretical understanding? Driver education, premised on the public interest in traffic safety, leads no one to exalt "driver science" to the level of a New Basic Skill, along with English and mathematics, as *A Nation at Risk* does for computer science.[7] Yet if only operational facility is involved in either case, why the disparity? It might be suggested that the level of operational understanding required of the computer consumer is significantly higher than that required of the automobile consumer, but a detailed argument would have to be made to this effect. In any case, it would further need to be argued that the school is the preferred locus for acquiring such understanding, rather than out-of-school experience. It is ironic that academic formalists, providing neither argument, often advocate a computer literacy that may require no formal schooling at all, or at best at a level comparable to that of driver education.

3. A third answer is that the computer would enhance the learning of traditional school subjects. Unlike the previous two answers, which urged the importance of learning *about* the computer, the present answer advocates *using* the computer to learn about other things. The idea is to have the computer pick up the rote and repetitive aspects of traditional learning, providing as much individualized drill, practice, feedback, and evaluation as may be needed for students to reach suitable levels of mastery. The computer is here thought of as a mechanical drill sergeant or, more generally, a mechanical teacher's aide.

As such, the computer has undoubted assets. It can connect with the student's learning process at any level and carry it further, in a manner unhampered by personal biases or social prejudices. It is also enormously patient (so to speak), providing as much practice and response as may be needed by the student to achieve any degree of mastery of school subjects. Behind some of the recent talk of computer literacy lurks perhaps this idea as well: that facility with the computer will enable its use to drill students in the basic skills associated with academic subjects.

Whether such use would indeed be generally effective in developing skills and improving academic learning is an empirical question on which I am glad to defer to educational practitioners and researchers. I consider here only whether an affirmative answer would imply that schools should adopt such use forthwith.

Effectiveness would not in itself, I suggest, warrant such a conclusion. Any means effective in achieving a given end will have costs, side effects, further consequences, and alternatives, all of which require consideration. A recent *New York Times* article reports the insight that flashcards may rival the computer in teaching rote materials.

Children may initially be more willing to learn their multiplication tables with a computer-graphics program than with flashcards because of the novelty of the learning device. But the motivation often wears off quickly because the process of rote learning is no more creatively addressed on the screen than it is with cards.[8]

In general, one would at least need to consider such questions as the following before moving directly from computer effectiveness to school adoption. What alternative methods might be employed to the same end? What would be the relative social and economic costs? What would be the expected effects on equal access for all children? What consequences might be anticipated for school structure, student motivation, teacher training, school curricula, and the social and moral climate of learning? These questions are not meant to be rhetorical. I list them not as a way of rejecting the proposed use of the computer in the school, but only to argue that they require consideration. Such consideration might well sustain the proposal in question. But it would do so on grounds that go beyond the mere effectiveness of the computer in drilling students in basic skills.

One potential side effect is worth special mention. Effective use of the computer in the manner proposed here might encourage complacency with respect to basic skills; such complacency might, in turn, scant other uses of the computer for education in higher level skills. A related effect seems already to have occurred in connection with the general recent emphasis on so called basics. The *New York Times* of April 14, 1983 thus describes educators as interpreting the recent mathematics survey of the National Assessment for Educational Progress as showing "an emerging trend in the nation's schools: younger students are improving in the basics and older students are doing worse in high-level skills." The report attributed "much of the positive change . . . to improved performance on rather routine items." However, "in general, students made much more modest gains, or no gains at all, on items assessing deep understanding or applications of mathematics."[9]

The president of the National Council of Teachers of Mathematics, Stephen S. Willoughby, was quoted by the *Times* as saying that "the only things we see improvement on—basic calculations—are things that a calculator can do better than a person. There is no way we can survive if kids do well only on "trivial skills and don't show an understanding at a high level." In both reading and mathematics, there seems to be a similar pattern, according to Mary M. Lindquist, quoted in the same *Times* report: "In both subjects, we may be concentrating on those skills that are easiest to teach and learn and neglecting the thinking skills that are not so easily taught and learned."[10] The moral seems to be that while basic skills need to be learned, higher skills also require nurture. Putting the computer to work on effective drilling in the basics ought not to fill us with such educational self-righteousness that we forget about developing higher level capacities.

4. This leads us to the fourth answer to our main question. This answer is that the computer should be used to help develop creative problem-solving abilities. Rather than serving primarily as an adjunct to the traditional academic subjects, the computer is to be used to promote logical, cognitive and reasoning abilities—what may be called, speaking generally, critical thinking, inclusive of inventive approaches to problems. The computer is to be not a drill sergeant but rather a trainer or coach in developing the student's capacity to solve problems.

This proposal has several of the same advantages as those of the previous one. Its interaction with the student is free of biases, it can be prolonged to any degree necessary for the learning task in question, and it lends itself to individualization of instruction. The question of its effectiveness in promoting critical thinking is, as before, an empirical question. But the setting of suitable criteria of success is here more controversial than in the case of drilling for mastery of basic skills, and involves more urgently the question of transfer. And, assuming the method to be effective by any suitable criteria, questions analogous to those raised for the previous case would be relevant here as well, e.g., questions of cost, alternatives, side effects, and further consequences.

On one issue, the present idea has an advantage over the last one. It places emphasis upon higher level, creative capacities, offering a maximal rather than a minimal vision of cognitive competences to be fostered. It tends in this way to counter the image of education as bounded by the familiar academic *subjects,* and to import the notion of *problems* as primary. Thus it moves to break out of the formalist mold which associates the computer with a hard education in the traditional subjects. But empirical evaluation remains to be dealt with, i.e., are there determinate criteria of success by which the computer can be shown to offer advantages in promoting creative problem-solving capacities?

Indefinitely many further applications of the computer to education might be devised. Nothing I have said implies that only the above four are possible or that they are the most desirable. I have used these four examples to illustrate the point that no computer use is inevitable and that every such use ought to run the gauntlet of questions ranging beyond considerations of effectiveness.

Computer language

I want now to consider a large-scale side effect of computer use—the impact of computer language on our conception of educational ends. Specifically, I address the potential constriction of such ends through our hypnotic fascination with the computer.

The question to be raised here is not one of efficiency in achieving the ends designated; I concede, for the sake of the present argument, that the computer has been empirically shown to be effective in any or all of the ways previously discussed. Precisely if our means are effective in achieving certain ends are we tempted to lose sight of other and more elusive ends of ours. I have already mentioned the emphasis on basic skills as having encouraged the neglect of higher-level capacities. Similarly, "teaching to the test" is easier than teaching for understanding; teaching facts and habits easier than teaching methods and dispositions. I spoke earlier of the *absolutizing of means*. What concerns me now is the *expansion of means* at the expense of ends.

Nor is this tendency peculiar to education. We naturally tend to shrink our vision of the world to our mode of access to it. As infants, we have to learn that there are objects beyond our field of vision and, as we grow, continually to expand our imaginative construction of the world beyond experience. Throughout life, our perception favors those things assimilable to our categories, rubrics, and models; what does not fit is noted only with difficulty. As researchers, we tend to identify our problems with those questions answerable by our chosen methods. It is no wonder that the phenomenon repeats itself again and again in the field of education.

*The general point is this: as the computer's presence grows, the whole array of our educational ends tends to shrink to what is achievable or supposed achievable by computer. Instead of understanding the computer as a means to goals independently sought, we tend to redefine our goals so as to match what computers may do. From its initial status as a technology for promoting independently specified educational values, the computer thus becomes transformed into a general criterion of value. And the whole process is facilitated by language transfer.

Even without hard evidence for the educational efficacy of the computer, the mere promise of such efficacy promotes the transfer of computer language to education. Such transfer tends to filter out ends and values that do not fit the metaphor—for example, ethical sensitivity, social perceptiveness, artistic expressiveness—so that the efficiency of the computer is expanded by definition. For it is the merest tautology that ends achievable by the computer are achievable by the computer. It is, however, far from tautologous that all educational ends are indeed achievable by the computer. Indeed, it is false, and improverishes education in fundamental ways.

There is a certain irony in this development. While computer language has promoted a reductive view of the realm of teleological and mental process, teleological language has enriched the view of computer processes. Thus, computer scientists and cyberneticists have increasingly employed teleological and, indeed, anthropomorphic language in working with the computer. They have also tried to simulate certain mental processes with their admittedly partial models, then transferring the unreduced teleological descriptions of such processes to these models. At the same time, researchers and educators have increasingly applied computer terminology to the mind, and tried to reduce mental functions to those of the machine, the whole reductive effort threatening to run in a logical circle.[11] How far we now are from a *genuine* reduction of mind may be illustrated by a recent comment of Shimon Ullman, head of the Weizmann Institute's National Center for Artificial Intelligence. According to Ullman,

> The main message of AI research seems to be those areas once considered inordinately difficult—such as designing a computer that can play world class chess—have proven relatively simple, whereas teaching a computer elementary tasks such as understanding English or visually discerning shapes, have proved nearly impossible. The main objective is to learn more about the brain through this research. The reason we're not sure just how to make computers intelligent is that we still aren't certain what goes on in the brain.[12]

Look at from the point of view of research, the transfer of languages from one realm to another exemplifies a creative strategy, often leading to progress. Certain analogies are suggestive enough to justify such transfers in the present case even if computers do not literally think and the mind is not literally a computer. One needs only to avoid making circular reductive claims. But looked at from the point of view of educational practice, the matter is more serious. For the computer metaphor acts to screen out what may be of the first importance, educationally speaking. The challenge confronting educators is to adopt whatever advantages computer uses may be shown to offer, while holding fast to their independent vision of educational values.

"The computer metaphor," as I intend this phrase, is actually a cluster of several related metaphors, operating in different ways and at different levels. Nor—and I emphasize this—is the computer metaphor bound to the strict understanding of the computer by the experts. It generates its force also, or even largely, from public conceptions of the matter, whether accurate or not. Now I want in what follows to concentrate on one major metaphor belonging to the cluster, that centered on the notion of *information*.

The notion of information

A prevalent public image of the computer is, surely, that of an information processor. Information comes in discrete bits, each expressing a factual datum. Data may be entered and stored in the computer's memory, retrieved from memory, and processed in simple or complex ways according to various programs, which instruct the computer exactly what functions to perform. These functions are in the nature of algorithms, specifying determinately how the data are to be transformed. The human operator determines that the solution to his problem might be computed by program from input data, punches in his instructions to the machine to institute the relevant program, and eventually sees the solution displayed on the screen before him.

Now to think of learning, generally, in these terms is undeniably suggestive. But see how much is left out of the picture. Learning takes place not just by computing solutions to problems, not even just by exchanging words, but by emulation, observation, identification, wonder, supposition, dream, imitation, doubt, action, conflict, ambition, participation, and regret. It is a matter of insight and perception, invention and self-knowledge, intimation and feeling as much as of question and answer. Even the understanding of an answer in everyday life involves catching not just the information literally conveyed by the words, but also what is expressed by their overtones and nuances and what is carried between the lines or in the silences. Such understanding is not, in general, reducible to computation.

The activity of the computer operator, in the public's mind, is isolated and cognitive, its vehicles the finger and the eye. But even our cognitive skills are social. They grow in the first instance out of interactions with others more skilled than we, in continuous processes of discussion, demonstration, and exchange. The activity of a learner involves all of his being. It is moral and muscular, visceral and vascular, social and historical, proceeding, in Dewey's words, by trying and by undergoing.

Learning advances not alone when new answers are gained but when old answers are lost, not alone when problems are solved but when solutions turn problematic. Indeed, the categories of question-answering and problem-solving are too meager to contain such educational successes as new competences formed, new attitudes crystallized, new loyalties shaped, new discriminations made, new appraisals formulated, new emotions felt, new insights gained, new challenges undertaken, new purposes assumed. Interactive technology is but the tiniest sliver of interactive life. Unless, indeed, the computer operator had been learning all his life and in multifarious ways before his first approach to the machine, he could hardly learn anything *from* the machine. What questions could he put, what purposes could he have, what significance could he possibly attach to the answers received?

The computer metaphor, as just considered, projects the situation of the computer operator upon the learner generally. Now consider another, and deeper, application of the metaphor, in which the learner is seen not as the operator but as the computer itself. Like the computer, he acquires information, stores it in memory, ready to retrieve and process it in order to solve the problems put to him. But here is the catch: the computer does not pose its own problems to itself, but requires an operator to do so, an operator with needs and purposes of his own. Without such needs and purposes, what constitutes a problem? What data require retrieval, and to what end? What functions ought to be activated, what needs fulfilled, what lacks satisfied? What can be the significance of information without appraisal in light of aims? Knowledge of one's enduring aims and purposes is, furthermore, not just another body of information, but a form of insight into the patterning of one's chosen problems, the setting of one's life tasks.

To speak of information and memory, not to mention knowledge, in reference to the computer, is itself a metaphorical transfer from the human case. To transfer such terms back from the computer to the mind, now emptied of the connotations of human activity, interpretation, need, and purpose, is an example of the irony I mentioned earlier. This double transfer in the context of practice leads us unwittingly to shrink our initial ideals of education and our conceptions of mind and schooling.

The everyday notion of information refers to material we can understand and interpret in context. Grasping what it expresses, we can paraphrase it and evaluate its contextual relevance, criticize and reject it, or back it up appropriately, respond to it with feeling, sense its metaphorical echoes, appraise its bearing on our purposes, and apply it in our activity. The computer itself cannot be properly described as doing any of these things, in the everyday senses of the terms involved. To characterize the electronic state of computer circuitry in terms of "information" is to employ the word under a different interpretation. Further to construe the mind in terms of "computer information" empties the human notion of virtually all its content.

It is important to emphasize that, even in its full-blooded human sense, the concept of information is far from capable of adequately expressing our educational aims. This is so even if we concentrate on the purely cognitive aims of schooling, as they relate to the enterprise of problem-solving. For although information is certainly essential to education, it is only part of the story. Consider: you can have been given a piece of information but fail to realize its significance either for the problem at hand or for action, more generally. You can accept that such and such is the case but be totally unable to give any good reasons for it, thus disqualifying yourself as really knowing that such and such is the case. You can know it but not recall it at the fitting moment, or recall it but be unable to apply it intelligently to the problem under consideration. You may indeed be *able* to apply it without being in general *disposed* to do so, not having formed the suitable inclination or character trait. The suggestion that at least the cognitive side of education can be fully expressed in terms of information transfer, storage, and retrieval would not be worth a moment's consideration were it not that it is implicitly conveyed by the current formalism, coupled with the public's awe of scientific facts.

To know a fact requires, however, as Gilbert Ryle has put it,

> having taken it in, i.e., being able and ready to operate with it, from it, around it and upon it. To possess a piece of information is to be able to mobilize it apart from its rote-neighbors and out of its rote-formulation in unhackneyed and *ad hoc* tasks.[13]

Now the Baconian image of science as an increasing accumulation of facts has independently distorted the ideal of education since well before the computer age. With "facts" now translated into "bits of information," the Baconian image is given modern dress. Just see how contemporary Mr. Gradgrind sounds when his little speech in Dickens's *Hard Times* is altered by replacing the word "fact" with "information." He is explaining his educational views to a teacher in the school he manages. I reproduce here the original passage, but you can mentally make the replacement at each occurrence of the word "Fact" or "Facts":

> Now what I want is Fact. Teach these boys and girls nothing but Facts. Facts alone are wanted in life. Plant nothing else, root out everything else. You can form the mind of reasoning animals upon Facts; nothing else will be of any service to them.[14]

The teacher addressed by Mr. Gradgrind agrees. He has learned and proposed to teach his students

> about all the Water Sheds of all the world; and all the histories of all the peoples, and all the names of all the rivers and mountains, and all the

productions, manners and customs of all the countries, and all their boundaries and bearings on the two and thirty points of the compass.[15]

Mr. Gradgrind considered the learning of such facts to be hard work. Current formalists think it can be made fun. The educational game selected as the best of 1984 by *Electronic Games* magazine, according to the *New York Times,* is one in which the player "must destroy the Fuzzbomb before it spreads across the entire nation. To confront the Fuzzbomb, the player or agent takes trains from city to city to get to the Fuzzbomb's location, which continually changes."[16] The presumed charm of this game is supposed to facilitate the student's learning to identify the state capitals. The same principle could no doubt be applied to the Water Sheds of all the world, and other such important facts.

Facts are, however, not the sorts of things imagined by Gradgrinds past or present. They are expressed in language, clothed in concepts, organized and transformed by theory, appraised by criteria of value, and intelligently or stupidly employed in the conduct of life. Neither the concepts nor the values we possess are automatically derivable from hard facts or data; they serve rather to mould the forms in which our putative facts are cast. These facts provide tests of our theories through their own credibilities but they do not generate these theories by any kind of routine processing. They are, in turn, responsible to our theories and tested by them. That we have the theories and facts we do is therefore a reflection not only of our mental capacities or of the "real world," but of our history and our intellectual heritage.

Even the capacity for *intelligent use* of information will not suffice to express our educational aims relative to problem-solving. Drawing on accumulated data is inadequate for accommodation to future change. What is wanted in addition is the generation of new information—information, moreover, that does not result simply from applying old categories to new circumstances. Devising new categories, composing new classifications, postulating new entities, guessing at new connections, inventing new languages and calculi are desiderata of the highest importance.

Problem-solving, further, needs not just the recognition and retention of facts but the recognition and retention of difficulties, incongruities, and anomalies. It does not simply affirm truths but entertains suppositions, rejects the accepted, conceives the possible, elaborates the doubtful or false, questions the familiar, guesses at the imaginable, improvises the unheard-of. An intelligence capable only of storing and applying truths would be profoundly incapacitated for the solving of problems.

When we move beyond problem-solving to consider educational aims in general, we find the computer metaphor based on "information" even more clearly inadequate. For we here encounter provinces long cultivated by rival metaphors, alien to the impression or transmission of facts. What I have elsewhere called the *insight model* is one such rival metaphor.[17] It speaks not of information but of insight and perception, vision and illumination, intuition of nuance and pattern, grasp of overtone and undertone.

A second such rival metaphor is that of *equipping,* or the provision of skills and capacities.[18] This is not a matter of storing answers, whether linguistic or numerical, it cannot be accommodated solely in information-theoretic terms. It concerns rather the forming or strengthening of abilities, the know-*how* commanded by a person, rather than his know-*that,* his capability to deal with the tasks and challenges of practice in the various domains of life. Nor is every bit of **know-how** accessible to algorithm, witness the comic's ability to make us laugh, the actor's capacity to make us weep, and the metaphorical ability itself, beyond the regimented interpretation of literal codes.

A third such rival metaphor is represented by what I have called the *rule model.*[19] This metaphor focuses on norms rather than capacities, on the pronenesses, likelihoods, tendencies, and dispositions of a person rather than on his mere abilities and skills—on what he *does* do rather than what he *can* do. In this realm we have again left the notion of information behind. For what is involved here is not the storing or transformation of data, but the shaping of habits of mind and feeling, the growth of attitudes and traits, the development of character. Our concern is not with knowing *that* nor even with knowing *how*. For we are dealing not with what people believe, nor with what they are equipped to do, but with what they can reliably be expected to do, with their predictable by typically unarticulated patterns of conduct, taste, and emotion. The inculcation of desirable patterns of this sort, beyond the reach of algorithms, is of the first educational importance, laying the foundations of mutual trust, common feeling, and shared value without which no community can stand, let alone thrive.

These various realms all require to be kept steadfastly in view as we make progress on any educational front. The whole array of ends must serve as the context within which we gauge our educational situation. Rather than cutting this array down to the size of our technology, we should strive to look beyond our technology, to determine the purposes and directions of our further efforts.

The computer has been associated with the recent swing to hard education, with the notion of raising standards, of higher achievement in academic subjects, of increased efficiency in the teaching of fact, of enhanced problem-solving capacity. All these matters are indeed important. There is no positive virtue in low academic achievement, inefficient teaching, or diminished problem-solving capacity. Whatever the computer may be able to accomplish in such areas is all to the good. No such accomplishment, however, should block our vision of equally vital educational goals, or shrink our highest ideals of learning. It is the task of educators to keep both means and ends in view.[20]

Notes

1 Israel Scheffler, "Concepts of Education: Reflections on the Current Scene," in Edward Landy and Paul A. Perry, eds., *Guidance in American Education: Backgrounds and Prospects* (Cambridge: Harvard Graduate School of Education, distr. Harvard University Press, 1964); repr. in Israel Scheffler, *Reason and Teaching* (London: Routledge & Kegan Paul, 1973), p. 59.

2 Peggy Schmidt, "What to Look for in Educational Software," *The New York Times,* Section 12 (Education, Fall Survey), Nov. 11, 1984, p. 8.

3 John Passmore, *The Philosophy of Teaching* (Cambridge: Harvard University Press, 1980), p. 115.

4 See Merry I. White. "Japanese Education: How Do They Do It?" *The Public Interest 76* (1984), pp. 87–101. White writes, "Computers and other technology do not play a large role in (Japanese) schools. . . . There is no national program to develop high technology skills in children. Americans spend much more money on science and technology in the schools; the Japanese spend more on teacher training and salaries" (p. 90).

5 In an address to the Philosophy of Education Research Center, Harvard University, Fall 1983. I am grateful to Professor Weizenbaum, whose pioneering critical reflections on the computer have taught me much. See especially, his book *Computer Power and Human Reason* (San Francisco: W. H. Freeman, 1976).

6 See Henry M. Levin and R. W. Rumberger, "The Educational Implications of High Technology," Project Report No. 83–A4, Institute for Research on Educational Finance and Governance, Stanford University, February 1983. These authors argue that "the expansion of the lowest skilled jobs in the American economy will vastly outstrip the growth of high technology ones" (Abstract).

   See also *The Boston Globe,* November 26, 1984, p. 42, which also quotes Seymour Papert as called "absurd" the "fear that children will be unprepared for the job market they face on graduation unless they have become 'computer literate'."

7 *A Nation at Risk,* U.S. Department of Education, Washington, D.C., April 26, 1983.

8 Schmidt, "What to Look for in Educational Software."

9 *The New York Times,* April 14, 1983.

10 Ibid.

11 Cp. the pioneering paper of Arturo Rosenblueth, Norbert Wiener, and Julian Bigelow, "Behavior, Purpose, and Teleology," *Philosophy of Science,* 10 (1943), pp. 18–24, which argues that the concept of "purposefulness" is "necessary for the understanding of certain modes of behavior" and that its

importance has been slighted owing to the rejection of final causes as explanatory; the authors then go on to interpret purpose in terms of negative feedback.

In my paper "Thoughts on Teleology," *British Journal for the Philosophy of Science,*[9] (1959), and then in my book, *The Anatomy of Inquiry* (New York: Alfred A. Knopf, 1963; repr. Hackett, 1981), I argued that if the Rosenblueth, Wiener, and Bigelow paper simply extends teleological language to selected forms of behavior of independent interest, there can be no quarrel with them,

> for in such a case, they would not be setting forth an analysis of teleology so much as striving to improve the description of the behavior in question through increased use of teleological language. If, however, as appears to be the case, they intend also to provide an *analysis* of teleological notions, their proposal may properly be judged by seeing how satisfactorily the analysis accounts for acknowledged instances of teleological behavior (p. 112).

My argument was that the authors' reduction of teleology to negative feedback does not succeed. But they thought it did and so, by their lights, were not arguing in a circle. But on my view, the claim to reduce human purpose to machine purpose by their method can achieve plausibility only by so enriching the latter as to encompass the former. But the trends I discuss in the text are quite general and go far beyond the above illustrative reference.

12   See *The Forward,* March 8, 1985, p. 33.
13   Gilbert Ryle, "Teaching and Training," in R. S. Peters, ed. *The Concept of Education* (London: Routledge & Kegan Paul, 1967), p. 111.
14   Charles Dickens, *Hard Times,* 1854, ch. I.
15   Ibid., ch. II.
16   Schmidt, "What to Look for in Educational Software."
17   Israel Scheffler, "Concepts of Education," pp. 71ff.
18   Cp. Gilbert Ryle, *The Concept of Mind* (London: Hutchinson, 1949), p. 310: "In a word, teaching is deliberate equipping."
19   Scheffler, "Concepts of Education," pp. 76ff.
20   I should like to call attention to the Summer 1984 issue of *Teachers College Record,* 85:4, which is devoted to discussions of the computer and education. Douglas Sloan's editorial introduction to the issue carries the admirable title, "On Raising Critical Questions about the Computer in Education."

CHAPTER 7

The design process
Donald A. Schon

Design, ambiguously signifying both process and product, is an exten-
sible term that has been stretched, of late, to include not only the design
of physical objects like buildings and tools, the traditional province
of the so-called design professions, but organizations, plans, policies,
strategies of action, behavioral worlds, and theoretical constructs—in
short, the entire range of artifacts made by human beings.

In the very broadest sense, designing is the process by which things
are made. In a sense only slightly less broad, designers make representations of things to be built. They shape materials to function in some
context through a web of deliberate moves and discovered consequences,
often unintended. Materials resist the imposition of form and it is a rare
move that has only its intended consequences.

Designing, so considered, has a flavor of ancient Greece. Its study is
a branch of poetics, derived from the Greek *poiein,* "to make." The
casuality of the design process suggests the interplay of Aristotle's
materials, formal, efficient, and final causes—as we might expect, given
Aristotle's understanding of casuality under the metaphor of design.

What would *not* be designing, on this view? Random or purposeless
behavior; processes so proceduralized (like ringing up items on a cash
register) that little or no room for decision remains; or the sort of
action on materials (like the weathering of a rock) in which deliberate
intervention plays a negligible part. We may design without knowing
that we do so, but not without forming materials to function in some
task environment.

In his well-known *The Sciences of the Artificial,* Herbert Simon has
proposed a view of design broad enough to encompass the making of
all varieties of human artifacts and a science of design that he character-
izes as a "science of the artificial."[1] He regards this science as the primary
basis for intellectual rigor in the professions, all professions, and he
distinguishes it from the natural sciences. Whereas the latter are concerned, in his terms, with "how things are," the science of design is
concerned with "how things ought to be, with devising artifacts to attain
goals,"[2] and, so construed, makes up "the core of all professional activity
. . . the principal mark that distinguishes the professions from the sciences."[3]

In all these respects, Simon has done a great deal to lay the groundwork for a much-needed epistemology of professional practice. The difficulty I have with his contribution is not the role he wants to create for a science of design but his approach to its definition. In this, moreover, Simon stands in a long tradition of theorists of design, decision-making, and problem-solving, a tradition that also includes, as I shall try to show, theories of biological, societal, economic, and policy change built on the metaphor of design. Adherents to this tradition have adopted certain fundamental strategies of analysis that seem to me to be radically incomplete. Through a critical analysis of Simon's theory, I want to explore how a more adequate theory of design might be developed.

In brief, Simon sees design as a problem-solving process. For him, design problems are instrumental problems in which one selects from available alternatives the best means for achieving some set of purposes, expressed in a "utility function." The designer transforms an existing state of affairs, a problem, into a preferred state, a solution. When his process is rational, it takes the form of a series of rule-governed decisions. Interestingly, natural science investigations and the discovery of mathematical proofs both qualify as design processes, in Simon's sense of the term, even though their subject matter has to do with the way things are rather than the way things ought to be.

The model of design as rational decision seems to me to be incomplete in three main respects, the first of which hinges on the idea of a design structure. A designer forms a representation of some initial design situation, framing a design problem that includes, when it is "well formed,"[4] elements from which to construct design options, a description of the situation in which options may be enacted as moves, and criteria sufficient to evaluate the effectiveness of proposed solutions. The design process is a series of transformations of such a representation according to rules that guide the sequencing and direction of design procedures. By design structure, I mean the designer's representation of a problem together with the rule-governed procedures that guide his transformations of it. In order for a design problem to be solvable, representation and procedures must be congenial to each other. In the case of Simon and others who hold the model of design as rational decision, the design structure is assumed to be given with the presented problem. For a rational decision process, in the sense required by the model, can occur only *within* such a structure. Hence the model does not explain how design structures are made and remade in the course of designing. In point of fact, well-formed problems and technical problem-solving tend to occur in actual designing only in later phases, after a basic design structure has stabilized.

Secondly, because of its division of designing into components of generation and selection, and because of its ways of conceiving of generation, the model of design as rational decision cannot account for important kinds of learning that occur within and across episodes of designing. In actual designing, designers often learn from earlier trials to reframe alternatives and even the problem itself. Moreover, each design project helps to prepare the designer for future projects. Designers "deuterolearn," in Gregory Bateson's phrase, to develop designs for designing.[5]

Finally, Simon, along with others of his general persuasion, tends to regard rational decision as a process that occurs within the mind of an individual. But actual designing is usually a social process, a dialogue among individuals in which different views of designing and different ways of framing design situations are pitted against each other. Design dialogues are dialectical unfoldings of conflicts among the views of design structure held by different parties to the dialogue. As design structures are made and remade in individual designing, so they are made and remade in design dialogues. Indeed, individual designing is often best understood as an introjection of design dialogue.

Design as rational decision

The model of design as rational decision depends on a strategy of analysis that divides designing into two main components, first the generation of alternatives (options for decision, or, as I shall call them, "design proposals", and second the selection of alternatives according to available decision rules. Rationality depends entirely on how selections are made. It is only a decision to select one option over others that *can* be rational or irrational, depending on its conformity or nonconformity to decision rules. Generating options is neither rational nor irrational but is best described as nonrational. In effect, the division of design processes into generation and selection is a strategy that separates out the one activity—decision making—that is presumed to be susceptible to rule-governed rationality.

A design process is considered rational, in the strongest and simplest case, if and only if its problem-solving steps are fully programmable under a set of designer rules. Simon illustrates such a case with his "diet problem":

> A list of foods is provided, the command variables being quantities of the various foods that are to be included in the diet. The environmental parameters are the prices and nutritional contents (calories, vitamins, minerals, and so on) of each of the foods. The utility function is cost (with a minus sign attached) of the diet, subject to the constraints, say, that it not contain more than 2000 calories per day, that it meet specified minimum needs for vitamins and minerals, and that rutabaga not be eaten more than once a week. The constraints may be viewed as characterizing the inner environment. The problem is to select the quantities of foods that will meet nutritional requirements and side conditions at the given price for the lowest cost.
>
> The diet problem is a simple example of a class of problems that are readily

handled, even when the number of variables is exceedingly large, by the mathematical formalism known as linear programming. . . .[6]

In cases like this, the design problem is an optimization problem solvable by the use of techniques derived from utility theory, statistical decision theory, and linear programming.

In more complex examples, the design problem has a larger decision structure made up of a series of decision nodes, each of which represents a finite set of options for action or information gathering. Depending on the decision taken at a node, new outcomes arise which yield further decision nodes, and so on, until the criteria of problem solution have been met. Again, such a process is considered rational if it is fully programmable, but in a somewhat different sense. Rules given from the outset must specify either the decisions to be made at each node in the structure or the procedures for calculating the benefits and costs of all possible options associated with each possible set of outcomes.

Consider, for example, a patient-specific process of medical care where, in a presented clinical situation, the patient is found to have pulmonary edema.[7] A basic treatment program specifies five responses: tourniquets, oxygen, aminophilin, digitalis, and diuretics. A fuller program specifies how the five responses relate to one another and to diagnostic conditions which could dictate exceptions to the simple program. For example, if digitalis has been given, or there is a prior history of digitalis, then diuretics are given and serum potassium is measured. If serum potassium is found to be low, potassium is given. If digitalis has not been given and there is no prior history of digitalis, then there need be no worry about potassium deficiency. The process can be represented by the following schema:

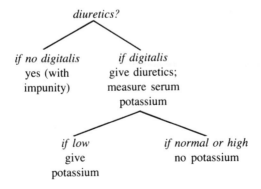

Figure 7.1

In the diet problem, where the starting information is complete, rules specify procedures for selecting the best option. Where outcomes or information relevant to decisions are not fully known in advance, as in the clinical problem, additional information can be gathered by following rules specified in the decision structure. In both cases, a decision structure fully articulates procedures for information gathering and treatment. It specifies all possible interventions and their connections to outcomes, and all possible information-gathering steps and their connections to categories of resulting information. The clinical example illustrates how the design process may be rational, in the sense of fully programmable, even when the starting information is incomplete.

Generating possible options for decision

The model of design as rational decision assumes a fully articulated decision structure given with the design situation. But most actual design situations fall short of this ideal. For example, existing medical knowledge may not enable us to predict all relevant outcomes and options for information gathering or action; or the co-presence of multiple diseases may present decision problems for which we are unable to formulate an adequate set of decision rules. For investigators committed to the model of rational decision, it is tempting to peel back the layers of this onion: if certain features of a decision structure are missing in real-world design, it may be possible to separate them out, one by one, and specify programs to create them.

Simon follows such a strategy. Beginning with simple cases like the diet problem, he gradually moves toward the complexities of real-world design, considering, first, a problem in which the decision structure is completely given except for a full set of options. "We cannot, within practicable computational limits, generate all the admissible alternatives and compare their respective merits. Nor can we recognize the best alternative, even if we are fortunate enough to generate it early, until we have seen all of them."[8] Here, Simon makes explicit the analytic strategy by which he splits the design process into components of generation and selection. Once all the admissible alternatives have been generated, the problem can be solved by selecting ("recognizing") one alternative as the best according to rules based on principles of utility and statistical decision theory. But what about the generation of admissible alternatives? How are we to understand it, too, as a rule-governed, programmable process? To this question, the design literature offers two main answers: random generation of combinations of given elements, or systematic search. Both answers link theories of designing to theories of biological and social evolution that were originally developed, as I shall suggest, under the influence of a metaphor of design. Both answers seem to me to leave unexplained what is most in need of explanation.

Random generation

Randomness has often been used as an approximate substitute for creativity in theories of problem solving, especially in the heuristic programming favored by Artificial Intelligence. But the idea is of much older provenance. Theories of biological, social, and economic evolution, of policy formation, of the psychology of creativity, and of organizational innovation have all relied, at various times, on a model according to which randomly generated design "proposals" are subsequently "disposed of" according to various criteria of selection. The beauty of this model is that one need not claim to know much about the generative process; ignorance is acceptable. Its cost is that one cannot identify particular proposals in advance but only the elements from which they will be constructed.

Here, the designer is assumed to have access to elements of design given with the design problem. Design options are combinations of elements, randomly generated (for example, by using a table of random numbers). Once generated, they are screened on the basis of criteria that are also presumed to be given with the design problem.

In some cases, theorists do not explicitly introduce the idea of randomness but treat the generation of combinations of elements as a blind, essentially mysterious process *as though* it were random.

Darwin's theory of the evolution of biological species asserts that random genetic variations yield a continuing supply of biological possibilities which are selected or rejected on the criteria of their fit with a changing environment. The evolving design of biological species results from many cumulative increments of generation and selection, "proposal" and "disposal." Although the great majority of proposals generated are inappropriate under given criteria of selection, some few turn out to be adaptive; their incremental incorporation into the genetic store of a species accounts for its evolution.

Darwin first applies this formulation to man's breeding of preferred varieties of plants and animals:

> . . . A high degree of variability is obviously favorable, as freely giving the materials of selection to work on; not that mere individual differences are not amply sufficient, with extreme care, to allow of the accumulation of a large amount of modification in almost any desired direction. But as variations manifestly useful or pleasing to man appear only occasionally, the change of their appearance will be much increased by a large number of individuals being kept. Hence the number is of the highest importance for success. . . . But probably the most important element is that the animal or plant should be so highly valued by man, that the closest attention is paid to even the slightest deviation in its qualities or structure.[9]

He went on to explain the mechanism of biological evolution in terms of the metaphor of "natural selection":

> If then, animals and plants do vary, let it be ever so slightly or slowly, why should not variations or individual differences which are in any way beneficial, be preserved and accumulated through natural selection, or by survival of the fittest?[10]

Social Drawinists applied a version of Darwin's theory to explain the evolution of societies. In *Social Change,* for example, William Ogburn spoke of the "selective cumulation" of customs:

> The material cultures possessed by a people in a particular location will, over a long period of time, show a large proportion actually lost. This would not be true to so great an extent for the world as a whole, though. However, it is certainly more accurate to refer to this particular cultural process as selectively cumulative; and by selective accumulation is meant the fact that new forms of material culture are added and some old ones discarded, there having been a selection. The additions have exceeded the discards, so that the stream of material culture of a particular people has widened with time.[11]

And economists, from Adam Smith onward, have relied on a model of the free market economy according to which the hidden hand of the market selects among products and production methods generated by firms, in ways unspecified by the theory, in order to secure the firm's competitive advantage—a process whose collective, cumulative result is economic progress.[12]

Christopher Alexander adopts a variant of this model in his description of processes of cultural design, by which a culture's artifacts reach what Alexander calls "an equilibrium of well-fitting forms":

> The basic principle of adaptation depends on the simple fact that the process toward equilibrium is irreversible. Misfit provides an incentive to change. Good fit provides none. In theory, the process is eventually bound to reach the equilibrium of well-fitting forms.[13]

By way of illustration, Alexander offers his well-known example of Slovakian peasant shawls:

> The Slovakian peasants used to be famous for the shawls they made. These shawls were wonderfully colored and patterned, woven of yarns which had been dipped in homemade dyes. Early in the twentieth century aniline dyes were made available to them. And at once the glory of the shawls was spoiled; they were now no longer delicate and subtle, but crude. This change cannot have come about because the new dyes were somehow inferior. They were as brilliant and the variety of colors was much greater than before. Yet somehow the new shawls turned out vulgar and uninteresting.

Now, if as it is so pleasant to suppose, the shawlmakers had had some innate artistry, had been so gifted that they were simply "able" to make beautiful shawls, it would have been almost impossible to explain their later clumsiness. But if we look at the situation differently, it is very easy to explain. The shawlmakers were simply able, as many of us are, to recognize *bad* shawls, their own mistakes.

Over the generations, the shawls had doubtless often been made extremely bad. But whenever a bad one was made it was recognized as such, and therefore not repeated. And though nothing is to say that the change made would be for the better, it would still be a change. When the results from such changes were still bad, further changes would be made. The changes would go on until the shawls were good. And only at this point would the incentive to go on changing the patterns disappear.

So we do not need to pretend that these craftsmen had special ability. They made beautiful shawls by standing in a long tradition and by making minor changes whenever something seemed to need improvement. But once presented with more complicated choices, their apparent mastery and judgment disappeared. Faced with the complex unfamiliar task of actually inventing forms from scratch, they were unsuccessful.[14]

Alexander does not use the word 'random.' He suggests something like it, however, when he speaks of generating changes in shawls, without saying how they are generated, and observes that changes are as likely to be for the bad as for the good. In order to account for an eventual equilibrium of well-fitting forms, he need postulate only the shawlmakers' ability to recognize needs for "improvement," generate new combinations from variables of color and pattern, distinguish good from bad changes, and store in cultural traditions the know-how to produce shawls that retain good changes.

Like Alexander, proponents of an incrementalist approach to planning and policy making—Charles Lindblom, for example[15]—take minor changes as the units of design. On this view, planners and policy makers always begin with an existing design; their limited knowledge and constrained situations prevent them from designing new forms from scratch. They initiate minor changes out of a confused sense that something needs improvement. According to some versions of incrementalism, policy changes, *ex ante,* are just as likely to be bad as good, but the good changes are more likely to be retained. The process of selective retention is sometimes attributed to planners (who, like the shawlmakers, are assumed to recognize bad changes when they see them) and sometimes to a kind of natural selection operating in the policy environment, leading in either case to a gradual, cumulative progress in policies and plans.

I have noted elsewhere that an analogous process was common to research and development practice in business firms during the late 1950s and early 1960s.

Those to whom the entrepreneurial task had been delegated confronted the new problem of innovation from within the corporation. They had no authority

to take leaps of decision on insufficient information which are essential to innovation. Instead, they could only propose upward to the boss, who disposed . . .
Those below proposed; those above disposed.
The process of innovation still had in it all the randomness and uncertainty . . .
[the subordinate] was continually floating balloons to the top of the company.
He would find the balloons, inflate them, let them go, and wait to see whether
they were shot down. Usually . . . they were. He would then have to infer, from
inspection of balloons shot down and those allowed to go up unimpeded, just
what would make a new development "go" in his company. . . .[16]

Here we also find a random, or at any rate unspecified, process for
generating many proposals, together with a tightly controlled method
(the boss's judgment) for selecting a few of them, on the basis of criteria
not necessarily fully specified in advance. In the '50s, managers not
only used the propose/dispose system but touted it as a superior means
of achieving product innovation.

When the model of random generation/programmed selection is carried to the workings of an individual's mind, we have theories of creative
problem-solving like that of Henri Poincafe, who proposed a stage theory
of mathematical invention: first, conscious work on a problem; then a
period in which ideas are incubated; sudden illumination; and finally a
new round of conscious work that confirms and develops the original
insight.[17] Poincafe is particularly concerned to explore how unconscious
work can produce illumination:

It is certain that the combinations which present themselves to the mind in
a sort of sudden illumination, after unconscious working somewhat prolonged,
are generally useful and fertile combinations. . . . all the combinations would
be formed in consequence of the automatism of the subliminal self; but only
the interesting ones would break into the domain of consciousness.
. . . Among the great numbers of combinations blindly formed by the
subliminal self, almost all are without interest. . . .[18]

Triggered by conscious work on a problem, conceptual elements are
blindly combined in a "subliminal" process like the swirl of molecules
in a gas (to use Poincafe's analogy). Only "useful and fertile" combinations rise to consciousness, the others being preconsciously screened out
on the basis of aesthetic criteria: ". . . only certain ones are harmonious
. . . and capable of touching this special sensibility . . . which, once
aroused, will . . . give them occasion to become conscious."[19] Illumination occurs, then, when random combinations of ideas, generated unconsciously through processes set in motion by conscious work, are subjected to conscious screening. Only the "fertile" combinations—happily,
the aesthetically pleasing ones—are presented to consciousness for further employment in conscious problem-solving.

All theories of random generation/programmed selection show striking similarities, as well as instructive differences. First, they are all, on our criteria, descriptions of designing. Only Alexander, it is true, speaks explicitly of design; but all of them—theorists of biological, social, and economic evolution, organizational innovation, and creative problem-solving—present descriptions of processes in which actual situations are changed into more desirable ones as initially given materials are formed, through the generation and selection of alternatives, into artifacts suited to their environments.

It is a moot point whether, in all these cases, designing is seen as a deliberate, purposeful activity. Interestingly, however, even theorists of social and economic evolution are drawn to the metaphor of an intentional, supra-individual designer: "society" selectively accumulates, the "hidden hand" of the marketplace chooses. And—as we have already noted—Darwin's theory of natural selection owes a great deal to his observations of breeding practices in common use among the English farmers of his time.

All of these writers regard many iterations of the generation/selection process as conducive to progress of a sort, though the meaning of progress shifts with the domain under consideration.

All of them share a model under which new possibilities for decision, generated out of known elements through an unknown or unknowable process, are subjected to selective screening on the basis of some established procedure. For all of them, that procedure has to do, in one way or another, with the detection of design proposals fit or misfit in relation to some environment. But the writers have different ideas about the nature of environment and of the processes by which fit or misfit is detected. Poincaré, for example, posits a preconscious screen that operates on the basis of aesthetic criteria. For Darwin, fit or misfit depends on whether or not a variation or individual difference enhances an organism's chances of survival in its biological environment—a criterion that depends, in turn, on the particular characteristics of the organism, its changing environment, and the organism/environment transaction. In theories of the evolution of societies, markets, cultures, or policies, fit or misfit is determined by certain individual and collective judgments or preferences. The theories need not (and usually do not) describe the bases on which such judgments or preferences are exercised. The problem is shifted, as it were, to the individuals in question.

The existence of such a diverse group of adherents, operating in such varied domains, suggests how wide-ranging has been the influence of the model of random generation/programmed selection. Clearly, it is very attractive. Nevertheless it presents serious difficulties, especially when it is taken not only as an after-the-fact account of design processes but as a normative, prospective model for designing. All of these difficulties hinge on discrepancies between certain of the model's assumptions and the characteristics of actual design processes.

In brief, the model assumes that design proposals are simple or merely additive, independent of one another, and incremental in their impact on design structures. But in actual designing, design proposals are often complex, interdependent among one another, and significant in their impact on design structures. Moreover, the model assumes that design structures are given with the design situation, whereas in actual design processes, structures are frequently made and remade in the course of designing. Each of these arguments requires elaboration.

First, let us consider the question of simplicity and complexity. In Simon's diet problem, foods are "simples" (considered, for the sake of the problem, as undecomposable units of design) and "diets" are complex in the sense that they are combinations of quantities of foods. Their complexity, however, is of a combinatorial or merely additive kind. When a particular food is added or subtracted, the diet is assumed to be changed only to the extent of that addition or subtraction. This is in contrast to the kind of complexity I will call *figural,* where addition or subtraction of one element changes the functional meanings of other elements with the result that the proposal must be considered different *as a whole.* Examples of figural complexity are to be found in the familiar drawings of the Gestalt psychologists; in music or painting, where the addition of a single note to a melody or a single patch of color to a composition can change the meaning of the design; or in systems—machines, buildings, computer programs, or human organizations, for example—where a change in the position, features, or functions of one element can produce significant changes in other elements and in the system as a whole.

The question of simplicity and complexity is closely linked to that of independence and interdependence. Two design proposals, or two elements of a proposal, are independent when one element's fit or misfit in a design structure does not depend on the presence or absence of the other. They are interdependent when the fit or misfit of their conjunction differs from their fit or misfit when they are taken alone. In an additively complex proposal, elements are independent of one another; in a figurally complex proposal, they are interdependent.

The model of random generation/programmed selection depends on the assumption that design proposals are simple, or merely additive, and independent of one another. Otherwise, the idea of random generation does not make sense. For if the elements of design proposals are interdependent, then they are objects of design in their own right. If such proposals are explainable by random generation, then why not the design structure as a whole? The design process would then be conceived as a series of mysterious, essentially unknowable guesses at complete solutions—a black box that would leave unexplained what is most in need of explanation.

But in much actual designing, proposals are figurally complex. To return to the clinical example given earlier, digitalis, diuretics, and potassium are functionally interconnected: diuretics reduce body fluids so that the heart has less work to do, and digitalis stimulates the heart muscle, but at the risk of reducing serum potassium below normal levels. Hence the competent clinician considers diuretics, digitalis, and potassium as interdependent elements of a figurally complex proposal for treatment, and an adequate theory of actual designing must explain how such proposals are constructed.

A similar argument can be made in the case of biological evolution. The familiar example of the giraffe's long neck is misleading. For the long neck is part of a giraffe system which includes a long and prehensile tongue capable of grasping food at the tops of trees, long legs which add to height and are designed for flight, and a digestive system attuned to the kinds of food best found with the help of the long neck. It is unlikely that one of these features would be adaptive in the absence of the others and therefore unlikely that they would emerge in their present systematic relations to one another through a process in which they were generated and selected in complete independence of one another. It would be more plausible to say that "design options" consist of alternative states of the total system.

Of course, one might posit a giraffe system consisting of all the elements and relations described above *except* for the long neck. Then a random genetic variation that contributed to a longer neck might be adaptive. But this sort of posit raises the question of the origins of basic design structures, to which we will return below.

When do conditions of independence and simplicity, or additive complexity, hold true? They hold for problems artificially constructed to *make* them hold. The diet problem is such a case, though even here it is interesting to note in recent nutrition science indications that foods contained in a diet may affect one another's nutritional value. These conditions also hold for certain classes of operations research problems where, as Simon points out, a large number of independent variables can be handled by the mathematical formalism of linear programming.

A further class of examples where these conditions may hold consists in processes where structures are built up from scratch through the combination of regular geometric solids. Certain biological forms, like honeycombs and wasps' nests, may fall into this category, along with self-organizing systems like crystal growths and structures formed by the close packing of certain regular solids. In these instances, the design structure consists in an array of more or less identical objects, each of which has a great deal of design built into it. Here, there are very few ways in which elements can combine and the resulting combinations set precise requirements for the addition of the next element.

In actual human designing, these conditions tend to be met only in later phases of a design process when the central features of a design structure are presumed to be set and stabilized, and only peripheral details remain in question. One might imagine, for instance, that the formula for a fabric softener has been fully defined and there remains only the question of its perfume. Or one might consider a machine that has been fully designed except for the color and texture of its housing. Even in such cases as these, however, the addition of final touches sometimes affects central features of a design structure in unanticipated ways, sending designers back to the drawing board.

If the model of random generation/programmed selection is limited in its applications to cases like the ones described above, then it is limited indeed! It holds only for a narrow range of artificially constructed problems, perhaps for certain examples of self-organizing systems, and for the later phases of certain other design processes. The attempt to apply the model more generally rests on the mistaken notion that the initial development of a design structure follows a pattern that actually holds only for the structure's final elaboration. Moreover, when the model is made into a normative prescription for effective designing, it becomes a recipe for conservatism. Designing, the theory then states, *should* proceed through the random generation and programmed selection of minor changes.

Just as the model of random generation/programmed selection cannot explain the figural complexity of design proposals, so it cannot explain the figural complexity of design structures. But in actual designing, figurally complex design structures come into being not only at the inception of the design process but, characteristically, over and over again throughout the process.

The making and remaking of figurally complex entities—proposals and structures—occur in several different ways, all of which derive from the designer's experience in the process, and are understandable as kinds of learning. What must be explained, then, are the kinds of learning on which skillful designing depends.

Let us consider this issue in the light of Alexander's shawlmakers. Figure 7.2 is a schema of the design process Alexander describes:

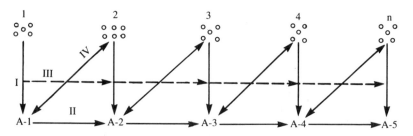

Figure 7.2

In this schema, the Arabic numerals refer to trials in which a designer introduces a particular change in pattern and/or color. Each trial is presented as a selection of one design option from a range of possible options (though, of course, no such choice is necessary; the shawlmaker might simply make what seems to be the 'right' move, without any conscious consideration of options), with the selected option indicated by a darkened circle.

When a designer introduces a change in color or pattern, the shawl changes. It is different just to the extent that it now incorporates the change which the designer has introduced—a difference, I claim, that often involves a change in figural, not only additive, complexity. The shawl is changed not only by the addition or subtraction of one element of color or pattern but changed as a whole figure, just as a melody can be changed as a whole by a shift in the duration or pitch of one or more of its elements. A–1 through A–n signify the changed states of a shawl consequent on each of the designer's moves. I label these symbols "representations" in order to be consistent with my view of designing as a process in which the designer's *representation* of a design situation undergoes a series of transformations. One might think of A–1 . . . A–n as standing for the designer's changing internal representation of the shawl, or one might think of the actual shawl as a representation of itself.

A–1 . . . A–n might also stand for different shawls, made at successive times, where the making of A–2 is informed by the designer's appreciation of A–1, and so on. Alexander's description of successive trials, and successive perceptions of fit or misfit, seems to lend itself to either of these interpretations.

The arrows in Figure 2 stand for different processes of enactment, change, or learning. The arrows labelled "I" stand for the enactment of a design option, the move by which the designer introduces the change she has selected. The arrows labelled "II" stand for processes of transformation: the process for example, by which A–1 becomes A–2. The arrows labelled "III" and "IV" stand for paths of learning, their different starting- and end-points signifying different ideas of the learning process, an issue to which I shall return shortly.

With each new trial, 1 through n, the designer selects a new element of color or pattern, and makes her judgment—according to Alexander's description—on the basis of its fit with the existing state of the shawl. The designer selects a change that fits that state and rejects the ones she perceives as misfits. But each such judgment differs from the previous one, not only because new design options are now in question but because the shawl is now perceived (represented) as a new entity. Judging whether a given design proposal fits A–2 is not the same as judging whether it fits A–1. In my terms, the criteria of fit have changed because the design structure has changed. Now Alexander attributes to the Slovakian peasant shawlmakers a capacity to make just such shifting judgments of fit and misfit, but it is not part of his intention to say how they do it. They *recognize* fit or misfit under continually changing conditions (so long as dyes, yarns and patterns sufficiently resemble the ones they are used to). If, on the other hand, one wished to give a formal description of the criteria under which successive judgments of fit or misfit were made—in order to construct a computer program to design shawls, for example—then it would be necessary to formulate rules and/ or procedures by which to determine, for each state of the shawl, which of a given range of design options fit that state. The strategy of such a description, or program, would consist either in specifying from the outset all relevant criteria of fit for all possible shawl-states, or in devising rules and procedures by which, given any particular state of the shawl and any set of design proposals, fit or misfit could be determined. This level of cognitive complexity must be incorporated in the process I have called "programmed selection," once we recognize that design proposals interact with design structures in a figurally complex way.

In actual designing, successive trials are not independent of one another, as in the familiar idea of "blind" trial and error where one keeps on trying things *(any*thing, in the end-case of a blind process) until something "works." The designer's choice of a new color or pattern is likely to be influenced by previous judgments of fit or misfit, that is, by learning from previous trials, and paths of influence may differ depending one one's view of the actual learning process.

In what is perhaps the simplest case of learning, the shawlmaker might judge among options at 2, as I have described above, on the basis of fit or misfit with the new state of the shawl that had resulted from trial 1 (as indicated by the arrows labelled "IV"). In this case, one might conceive of the shawl itself as a repository of learning derived from previous trials; each new state of the shawl, as perceived by the shawlmaker, provides a new context in which the next judgment will be made.

In a second case, one might conceive of the shawlmaker as making a judgment at the moment of any given trial on the basis of her appreciation of the previous trial (as indicated by the arrows labelled "III")—or on the basis of *all* previous trials. In each such instance, she would be seeing the presented situation as a version of the preceding—saying to herself, for example (if one imagines spelling out in discursive reasoning the judgment she probably makes immediately and tacitly), "Just as a contrasting color worked there, so it may work here," or, "Just as I intensified that pattern at the corner with a gold thread, so I should match it with a gold thread here."

All such learning depends on the designer's perception of the earlier trial(s) and the present one, and on her appreciation of the significance of the earlier trial(s)—their implications, potentials, constraints—for the present one. These relationships also involve figural complexity. One might imagine the designer entertaining, in her mind's eye, the juxtaposition of an earlier trial and a possible future one, judging some of these conjunctions as "fits" and others as "misfits."

In short, actual design proposals are generated *and* selected through processes of learning that involve appreciations of figural complexity. When they are enacted, they change design structures in ways that set new conditions for the judgment of fit or misfit. These observations hold, I suggest, not only for examples like shawlmaking but for designing the full range of human artifacts. And they are not described or explained by the model of random generation/programmed selection.[20]

Systematic search

An alternative approach to the generation of design options, or proposals, is that they are the results of a designer's systematic search. With this explanation, the underlying metaphor shifts from the random or blind combination of design elements, given with the problem, to the intelligent exploration of a terrain—or, as Simon calls it, a "problem space."

During World War II, the U. S. Navy's Weapons Evaluations Group addressed the problem of submarine search, which was one of the first to be approached through the new techniques of applied mathematics. It became a formative problem for the developing science of operations research and gave rise to a branch of applied mathematics called search theory. Given the metaphor of search (as in "searching for answers"), already built into ordinary language, it is no wonder that efforts should then have been made to extend search theory broadly to processes of problem solving and design.

Simon presents the view as follows:

> When we take up the case where the design alternatives are not given in any constructive sense but must be synthesized, we must ask once more whether any new forms of reasoning are involved in the synthesis, or whether again the standard logic of declarative statements is all we need . . . once we have found a candidate we can ask: Does this alternative satisfy all the design criteria? Clearly this is also a factual question and raises no new issues of logic. But how about the process of *searching* for candidates? What kind of logic is needed for search? . . .
>
> GPS [a problem-solving program developed by Simon and his colleague, Allan Newall] is a system that searches selectively through a (possibly large) environment in order to discover and assemble sequences of actions that will lead it from a given situation to a desired situation. . . .
>
> To represent the relations between the afferent and the efferent worlds, we conceive GPS as moving through a large maze. The nodes of the maze represent situations, described afferently: the paths joining one node to another

are the actions described as motor sequences, that will transform one situation into another. At any given moment, GPS is always faced with the single question: "What action shall I try next?" . . . It is characteristic of the search for alternatives that the solution, the complete action that constitutes the final design, is built from a sequence of component actions. The enormous size of the space of alternatives arises out of the innumerable ways in which the component actions, which need not be very numerous, can be combined into sequence.[21]

On this view, the paradigmatic process of problem-solving becomes search for the best path through a maze. The maze is a network of paths of action, similar to the network of a decision structure, within which each path leads to a particular modification of the original situation. The heuristics of search for the best path through a maze become broadly accessible for solving problems, including those not ordinarily seen as problems of search, just as in the previous case all problem-solving was seen in terms of the selection of randomly combined elements. In both cases, the effort is to subsume all problem-solving under the schema of a process we know how to program.

Simon adds, however, that

. . . problem solving systems and design procedures in the real world do not merely *assemble* problem solutions from components, but must *search* for appropriate assemblies. In carrying out such a search, it is often efficient to divide one's eggs among a number of baskets—that is, not to follow out one line until it succeeds completely or fails definitely, but to begin to explore several tentative paths, continuing to pursue a few that look most promising at a given moment. If one of the active paths begins to look less promising, it may be replaced by another that had previously been assigned a lower priority.[22]

Search for solution proceeds *via* search for the most promising paths to solution, which one must be able to compare and evaluate for relative promise early in the design process. Rational design depends not only on applying utility and statistical decision theories to alternatives within a fully articulated decision structure, be on the designer's ability to carry out an intelligent search for paths to solution.

Simon devotes several sections of his book to this topic. He begins by recognizing the interaction of component paths: "Actions have side consequences (may create new differences) and sometimes can only be taken when certain side conditions are satisfied (call for the removal of other differences before they become applicable)."[23]

Hence, one cannot usually construct an effective path to solution by adding the component paths that remove a unit difference between problem and solution states. It is necessary to "search for assemblies" which are "appropriate" in the sense of taking interaction of components into account.

Simon goes on to consider how designers should calculate the "costs" in expenditure of design resources and "benefits," in promise of solution, that may be associated with an assembly of paths. He presents Marvin Mannheim's proposal to organize problem space into a hierarchy of global and local paths to solution, which permits a progressive global-to-local search.[24] He makes reference to other search programs which assign values to assemblies, "as processes for gathering information about problem structure that will ultimately be valuable in discovering a problem solution."[25] And he considers programs which begin with the functional decomposition of a problem, such as building a house, in order to permit application of "generator/test" cycles to each of the functional components of the problem. He admits, however, that, "A theory of design will include principles—most of which do not yet exist—for deciding such questions of precedence and sequence in the design process."[26]

So long as design theorists explain the generation of design options in terms of the systematic search of a problem space, they must assume—whatever new principles they may discover—that a great deal of structure is given with the design problem. Consider Simon's image of moving through a large mass.

An actual maze has a structure. At the very least, it has an entrance, a way out, and a network of paths connecting entrance to exit. Some paths are blind alleys; others open onto other paths. Combinations of paths may also lead to dead ends, or to other assemblies, and at least one route through combinations of paths leads to the exit—so long as the problem represented by the maze is soluble.

When systematic search of a problem space is conceived in terms of the metaphor of running a maze, design options are taken to be paths or combinations of paths. They exist in the maze, and one must discover them in order to try them. But trying them does not change them. The maze runner is seen as learning *about* paths and interconnections of paths that are there to be discovered. As he tries one path after another, the maze runner may learn. His success in solving the problem depends on his learning to discover strategies for selecting and sequencing paths to be run and on his complementary discovery of the maze's structure, the spatial configuration in which paths are related to entrance, to one another, and to exit.

To the extent that actual design situations have this mazelike structure and lend themselves to these sorts of discovery, maze running may be a fruitful metaphor for generating and selecting design options. But his depends on a certain *objectivism*. For any particular maze, the same configurations of paths must dependably present themselves to anyone who chooses the same initial path. Just as the model of random generation assumes that design elements are given with the problem and treats combinations of these elements as objectively discoverable, so the model of systematic search assumes that paths are given with the problem and their subassemblies are objectively discoverable. The designer's discretionary freedom to invent and choose is limited to *strategies* of search whose consequences (discovery or non-discovery of subassemblies) are, again, implicitly given with the structure of the problem.

What sorts of problems fit these conditions? In the first instance, artificially constructed problems, like the well-known "Towers of Hanoi," and problems that lend themselves to the use of operations research techniques. Beyond these sorts of examples, any problem may be *made* to fit these conditions by giving it a well-articulated structure, so long as the problem solver sticks to that structure.

But the model of systematic search explains neither the development of design structures nor the development of figurally complex options in which the meaning of a given path changes significantly when it moves from one context to another. In this model, there is room for the designer's learning, but only for learning about subassemblies whose elements are presumed to be given with the problem and remain constant throughout the process. Hence, it does not account for kinds of learning—like the shawlmakers' learning, described above—where, in the process of designing, the designer comes to see the situation, design trials, and criteria of fit in new ways. Systematic search does not account for cases in which running the maze changes the maze.

Both models of generation, random combination and systematic search, lead to a dilemma. One must either forego the model's application to many of the most interesting cases of design, or assume as given a pre-existing structure that the model leaves unexplained. In this respect, Alexander's view of cultural design is like Simon's General Problem Solver. Both are partial theories of the design process, leaving unexplained how in the course of designing basic design structures and figurally complex design options are formed and transformed.

It is useful, of course, to explain what it means to be rational or effective *within* a design structure. One might even claim that we do not ordinarily have to create design structures from scratch, but only to modify existing ones. But for many kinds of problems—of organizational, policy, and program design, as well as design of the physical environment—even the modification of an existing design structure requires transformations that lie beyond the models described by Alexander or Simon.

It is for these processes of formation and transformation that I reserve the term "synthesis." And for synthesis, in this sense, there exists no adequate theory. There is not even a serious contender.

This I take to justify the very exploratory comments that follow. They are intended to suggest some of the things a theory of synthesis should be about, and some of the directions it might take. I shall draw my examples from social policy and service delivery systems, a field I know something about through my work with Martin Rein. However, other fields of design might equally well have been chosen.

Synthesis of design structures: the case of service delivery systems

Service delivery systems include services related to housing, criminal justice, health, welfare, education, and manpower—indeed, any service provided to a broad clientele, distributed through interconnected networks of agencies, under a system of regulations and policies, drawing on established funding sources.

It is difficult to make sense of data about a service delivery system in such a way as to yield coherent and persuasive recommendations for policy. Often, studies of service delivery systems result in assemblies of facts, clustered in one part of a report, and a set of unrelated recommendations in another. Prevailing notions of social science methodology play a particularly villainous role. Students, in particular, often feel that it is incumbent on them to generate "hypotheses" (for example, "Decision processes work more slowly in large organizations"), which they conceive as projected correlations of variables. They are puzzled when such hypotheses turn out to be unconfirmable or, if they are confirmed, turn out to lead nowhere.

Martin Rein and I have found it useful to ask our students, once they have immersed themselves in data about a particular system, to tell a diagnostic/prescriptive story about the system, one that indicates what is wrong with it and how it can be set right.[27]

Two such stories, in abbreviated form, are as follows:

There is a group of people in need of service. The services they need are varied and complex, consisting of many different kinds of specialized treatment. Their delivery must be differentiated according to the needs of different individuals, or the same individual over time, and they must be administered in a coordinated way so that services are linked to one another and easily accessible to clients.

In the past, these services were integrated and accessible. Now, however, they are fragmented; each type of service is offered in a different place by a different provider, with no coordinated interconnection among them.

This may have happened for any one of several reasons. Perhaps functions have become more specialized, as service providers have professionalized. Perhaps the clients themselves—families, or neighborhoods—have broken apart.

Whatever the causes of fragmentation may be, clients are now unable to get easy access to the services they need, nor are services delivered in a coordinated, continuous way. As a consequence, clients suffer. They do not get what they need in the way they need it.

The story may be told about social welfare services, in which case it refers to the decline of urban neighborhoods, the abandonment of neighborhood settlement houses and the subsequent establishment of many specialized social welfare agencies to which clients no longer have unified access. Or it may be a story about health services, and then it refers to the decline of the old-style family doctor, and the rise of medical specialists no one of whom really knows much about the patient.

> Some people need a kind of service they can now get only if they remain in institutions specially designed for its provision. But institutions are custodial; they restrict residents' freedom of action and isolate them from their natural home communities.
> Through prolonged residence in an institution, people become institutionalized. They adapt so well to the special requirements an artificial institutorial life that they become ill-adapted to life in the real world.

This story may be told about mental hospitals, prisons, old age homes, or centers for delinquent youths.

Stories such as these are archetypal. The crop up in discussions in many different fields of social policy. They underlie not only the responses of students but the work of researchers in the field.

They are also useful. They enable the storyteller to select for attention a very few features of the material which, however, fit into a pattern that is both descriptive and normative, diagnostic and prescriptive. The synthesis of "facts" about the system is also a way of pointing toward recommendations for policy.

In the first case, the story of fragmentation leads to a prescription of coordination. If services were once whole and now are fragmented, then the problem is how best to make them whole again.

In the second case, the diagnosis of institutionalization leads to a prescription for community care. If individuals are damaged through their segregation in institutions and their isolation from communities, then the problem is how best to reintegrate them into communities.

In each case, the story contains a basis for moving from diagnosis to prescription, from facts to policies, a movement that Rein and I have called the "normative leap."

In the first story, the basis of the normative leap is the notion of fragmentation. Services are seen as having been whole, as fragmented now, and as needing to be made whole again. But services do not literally fragment like a physical object that can be broken into parts. We are dealing here, then, with a metaphor—the metaphor of something like a bowl that can be broken and reassembled. It is a metaphor, moreover,

which embodies a normative idea. A bowl is *better* whole than fragmented and, other things being equal, if the bowl has been broken, it is
right for it to be made whole again. When this idea, drawn from the
realm of bowls and vases, is transposed to services, it yields the notion
that services are better off integrated than fragmented, and that it is right
to reintegrate services that have been fragmented. That the plausibility
of this recommendation derives from the metaphor of fragmentation can
be seen by substituting another metaphor for it. A story might have been
built around the idea of services growing from an early stage of mutual
dependence to a later stage of maturity in which they become independent. Would it be obvious, then, to say that it is better for them to be
"whole," where wholeness signifies mutual dependency?

In the second story, the metaphor is that of a building like a prison
which segregates persons and isolates them from a home community
outside. Given the familiar ideas that surround institutional buildings
and home communities, it is plausible—even obvious—that people are
better off in their communities than in isolated buildings. But what if
the metaphor were that of protection? Then it might seem obvious that
people are better off in institutions (like the early "reform schools"
in Massachusetts) where they can be protected from the dangers and
distractions of, for example, a dirty, crime-ridden urban neighborhood.
Or what if the institution itself were seen as housing a community? Then
it might seem obvious that people are better off as members of an
institutional community rather than as residents of a home environment
where they suffer from isolation or anomie.

Generative metaphor

The two stories facilitate the normative leap because they are built on
generative metaphors, families of familiar ideas carried over *(meta-
pherein,* in the Greek) to a new situation for which they serve as projec-
tive models.[28] The familiar ideas contain normative evaluations; they
describe things in ways that reflect what Geoffrey Vickers has called an
"appreciative system."[29] For example, as I have mentioned above, objects like vases and bowls are better whole than broken, at least under
ordinary conditions. Hence, when familiar ideas are carried over to a
new situation, the new situation comes to be evaluated as we evaluate
the familiar one. The metaphor generates a description of the unfamiliar
situation in which the normative leap is already made; facts carry normative weight. Once we are able to see a service system as fragmented,
we find it obvious that the system needs to be made whole. Once we see
an institution as an artificial environment that confines people and isolates
them from their natural communities, we find it obvious that people
should be freed up to return to their natural settings.

Generative metaphor produces a selective representation of an unfamiliar situation that sets values for the system's transformation. It frames the problem of the problematic situation and thereby sets directions in which solutions lie and provides a schema for exploring them.

Metaphors are simple notions, easily held in the mind, but they stand for complex families of ideas. The creation of a design structure requires precisely such a hybrid of simplicity and complexity. The metaphor of fragmentation, for example, refers to a phenomenon about which we already know a great deal. Hence, the simple metaphor of fragmentation is able to function as a formula that compresses a great deal of information. Everything we know about fragmented things can be transposed to the context of services. But each transposition takes the form of a question, rather like a riddle, because the things one knows about fragmented objects are not likely to be literally true of services.

For example one can ask, What are the fragmented services? Were they previously whole? How did they fragment? What does it mean for them to be made whole again—accessible under one roof, integrated in a single service-providing process (as when doctors and teachers work together to help a disabled child), or provided under the aegis of a single agency? What are the possible means and likely consequences of "making whole"? When two services are coordinated through the use of a single facility, for example, what can be projected as to their future use by clients and their influence on each other?

Such riddles give direction to inquiry. They help to determine what is worth investigating. Answers to them yield a new representation of the situation which defines the elements to be attended to, suggests their casual connections, and permits an inquirer to anticipate how the situation is likely to respond to intervention. By interrogating a generative metaphor, raising questions whose answers become hypotheses to be tested through further inquiry, the inquirer can elaborate a design structure, as in the following dialogue:

Teacher: Why do you say these services need to be coordinated?
Student: It's obvious.
T: Why is it obvious?
S: Well, clearly it's better for them to be connected together than fragmented.
T: What's lost if they're fragmented?
S: A number of things. For one thing, it's hard for a person, particularly if he is old or disabled, to get what he needs if he has to go to many different places and deal with many different agencies.
T: But this happens all the time. You go to one place to have your shoes repaired, another to buy insurance, and still another to have your teeth fixed. Are these services "fragmented," too?
S: It's not the same thing. Take the case of an old person who is blind. He's apt to have many other needs associated with his blindness. He may need medical care, help with transportation, training for a

job, or psychiatric counseling. And these are likely to be connected needs. He is a whole person, with one interconnected set of problems, and he needs a service system that can respond to him as a whole person.

T: But were these services ever integrated in a single agency?

S: No, but that's irrelevant. The problem is to treat him as a whole person rather than as a series of disconnected needs.

Here, the student begins with the statement that services are better whole then fragmented, a statement whose obviousness rests on the as yet unexamined metaphor of fragmentation. The student first translates "wholeness" into "single access to different services," but rejects this idea when he sees that different services are often provided satisfactorily under multiple auspices. In his second attempt at translation, he suggests that it is the person, rather than the services, that must be made whole. And he rejects the proposition, also derives from familiar knowledge about broken things, that fragmented services must once have been whole. If he were to follow up this line of inquiry, he might go on to explore just what services need to be connected, and how best connected, in order to respond to the client as a whole person.

In order to create a design structure, it is not enough to make a metaphor, like the metaphor of fragmentation and wholeness, for the riddles generated by the metaphor may be answered in many different ways. It is the metaphor plus the dialogue of its translation that yields design structure.

These examples of the metaphorical generation of design structures are from the field of policy formation, and they contrast with such accounts as Lindblom's disjointed incrementalism. It is interesting to speculate on the ways in which generative metaphor might substitute for the model of random generation/programmed selection in other fields. For example, Poincaré, in his model of the creative process in mathematical invention, already hints at a metaphorical explanation when he mentions his sudden recognition of similarity, first, between "the transformations I had used to define the Fuchsian functions" and those of non-Euclidean geometry and, subsequently, between the latter and "the arithmetic transformations of indeterminate ternary quadratic forms."[30] Although Poincaŕe goes on to explain these sudden illuminations through the random generation and aesthetic screening of combinations of unitary concepts, his insight consists in seeing an unfamiliar set of transformations as a familiar one.

In place of Ogburn's "selective accumulation" of social customs, we might imagine a theory of societal change that would explain the generation of new cultural forms through the metaphorical transformation of existing cultural types—that is, through the idea of a cultural repertoire transformed through its transposition to a new context. Alexander's account of the evolution of new shawls is, in fact, vague enough to include a metaphorical explanation of development. The changes introduced by the shawlmakers might consist of just such transformations of familiar types as I have hypothesized in my discussion of a shawlmaker's learning from one trial to another.

How generative metaphor might become part of an account of biological evolution I do not dare guess—though I find the prospect intriguing.

In all these fields of design-like evolution, the idea of synthesis through generative metaphor raises many more questions than it answers. Some of these suggest interesting directions for further inquiry, as I shall illustrate in the area of social services.

How does storytelling reveal and elaborate generative metaphor?

Students are often surprised at the stories they tell, and even more surprised at how useful their stories turn out to be. Where do their stories come from? And why is storytelling so often accompanied by a sense of discovery? On one view, the storytelling context leaves us relatively unconstrained by fear of criticism, allows us to "speak before we have anything to say," and thereby enables us to tap into our store of tacit knowledge—things we have known about this situation and its relations to other situations but had not made explicit to ourselves. Or perhaps storytelling enables us to piece together bits of knowledge we already possessed but had never assembled.

We seem to possess a narrative or dramaturgical impulse to make sense of unfamiliar situations by telling stories about them. We continually seek to make sense of things strange to us by fitting them into versions of familiar stories. Hence, when we ask someone to tell a story about a new situation, we ask him to pay conscious attention to a sense-making process in which he is already tacitly engaged.

Given some such narrative impulse, is there a pattern to the stories we tell? Do we draw from a limited repertoire of stories which we adapt, now to one situation, now to another? How does the process of selection, fitting, and adaptation work?

It is intriguing to speculate on the counterparts to storytelling that function in contexts that lend themselves less obviously to narration, for example, graphic design. Just as we might imagine a designer of social service systems having access to a *repertoire* of metaphors from which he can generate problem-setting stories, so we can imagine a graphic designer having access to a repertoire of visual images any one of which can serve as a basis for the representation of a design situation. Stories and visual images may function like prototypes, each a source of a different way of seeing the situation.

How are generative metaphors found and selected?

Encounter with an unfamiliar situation provokes a search for connections with familiar ones. This is not Simon's search for paths to solution, but a search for ways of constructing design structures within which paths to solution may later be discovered. Nevertheless, it is search of a sort. Perhaps it takes the form of a scanning of the designer's repertoire of prototypical stories or images, prototypes whose use is characteristic of what might be called a "design culture" or perhaps of an individual designer's idiosyncratic style. Often, we *find* ourselves with a metaphor, without having been aware of looking for one.

Common usage suggests that designers scan their repertoires for similarities between a new situation and situations represented in the inquirer's memory store. But in this respect common usage may be misleading. At first, we are more likely, in Thomas Kuhn's phrase, to perceive a similarity without being able to say similar with respect to what."[31] Only later, then a metaphor has been made—when we have already begun to speak of services as fragmented, for example—does the question of similarity arise. Then, as we consciously juxtapose fragmented services and broken bowls, we may arrive at explicit descriptions of their similarities and differences. This process may lead us to propose a general theory of fragmentation that includes among its instances both service systems and bowls. Reflection on the metaphor of fragmented services may work backward, as it were, to reshape our ideas about the sorts of things that may be whole, broken, and made whole again.

How do we come to select one generative metaphor rather than another? One kind of answer is semantic. The metaphor of fragmentation is already in our ordinary language; we are in the habit of describing things other than physical objects as broken or whole. But we are also used to other habits of metaphorical description—metaphors, for example, that hinge on the distinction between the natural and the artificial, high and low, strong and weak. What leads us to choose just *this* metaphor?

Another kind of answer draws on sociology of ideas. If we were to trace the idea of fragmented services to its origins, we would uncover a network of practitioners and analysts who have participated in a kind of social movement organized around the reform of service systems through coordination. Indeed, the very notion of "system," borrowed from the weapons systems of World War II, may lie somewhere near the origins of this movement. In the case of the metaphor of artificial institutions and natural communities, it may be possible to trace these ideas back to the eighteenth century and perhaps to an individual, Jean-Jacques Rousseau, whose theories of natural man corrupted by artificial institutions penetrated deeply into the mainstream of Western social thought.

In cases such as these, the use of a metaphor reflects the operation of social movements that have brought particular ideas of reform into currency. An individual may find himself thinking of fragmentation and coordination when he thinks of service delivery systems, without knowing how he came to do so, because that metaphor has become powerful for thought and action in the society of which he is a part. But more than one metaphor capable of influencing our thinking about reform exists already embedded in our everyday language and in our stock of ideas in currency. There remains the problem of understanding the interaction between broadly shared domains of language and ideas in currency and the thinking of a particular individual engaged in a process of design.

Is there a basis for saying that one metaphor is better than another?

Through generative metaphor, we set problems whose adequacy can be judged in terms of our ability to solve them. Have we set a problem we can solve? Beyond this fundamental question, however, we can also ask whether we have set the *right* problem. When we set the problem of service system design in terms of fragmentation and coordination, for example, we are apt to think exclusively in terms of existing services, without attention to their quality or their appropriateness to changing circumstance. Needs for services may change as social contexts change. Old people, for example, tend now to be deprived of the supports once provided by an extended family. Or the creation of new resources may provoke a change in perceptions of needs for service, as people learn, for example, to "need" the most advanced medical technologies. The metaphor of fragmentation and coordination may yield an inadequate problem formulation because it induces us to overlook such changing needs.

Each generative metaphor suggests particular strategies of selective attention and inattention. It is, in the final analysis, on the basis of our appreciative systems, the values we place on things attended to or overlooked, that we judge the adequacy of a way of setting a design problem.

Designing as reflective conservation

Once we conceive of designing as a process that begins with the designer's construction of an initial design structure, then we are also likely to pay attention to the ways in which design structures evolve. Having framed the reform of a service delivery system in terms of de-institutionalization, for example, we may discover, by trying to solve the problem we have set, just how inadequately we have framed it. The caring networks of natural communities may fail to materialize, once people are released from mental hospitals stigmatized as snakepits or from prisons vilified as schools for crime. The costs and difficulties of "community care" may appear overwhelming, once we actually try to implement de-institutionalized service systems.

From this perspective, the design process is a frame experiment.[32] Beginning with one way of framing the problem, derived from a particular generative metaphor, we invent and implement solutions whose unanticipated effects make us aware of the selective attention or mistaken assumptions built into our initial frame. We become aware of values we did not know we held until we violated them.

Our frame experiments are dialectical, or—as I prefer to say—they are "conversations" with the materials of a situation. When we frame a situation and create an initial design structure within which we begin to invent and implement solutions, we become newly aware of conflicts within our own appreciative system. In the extreme case, these conflicts may present themselves as intractable, and the design problem becomes a dilemma.

In the case of service delivery systems, design dilemmas may take quite predictable forms. Every service delivery system represents answers to questions such as these: who is to get what service? under what auspices? how are services to be funded, controlled, sequenced, and evaluated? Characteristically, answers to these questions consist in strategies that conflict with one another.

We tend to place a high value on the equitable provision of services, but under conditions of limited resources, a high priority on equity may mean that no one gets enough. In order to make service systems more consistent and efficient, we may opt for a strategy of centralization, which interferes with norms of responsiveness, diversity, and community participation, all of which militate toward a strategy of decentralization. For the sake of learning, we may emphasize small-scale experiments, which can be seen as discriminatory or elitist. A priority on quality may lead to an emphasis on professional expertise that conflicts with values of community control.

Sometimes, a designer becomes aware of conflicts like these as his design process unfolds; he discovers the narrowness of an original design structure as he tries to implement solutions derived from it. Sometimes a potential for conflict is inherent in the discrepant frames held by different designers. Then, in the literal sense of the word, designing can be understood as a "conversation," a dialogue among individuals who frame a design situation in different ways, employ different generative metaphors, operate from different appreciative systems.

For example, frame conflict may stem from the different perceptions of different professionals, all of whom are involved in designing; or it may stem from the different perceptions of interest groups who have different stakes in the design. To take a recent instance, the design of systems of medical care involves not only physicians, but providers like nurses and paraprofessionals, health workers' unions, health policy analysts, hospital administrators, health maintenance organizations, health insurance agencies, and advocates for special groups of patients like the elderly or the poor. Not only are participating groups likely to frame the problem of health service delivery in different ways; the very words used to describe problems and solutions are likely to have different meanings for them. So, for example, a word like "centralization" may hold connotations of efficiency for one group and coercion for another.

In their design conversations, participants often talk across discrepant frames, unaware that they are doing so. Apparent agreement can mask conflict that emerges later on, when proposed solutions are implemented. Disagreement can disappear when individuals discover what they mean by what they say. The discovery of an authentic design dilemma—one that owes its existence to actual frame conflict—may come as a result of individuals working hard to communicate with one another, learning to create the conditions for valid inquiry into one another's frames.

Once a design dilemma has emerged, it may be resolved or dissolved in a variety of ways. Resolution may take the form of an invention that satisfactorily meets requirements which had seemed, until the moment of invention, to be interactably inconsistent. Or it may take the form of a mixing of values so that all may be achieved at some satisfactory threshold, though none is optimized. Or a dilemma may be resolved by deciding that some values take priority over others. Utility theory offers a way of treating values as comparable and additive, translating the terms in which benefits and costs of alternatives are variously described into the common currency of utility. But utility theory does not provide a means for deciding among conflicting values judged to be incommensurable, or for resolving conflicts about the weights that should be assigned to different values.

Sometimes design dilemmas may be dissolved by reference to values that pertain to the process of designing itself. In a real-world setting subject to real-world constraints, there is an economics of designing, related to the allocation of scarce resources of time, energy, and intelligence. A typical event in the life of a design team is the discovery that the deadline for completion of the work is imminent and a solution must be produced. The resulting pressure for solution may trigger the invention of new design options, or it may provide an incentive for making hard choices that had been deferred or bypassed.

Designing, in the dual sense of dialogue among individuals and transaction with the materials of a problematic situation, is a process in which communication, political struggle, and substantive inquiry are combined. The adequacy of a generative metaphor, or the problem setting that results from its use, should be considered in the light of the metaphor's functioning in the full process of design. A generative metaphor may be judged appropriate, for example, if it leads to the creation of a design structure that directs inquiry toward progressively greater inclusion of features of the problematic situation and values for its transformation. A good design process gives direction to inquiry while at the same time it leaves design structure open to transformation.

Conclusion

In this paper, I have explored the very widely and deeply held model of designing as rational decision, with its division of the design process into generation and selection, and its alternative views of generation either as random combination of given elements or as systematic search of a problem space. On the one hand, I have wanted to show how this model is entrenched not only in theories particular to the design professions but in theories of psychological, social, economic, and biological development built on the metaphor of design. On the other hand, I have wanted to identify sources of incompleteness inherent in the model. It cannot explain that initial creation of figurally complex design structures and options. It cannot account for the dialectical trans- formation of structures that we observe when we attend to the ways in which designers learn through designing. Hence, it is limited either to the special class of problems—for the most part, artificially con- structed—where design structure is given from the outset, or to the later phases of actual processes where designing takes the form of technical problem-solving within a stabilized structure.

I have proposed an alternative view of designing based on generative metaphor. Here, the focus is on problem setting, as well as problem solving. The split between generation and selection no longer holds, for the metaphorical development of a design structure determines both the general character of options and the criteria by which to select among them. Designing is seen as a conversation with the materials of a situation within which new trials are often based on learning from earlier ones. It is seen, for the most part, as a social process in which different designers frame the situation in different ways and learn, when they are successful, to talk across divergent frames. The idea of a designer's repertoire of types, images, and metaphors plays a central role on this perspective, as does the idea of design dilemmas, on whose resolution or dissolution the possibility of problem solving depends.

From this vantage point, there are significant implications for the theory of designing, as well as for design education and the development of computer-based design assistants. Attention must now focus on the formation and reformation of structures within which unitary elements and relations are given. One can no longer rely on the positing of elements and relations, presumed to remain constant throughout a design process: only the least interesting processes conform to these conditions. One must account for the kinds of learning in which designers transform structure by implementing design proposals and continually see situations and options in new ways. One must forego objectivism and attend to designers' perceptual construction of new design entities.

Design education must give a central place to such processes as the framing of design situations, the development of a repertoire of types and images, skill in the metaphorical process of seeing-as, and reflection on divergent frames.

Once the figural complexity of actual design structures and options moves to center stage, it must seem extraordinarily ambitious to build computer programs capable of reproducing the cognitive complexity of actual designing. It is quite another matter, however, to envisage computer assistants for designers—computer environments able to track a complex design process, assist in handling the additive complexity of technical problem solving within a given structure, or provide access to a store of examples, images, and descriptions.

Finally, although an understanding of designing based on generative metaphor and conversation may no longer deserve to be called a "science" in Simon's sense, it can still contribute to an epistemology of professional practice. Simon's insight into the design-like character of practice holds true, even though the model of design as rational design does not.

Notes

1 Herbert Simon, *The Sciences of the Artificial*, MIT Press, Cambridge, MA, 1971.
2 *Ibid.* pp. 58–59.
3 *Ibid,* pp. 55–56.
4 A well-formed problem, in Simon's terms, is illustrated by the "diet problem," described below.
5 Gregory Bateson, *Steps to an Ecology of Mind*, Ballantine Books, New York, 1972.
6 Simon, *op. cit.*, p. 61.
7 As analyzed by Dr. William B. Schwartz, of the New England Medical Center, and by Anthony Gorry. The example given here has been taken from conversation with Dr. Schwartz.
8 Simon, *op. cit.*, p. 63.
9 Charles Darwin, *The Origin of Species*, Mentor Edition. New York, 1958; p. 55.
10 *Ibid*, p. 74.
11 William Ogburn, *Social Chance*, Viking Press. New York, 1922; pp. 76–77.

12 Adam Smith, *An Inquiry into the Nature and Causes of the Health of Nations*, Modern Library Edition. Random House, New York, 1937; originally published in 1776.

13 Christopher Alexander, *Notes on the Synthesis of Form*, Harvard University Press, Cambridge, MA, 1964; p. 50.

14 *Ibid*, pp. 53–54.

15 Charles E. Lindbolm, *The Intelligence of Democracy*, The Free Press, New York, 1963.

16 Donald S. Schon, *Technology and Change*, Delacorte Press, New York, 1966; pp. 78–79.

17 Henri Poincafe, "Mathematical Creation," in Brewster Ghiselin, ed, *The Creative Process,* Mentor Books, New York, 1955.

18 *Ibid*, p. 39–40.

19 *Ibid*, p. 40.

20 Most recent attempts to design computer programs that "learn" also depend on the existence of design elements and criteria of selection that are assumed to hold constant throughout the design process. For example, one popular model of "learning" programs employs probabilistic analysis to reinforce combinations of elements that are qualified, according to some established test, as "hits."

21 Simon, *op. cit.,* pp. 67–68.

22 *Ibid*, p. 69.

23 *Ibid*, p. 68.

24 Marvin L. Mannheim, *Hierarchical Structures: A Model of Design and Planning Processes*, The MIT Press, Cambridge, MA, 1966.

25 *Ibid*, p. 72.

26 *Ibid*, p. 75.

27 Martin Rein and Donald A. Schon, "Problem Setting in Policy Research," in Carol H. Weiss, ed, *Using Special Research in Public Policy Making*, Lexington Books, D. O. Heath and Company, Lexington, MA, 1977.

28 See Donald A. Schon, "Generative Metaphor: A Perspective on Problem Setting in Social Policy," Andrew Ortony, ed, *Metaphor and Thought*, Cambridge University Press, Cambridge, England, 1979.

29 Geoffrey Vickers, *Responsibility—Its Sources and Limits*, Intersystems Publications, Seaside, CA, 1980.

30 Poincaré, *op. cit.,* p. 37.

31 Thomas Kuhn, "Second Thoughts on Paradigms," in F. Suppe, ed, *The Structure of Scientific Theories*, University of Illinois Press, Urbana, IL, 1974.

32 See Donald A. Schon, *The Reflective Practitioner*, Basic Books, New York, 1983.

CHAPTER 8

Will education contain fewer surprises for students in the future?

Paul A. Wagner

Three trends promise to have a major impact on public education during the next twenty or so years. While each reflects a distinct domain of experience, the three interact in such a way that their collective impact on education will be revolutionary. The first trend to which I refer are the current advances of those engaged in the research enterprise of cognitive science. While cognitive science has very little to offer in the way of practical advice to classroom teachers or educationists at the moment, it has created a great deal of enthusiasm for "control system learning theories,"[1] instruction in heuristics,[2] and so on. Cognitive science has come to dominate psychological research.[3] Partly because of the continued conceptual proximity of educational research to psychological research and partly because of the power evidenced by current cognitive science models, one can expect that educational research and subsequent practice will one day become greatly influenced by cognitive science. Indeed, one already finds the terminology of cognitive science research making its way into the educational literature.[4] Whole conceptual networks originating in cognitive science cannot be far behind.

The second trend likely to affect education is in part a social consequence of the first. In the past, the educational literature and folklore has revealed an inordinate concern for the "affective" domain of human learning. The concern for the affective domain has so dominated educational practice that teacher-training programs often seem to focus exclusively on procedures for getting students to "like" the elements and processes of schooling. Many student teachers have come to think that the most important measure of their teaching skill is whether or not the students "like" the teacher or, at least, the teacher's instructional techniques. And, finally, when the television news media does a story on an instructional innovation, the classic media technique is to show viewers children at work and then to ask one or more of the children, "How do you like (say) working with computers?" Student expression of satisfaction is then taken as adequate testimony of the effectiveness of the technique.

An earlier version of this paper was presented at the Harvard University Philosophy of Education Research Center. I want to thank Professors V. A. Howard and Israel Scheffler for their comments on the earlier version. Research for this paper was funded by the Melrose-Thompson Foundation.

Despite the history of concern for the affective domain of human learning, concern for such matters is likely to wane. There are several reasons for this. One is that, in response to current public pressure, schools are becoming increasingly concerned that students can demonstrate that they have acquired knowledge of important material. Thus, quantity of skill and information learned has become increasingly important as a measure of educational success. In addition, recent advances in neurophysiology and neuropharmacology suggest that human experience is little more than an event in an electro-chemical machine.[5] Smokers, dieters, phobics, and even schizophrenics find their experience is susceptible to what is apparently a strictly electro-chemical explanation. Finally, as current work in cognitive science advances, the importance of the affective domain in human learning diminishes. This is because reference to the affective domain of human experience always seemed to suggest the existence of an unexplainable and mysterious realm of human existence, and it is just such mysteries that cognitive science has set out to remove, either through theoretical advance or through definitional fiat.

In what follows, I will do three things. First, I will explain why the trends mentioned above can be expected to continue for quite some time. Second, because cognitive science plays a predominant role in each of the trends discussed in the first section of this paper, I will review the recent development of the research program that today comprises cognitive science.[6] In doing so I will explain the program's goals as well as its shortcomings. Finally, in the concluding section of the paper, I will argue that the advance of the cognitive science research program is likely to result in diminished attention to emotions by both researchers and educationists. Should this occur, both the explanatory power of the new psychology and the success of newly contrived instructional techniques will suffer. In short, I intend to show that the role of emotions is central to human mental life. In addition, any theory which neglects assigning a role to such phenomena fails as a scientific theory. More importantly, from the perspective of this paper, it fails as the kind of theory upon which it is reasonable to base recommendations pertaining to curricular design and instructional technique.

Educational practice and technology must resist adopting the vocabulary and conceptual scheme of the latest science of the mind until such time as it becomes evident that such notions will adequately pay their way. There are mental events that are central to human cognizing that are not captured by standard cognitivist theories. Indices identifying these events must be retained in the lexicon of the educational researcher and practitioner if education is to achieve its most central aims.

Current trends in cognitive science affecting education

The formal modeling of cognitive scientists has been successful in reducing the mysterious realm of human existence. For example, many problem-solving skills which had previously been attributed to the uncommon ingenuity of an exceptional individual have been reconstructed through computer simulation and made accessible to us all. Indeed, the successful construction of expert systems seems to represent a democratization of the talents of a (previously) elite intelligentsia. Even examples of creativity seem to fall one by one to the routinizations of the competent programmer. And even the programmer himself is not beyond the reach of the programmable. As much recent research has demonstrated, computers can both learn and create new programming moves and even new programming languages.[7]

In the age of cognitive science, the exotic display of genius now seems more commonplace. Genius may no longer be seen as an instance of inspiration or a flash of creative insight. Rather, genius seems more and more to be a mere function of additional programming. In a world of electro-chemical machines whose intellective life amounts to no more than what can be arranged on a suitably formalized and lengthy tape (a Turing machine), there is little reason to direct further attention to the affective dimensions of human learning. Rather, talk of the affective is increasingly seen as an awkward and contrived way for identifying input statements.[8]

Just as the second trend can be seen as partly a function of the first, so the third trend can be seen as a function of the second. To the extent that human learning can be identified with a set of programmable heuristics, the institution of learning ought to become predominantly occupied with instilling in children the most powerful heuristics available. Thus instruction in information optimization (inferential and evaluation techniques) will seemingly take center stage in public education. In the current vernacular, this amounts to the claim that techniques for efficient memorization and retrieval of information and courses in critical thinking will predominate. It is yet to be seen if critical thinking courses will attend to the study of discipline-specific heuristics and crossdisciplinary heuristics or some combination of the two.

Discipline-specific heuristics are those techniques of evaluation and inference-making limited to a single realm of discourse or family of language-related subjects such as (say) physics and the sciences, respectively. Crossdisciplinary heuristics are those techniques of evaluation and inference-making that seem to have an adjudicating force in nearly all realms of human discourse. They include such things as the basic laws of logic, the elements of induction and probabilistic reasoning, and many of the fallacies taught in informal logic courses. Of course, there is always the talk of the mystic, the lover, the romantic, and an occasional quantum theorist for which such crossdisciplinary heuristics seems inapplicable. However, such cases are of little importance, for it is not at all clear that such talk succeeds in conveying a body of information from one cognizing unit to another. In any case, in addition to an increased emphasis on memory skills, courses in critical thinking can be expected to increase in popularity. Indeed, there are already a number of research and training institutes sponsoring programs for either teachers or children in critical thinking.[9] In anticipation of the growing market in measuring discrete and identifiable critical thinking skills, there have recently been a proliferation of critical thinking tests such as the New Jersey Test of Reasoning, the Wason/Glasser Test of Reasoning, and the Ross Test of Reasoning. All this testifies to the emphasis currently being placed on critical thinking in education.

If nothing disrupts the three trends described above, there will eventuate a concept and practice of education very different from that realized anywhere else in the world today. The mind will be viewed as a Laplacean universe, persons as organic cognitive processing units, and schools will be little more than programming stations. I suggest this scenario not to frighten the reader away from some dreadful Orwellian future, but to caution against the uncritical acceptance of new research programs, against the abandonment of useful concepts, and against the adoption of educational practices of limited perspective.

Admittedly, educational theory as long suffered from a lack of rigor. Similarly, educational practice has typically been seen as a function of regional whim and fancy. This will not do. Teachers are morally committed to doing more for their students than merely introducing them to, or indoctrinating them in a capriciously selected set of conventions. Teaching is by its very nature a moralistic enterprise. Teachers are dissatisfied with the way children grow up in a state of nature. Consequently, they take it upon themselves, either individually or through some sort of institutional affiliation, to exorcise the student of undesirable natural tendencies and to instill in him or her instead the skills and world-view of the dominant civilization. No one knows for sure if the world-view of the dominating civilization is preferable to any of its current competitors. Nevertheless, by acquiring a powerful world-view, the student ultimately becomes, with nature, a co-architect of the world around him. By "dominant civilization" I do not mean to identify the nationalistic perspective of major geographic and political units. Rather, what I have in mind is something like the notion we currently associate with the term "Western World." A world-view is powerful to the extent that it extends the control of the student in his or her attempt to create and manage the world today and the world of tomorrow.

Teachers deem it a fundamental good to assist the student in becoming with nature a co-architect of the world. Individual teachers and groups of teachers may also want to instill in the student certain moral, social, religious, or political values, attitudes, or beliefs, but that is beyond my concern here. What I want to point out is what I take to be a logical point about the word 'teacher,' namely, that teachers are those who intentionally attempt to disrupt the natural intellectual development of the child for what they take to be a greater good. One so committed cannot well tolerate capriciousness or ambiguity in matters of value or matters pertinent to either pedagogical theory or practice. To treat educational prescriptions as if they were properly the stuff of fancy and conjecture is tantamount to abdicating one's role as teacher. When educational prescriptions are treated in a cavalier or abusive manner, teachers are duty-bound to object, "This just will not do." The educational influence of cognitive science is cause for teacher concern.

It was not until the advent of cognitive science that a science of psychology became distinct from more applied endeavors such as educational psychology, counseling psychology, industrial psychology, and so on. Cognitive science appears to possess all the scientific virtues psychological researchers have been seeking for over a century. It is uncompromising in its rigor and accessible to empirical test. It relieves psychology of the "ghost in the machine" and yet does not ignore the obvious phenomena of mental processing as did its immediate predecessor, behaviorism. Cognitive science's success as the research program of choice for psychology virtually insures that it will influence much of the theorizing in, and ultimately the practice of education in the future. Thus, before proceeding further, a sketch of current cognitive science is in order.

Cognitive science: its history, its promise, and its reality

The history

The term 'cognitive' has recently become quite fashionable in psychology. And, because of the close relationship existing between psychology and education, the descriptor 'cognitive' has become equally fashionable in education. Research funds from the National Science Foundation, the Department of Defense, and other large organizations continue to flow toward support of research labelled "cognitive" and away from research labelled "behavioral," "social," "psychological," or other "non-cognitive" approaches. The result of this drift of research funds and effort toward "cognitive" research has, in recent years, produced a sort of bandwagon effect. Researchers who only a few years ago were declaring themselves behaviorists, humanists, transactionalists, or some other such thing have recently begun re-describing their research or clinical approach as cognitive. In many cases there is no evident change in the researcher or the clinician's technique. In such cases, the shift to cognitivism represents little more than a shift in the label one uses to describe oneself, one's work, and one's collegial affiliation. Nevertheless, beneath this very noticeable shift in fashion, there does exist a school of thought and an evolving research program which Howard Gardner aptly describes in his recent book, *The Mind's New Science.*[10] Because it has become fashionable, and because it is, in fact, developing a powerful research program, there is every reason to believe that cognitivism will shortly become the sole dominating research program of psychology.

Cognitive science did not suddenly appear on the psychological horizon. Indeed, the scientific study of cognitive processes can be seen to date back at least to the empirical work of Ernst Mach.[11] However, cognitive science did not begin in anything like its present form until much later in the twentieth century when the four disciplines of linguistics, philosophy, psychology, and computer science began to recognize that they shared a common array of problems.

Although cognitive science today represents the efforts of four distinct disciplines, the central issues of cognitive science all can be said to originate in philosophy. For example, there is a very important sense in which the central concerns of cognitive psychology can be said to date back to Aristotle, those of computer science to Pascal, and those of linguistics to Thomas Hobbes. However, even from the perspective of cognitive science *as* a twentieth-century science, the roots of the emerging discipline are traceable to a few representative philosophers. For example, the work of philosophers such as Ludwig Wittgenstein, Rudolf Carnap, and Noam Chomsky is centrally featured in current approaches to the study of linguistics. Through the subsequent work of their students the problems posed by philosophers Yehoshua Bar-Hillel, Alonzo Church, and further back, Bertrand Russell have set the direction for much of the theoretical work prescriptive of current research in information theory and computer science.[12]

Since the relationship between philosophy and psychology has been both intimate and volatile, it is difficult to identify a few intellectual ancestors of cognitive psychology. On the one hand, the relationship between psychology and philosophy has at times seemed so volatile it is difficult to imagine any cross-fertilization of ideas between the two. On the other hand, individual philosophers and psychologists have frequently befriended one another because of their shared interests in mental activity and the usefulness of distinctions arising from contemplation of possible mind/body dualities. For example, the philosopher Gottlob Frege was nothing short of brutal when explaining why the psychology of judgment should be distinguished from the philosophical study of the structure of judgment.[13] In contrast, the psychologist Richard Gregory attributes to the philosopher Norwood Russell Hanson the inspiration leading to much of Gregory's empirical research.[14] Similarly, cognitivist Jerome Bruner credits philosopher Nelson Goodman for advising him of the merit of viewing each psychological subject as a world-maker.[15]

To identify a few philosophical heirs of twentieth century psychology would be impossible. Suffice it to say for now that the relation between the two has, despite appearances to the contrary, led to many important advances in psychology and, more recently, philosophy too has recognized the contribution of psychological findings to current philosophical research.[16]

While philosophical concerns may have prompted the direction taken by researchers in psychology, linguistics, and computer science, the contributions of each discipline, as well as the continuing contributions of current philosophy, remain unique in the evolving program of cognitive science. Consequently, if one is to understand the nature of cognitive science one must understand the goals pursued by each of the contributing disciplines immediately prior to the emerging synthesis of research programs.

As noted above, each of the varied research programs that have led to the current synthesis in cognitive science originated with a set of provocative philosophical problems and concerns. To give an adequate account of each of these would require a far more lengthy exegesis than I am able to provide in these few pages. In lieu of such an exegesis, I will briefly describe how the work of one philosopher, Ludwig Wittgenstein, either inspired or at least illustrated the sorts of interests that led researchers in philosophy, linguistics, psychology, and computer science to share a common set of goals.

Wittgenstein began his philosophical research by attempting to give an account of how a properly functioning language represents the world. This project led Wittgenstein to search for universal structures of linguistic practice that could be modelled and thus illustrate how a proposition can picture a piece of the world.[17] Wittgenstein saw in mathematical logic an appropriate tool for modelling the sorts of linguistic universals he believed existed. A competent engineer, mathematician, and logician, Wittgenstein soon began thinking about the characteristic features of languages other than those exhibited in linguistic expression. Most particularly, Wittgenstein thought about the language of mathematics. Eventually, Wittgenstein's philosophical musings led him to conclude that the search for stable and incorruptible meaning is a fruitless enterprise. Meaning seems to be no more than an expression's use. Change the expression's use and you change its meaning. There are no metaphysical substances of any sort that constitute the meanings of terms. There is no Protagorean foundation upon which our thoughts must be securely anchored.[18]

The consequences of Wittgenstein's philosophical trek are many for those engaged in cognitive science. For one thing, his work encouraged a sense of modesty among philosophers. No longer could philosophers pretend to identify important truths about the world merely by thinking carefully. Rather, what the philosopher could do best was to think about the tools of thinking, namely, the elements of language.

Wittgenstein's methods and concern for studying the tools of thought have largely been adopted by contemporary linguists. For example, Wittgenstein's claim that meaning extends no further than use lends considerable support to linguists' attempts to model linguistic practice schematically. In addition, Wittgenstein's original project, in which he set out to model universal characteristics of propositional expression, has been taken over and usefully extended to nearly all areas of linguistic practice by philosopher/linguist and now cognitive scientist Noam Chomsky.[19] Chomsky, of course, has developed modelling techniques and extended the search for language universals far beyond anything Wittgenstein ever imagined. Nevertheless, the inspiration for this work, however indirect it might be, can be plausibly identified with Wittgenstein.

Wittgenstein's work in the study of symbol systems may well have influenced early work in artificial intelligence. A young Cambridge mathematics student, by the name of Alan Turing, attended Wittgenstein's lectures on the foundations of mathematics. Turing, along with Norbert Weiner, Claude Shannon, and John von Neumann, became one of the founding theorists of the artificial intelligence movement. Turing was offended by Wittgenstein's reduction of mathematical structure to a mere anthropological phenomenon. To Turing, mathematics exhibited a reliability that could not be explained away by merely noting the development of appropriate social conventions.[20] More importantly, from the perspective of artificial intelligence, Turing came to believe that any systematic process such as exists in human thinking can be modelled by another computationally accessible model. Thus, Turing came to believe that the entire range of human cognition could be modelled by a single program. The term "Turing man" has been used variously to describe either the program which constitutes a model of human cognition, or, more generally, a view of man as a computer-like processing unit.[21] While Wittgenstein may have served only as a foil against which Turing learned to hone his arguments, the evolution of Turing's ideas continue to play a central role in artificial intelligence today.

In psychology, no less than in linguistics or artificial intelligence, Wittgenstein's work again played an inspirational role and illustrated themes which remain central to the research program of cognitive psychologists today. Wittgenstein deplored irresponsible speculation about the actual content of thoughts or how a thinker manipulates bits and pieces of thoughts before making an array of thought-material accessible to public scrutiny. In looking at what humans in fact do with things we call thoughts, we are limited to the evidence provided by the existence of our various symbol systems. There is, at present, no way we can know what is going on in the mind of a thinker. However, by analyzing how linguistic strings are associated with one another, we can learn all that can be learned about thought-processing. Thought-processing refers to the manipulation of symbols. Thinking may involve that and more.

Wittgenstein objected to the attempt to study the nature of thoughts as things-in-themselves. Such queries are, to Wittgenstein's way of thinking, meaningless. There simply is no way for distinguishing accurate from inaccurate accounts in such matters. The available data extends no further than the linguistic conventions actually employed in a given set of circumstances. Thus, the responsible study of thinking begins and ends with the overt data of actual language-use, not because there is no more involved in thinking, but rather because there is no more in thinking that can be plausibly explained.[22] While many behaviorists have at times found solace in such Wittgensteinian arguments, the arguments themselves do not preclude the attempt to model linguistic structures; in fact they tend to encourage it.[23]

Even though the researcher can never know the meaning a thinker assigns to a linguistic expression, the researcher can catalog the syntactic patterns exhibited by the expression in question as well as other associative expressions. Such catalogs of syntactic sequencing may ultimately be shown to exhibit a further underlying structure. To the extent to which a model of any underlying structure can entail the various entries in the catalog, then to that extent the model exhibits characteristic features of a similarly extensive range of human thinking.[24] In other words, while Wittgenstein admonishes the psychological researcher from speculating beyond what the data allows, he does not discourage the attempt to model the structure revealed in the data as a means for modelling human thinking.

As noted above, Wittgenstein is not necessarily the originator of all the themes motivating the disciplines which today comprise cognitive science. Rather, what we find in Wittgenstein is an array of concerns central to current cognitive science and representing the individuating interests of each of the several component disciplines. Indeed, the admonition to limit theorizing about mental processing to publicly accessible data originated with a predecessor of Wittgenstein's, namely physicist and psychological researcher Ernst Mach.

Unlike Wittgenstein, Mach was at times actively engaged in empirical research. His research was designed to depict features of actual mental processing. For example, in one study for which Mach gained considerable acclaim, he presented subjects with a spinning disk. The surface of the disk was painted in a checkerboard configuration. When viewing the spinning disk, subjects reported seeing bands of black and white and not a black-and-white checkerboard configuration. This series of experiments convincingly demonstrated that the mind does, in fact, process sensory excitation. Consequently, laws of human action would be incomplete if reference to such processing were omitted.[25]

While Mach's work was of unsurpassed originality and importance in its day, its effect on Anglo-American psychology was inconsequential. The principal reason Mach's work has little effect on subsequent Anglo-American psychology extends beyond mere nationalism—though that, no doubt, was also a cause. Mach's geographic locale led non-German researchers to regard his work as characteristic of other German introspectionists. When introspectionism was rejected in favor of behaviorism, experimental results associated with introspectionism were quickly forgotten or ignored. Psychologists by and large abandoned the study of mind.[26]

During the 1950s psychologists began reconsidering their commitment to behaviorism and their abandonment of so-called mentalistic psychology. Experimental work by psychologists Edward Galanter, Karl Pribram, and George Miller caused psychologists to question the explanatory power of the behavioristic paradigm.[27] For example, Miller's study of humans' inability to remember uninterrupted sequences of numbers beyond seven digits (plus or minus two) is often cited as a classic study in cognitive psychology. In particular, the study of the "magic number 7 (± 2)" demonstrated behaviorism's inability to account for a limitation of our mental facilities. Indeed, our ability to remember sequences of numbers should be as varied as our individual experimental histories. Furthermore, from the perspective of behaviorism there should be no reason why an appropriate reinforcement schedule could not be contrived which would extend a subject's ability to remember an uninterrupted string of numbers. That seems not to be the case however. Try as we might, we cannot liberate ourselves from the grip of the magic seven.[28]

The experimental work of cognitive psychologists has been accumulating at a frenzied pace since the 1950s. Where once the study of mental activity set one outside the mainstream of psychological research, today it identifies one as a pioneer in the burgeoning field of cognitive science. Image-processing is being successfully studied, as are the actual heuristics ordinary people use to address problems of risk-analysis, placing a wager, purchasing a product, and so on.[29] For most of its short history, psychology has had considerable difficulty in striking a balance between the accumulation of research data and the construction of adequate theories. Either the accumulation of data outdistanced the explanatory power of the research program (as in the case of early gestaltist programs) or the explanatory power of the theory, potentially all-encompassing, was, in fact, ill-suited to account for more than a very limited range of data (this was the case with the behaviorist program). For the moment at least, cognitive science is rich in both accumulated data and theoretical constructs.

The theoretical constructs of cognitive science are largely derived from the fields of computer science and information theory. The computer demonstrated that even a brute mechanical system could operate in a self-correcting, goal-directed manner. If a physical system such as the computer could operate in such a manner then there was no longer any reason to deny that humans might operate in a similar fashion or that the use of such terminology made theories suspiciously speculative. Consequently, accounts of human cognitive activity that made reference to teleological functions became, once again, respectable.

The promise

Information theory provided researchers with a mathematically rigorous tool for organizing data and subsequently modelling a wide range of processing activities. Particularly in the domain of cognitive processing, information theory has shown itself amenable to the parsing activities of linguistic activity, decision analysis under conditions of uncertainty, and image manipulation. Together with the programming power of the modern computer, information theory has provided the cognitive researcher with a means for providing rigorous and empirically adequate models for a whole range of cognitive activity.[30] The question that remains—indeed, the central question of cognitive science today, is whether or not such tools will prove to be effective for modelling the entire range of human cognitive activity.[31] While success in modelling cognitive processing has been achieved in an impressive array of conceptual domains, the primary focus of interest remains centered upon linguistic investigation. Since mature human thought is most commonly expressed in words, phrases, sentences, and the like, it is not surprising that this should be so. Furthermore, there is no question that cognitive science confronts its most serious challenge through the attempt to model the entire range of linguistic activity. Finally, since much success in modeling linguistic activity has already been achieved, there exists a powerful research tradition that promises much fruitful exploitation in the future.

The languages that cognitive science seeks to model are not the languages most speakers believe themselves to be familiar with. They are not the languages of description, action, conversation, or convention. They are not the sort of phenomena Wittgenstein discussed in his *Philosophical Investigations* or that structural linguists attempted to describe by observing the speech practice of speakers in various cultures. Rather they are the languages which Jerry Fodor describes collectively as *the* language of thought or, alternatively, Chomsky describes as "I-languages."[32]

If one is to acquire a genuine appreciation for the goal of cognitive science, it is instructive to have a thorough grasp of what Chomsky means by the term "I-language." Chomsky distinguishes I-languages from what he calls "E-languages." E-languages are about the world. Questions regarding the proper extension of a semantic unit in a given world are E-language questions. Chomsky regards such questions as probably unanswerable—at least in any scientifically rigorous way. On the other hand, it *is* reasonable, he believes, to study I-languages. For Chomsky, I-languages exist as a derivative biological fact. It is for Chomsky an indisputable phenotypic characteristic of human beings that such creatures are language users. Consequently, there must be some biological trait that is realized in the evolution of individual linguistic skill. Human languages are not the instinctive squeaks, growls, barks, and chirps that one finds in other species. Rather, human languages, ranging from mathematics to native tongues, exhibit a deep structure. It is the deep structure of such languages that cognitivists hope to model in a computationally accessible fashion.[33]

Already, as noted above, cognitive scientists have achieved several important, though admittedly modest, successes in their endeavor. For example, perhaps the earliest notable successes are Joseph Weizengaum's ELIZA and DOKTOR. Each engages in a sort of Rogerian counseling dialogue with "clients."[34] The fact that these computer programs produce linguistic responses compatible with the expectations of a native speaker is generally taken as an empirical verification of the fact that the program's structure is functionally analogous to the deep structure utilized by actual human speakers. On another occasion, Patrick Suppes and his associates at the Institute for the Mathematical Study of the Social Sciences at Stanford developed a computer-assisted instruction program for teaching one of the Slavic languages. It was later discovered that the same parsing configurations used for teaching the original language could be used to teaching another Slavic language. Though it was never Suppes's intent to model any aspect of a Chomskian alleged deep structure, his work does in fact lend credence to the notion that speech patterns manifest in a native tongue exhibit an isomorphic relation to other more subtle and elegant structures.[35]

The parsing configurations of programs such as ELIZA, DOKTOR, and Suppes's Slavic language program are free of semantic content. This is precisely the point Chomsky intends when he distinguishes E-languages from I-languages. E-languages are about the world. As such they are subject to all the whimsy and capriciousness of human social practice. I-languages, on the other hand, are algorithmic procedures for managing the transfer of information. If one's goal is to study cognitive activity then there is no reason to go beyond the study of I-languages. I-languages are the biological inheritance that enable us to learn, deliberate, think, perceive, and speak. I-languages are not learned; they are what makes learning possible. Consequently, to study and, ultimately, to understand human *thinking* one does not need to be concerned with how experience initiates either learning or thinking. How such things occur will remain a mystery for quite some time. Nevertheless, such concerns need no longer deter us from studying how thinking proceeds any more than a lack of knowledge about an individual programmer deters us from understanding how a computer operates. *Data entry* into the human thinking machine remains largely a mystery. Nevertheless, from the perspective of cognitive science it is not a mystery which fundamentally inhibits the study of thinking. Experience is a matter of data entry. The cognitive scientist begins with decoded data entry as a given and then sets out to model the processing structures that lead to predictable encoded outcomes.[36]

The reality

What Chomsky and other leading cognitive scientists have sought to establish is what cognitivist Stephan Stich describes as the Syntactic Theory of Mind.[37] The Syntactic Theory of Mind is an ontologically reductive program. Mental events no longer have meaning other than a discrete location in some syntactic system. Thoughts are syntactic strings. They have no real-world objects. Emotions play no role in thinking itself. Syntax, and syntax alone, comprises the ontology of mind.

Not all cognitive scientists are equally enamored with the Syntactic Theory of Mind. Nevertheless, it must be admitted that the Syntactic Theory of Mind represents a mainstream cognitive science, and cognitivist detractors are few and far between. For example, Weizenbaum, earlier mentioned as the author of ELIZA and DOKTOR, has joined forces with phenomenologically minded philosophers such as Hubert Dreyfus and John Searle in decrying the fact that computationally accessible models of human thinking fail to capture the phenomenological aspects of cognitive experiences.[38] This criticism is generally accepted by cognitive scientists but regarded as inconsequential. For example, one can easily imagine that there is a shift of feeling accompanying a monk's recital of his daily office after many years. He may feel more religious or he may fell less so. Nevertheless, repetition of the ritual rarely leaves the monk feeling unchanged. In contrast, a computer can be required to "say" its daily office more frequently and over a longer period of time and yet experience no change in feeling. Computers feel nothing; people do.[39] Even if one were to allow for a little creative engineering and an equally creative use of the word 'feeling,' we might be willing to admit that computers could have some feelings but the phenomenologists would still persist and inquire, "But do they feel things *as* people do?" However one might attempt to resolve this concern, it really matters little from the perspective of cognitive science. Even if humans are in a uniquely privileged position for appreciating human feelings, this matters little unless feelings play a functional role in cognitive processing. From the perspective of cognitive science, they don't.

Clearly people experience feelings. We think about what we feel. However, in thinking *about* what we feel we are processing data that has already been successfully decoded and entered into our information-processing system. Feelings do not, generally speaking (or so cognitivists claim), play a role in our cognitive processing. The sole exception to this is when intense feelings interrupt the operation of the human information-processing system. However, subsequent to any interruption, if the system has not been damaged, it will immediately return to its normal operating mode. Admittedly, the experience of intense feelings may result in new data entries. But new data entries, like old ones, are processed by the same I-language operating system.

Traditional phenomenologists seem satisfied with this portrait of cognition but other critics are not. For example, Patricia and Paul Churchland have been adamant about insisting that scientific psychology should tell us about how the mind interacts with the environment and not merely how it processes information.[40] Cognitivists recognize that a comprehensive account of the human animal should account for such things. As cognitivist Zenon Pylyshyn admits, "not everything pertaining to an organism is appropriately described at the symbolic level, at the level of symbol structures and information: some aspects of the system are appropriately described in the vocabulary of physics, chemistry, biology, electrical engineering and so on."[41] However, what Pylyshyn and other cognitive scientists deny is that psychology must accept responsibility for detailing the elements of the cogitating unit's information pick-up function. The information pick-up, or transducer function, as Pylyshyn calls it, is "a physical process. . . . Thus, typically it does not come under study by cognitivists who simply presuppose that an organism is equipped with transducer functions."[42]

The cognitivist sees the mind as an epiphemomenal construct manifest in the human organism. The task of the psychologist is to model the information-*processing* features that constitute the mind. To require the psychologist to give an account of the system's interaction with its environment is to require the psychologist to give a comprehensive account of the human animal itself. This, cognitivists claim, is an unreasonable demand to make of any scientific endeavor. Such a condition would require the psychologist to do, in Pylyshyn's words, "physics, chemistry, biology, and electrical engineering," as well as psychology. No one would suggest we make such demands on other sciences, so why should so much more be expected of psychology?

Pylyshyn expresses some sympathy for the Churchlands' concern and decries those cognitivists such as Chomsky who minimize the role of environment in learning to exercise certain language skills.[43] Despite the apparent dispute that exists between Chomsky and Pylyshyn on this issue one ought to be careful not to make too much of it. While admitting sympathy for the general question, "How does the system interact with the environment?" Pylyshyn remains as resolute in his methodological solipsism as Chomsky. For Pylyshyn, as well as for nearly every other mainstream cognitivist, cognitive science is appropriately limited to information-processing. The details of information acquisition, the transducer function, are best left for study by other more appropriate sciences acting, perhaps, in concert. By delimiting its scope, cognitive science is exhibiting one of the most treasured virtues of responsible scientific practice, namely, parsimony. Good scientific practice is, in part at least, a matter of identifying a limited range of theoretically related phenomena and constructing hypotheses descriptive of isolated instances of behavior. The research program of cognitive science secures parsimony in cognitivist research.

If one grants for the moment that cognitivist arguments successfully dispose of the criticisms levelled at cognitive science by traditional phenomenologists, such as Dreyfus, Searle, and Weizenbaum and neurophilosophers such as the Churchlands, there remains yet a third source of criticism. This third source does not represent a new school of thought. Nevertheless, for those who find themselves naturally disposed to labelling competing claims, the term "New Wave Phenomenology" might be a tempting descriptor for identifying the major themes in this third source of cognitivist criticism. Those who might be properly described as New Wave Phenomenologists claim that there is a phenomenology of cognitive elements that possess a causative role in human thinking. In short, New Wave Phenomenologists are principally concerned with disabusing the cognitivist of his solipsism.

As noted above, the methodological solipsism of cognitive science extols the study of syntactic structure and discredits any attempt to explain cognitive function which defers to the elements of experience of semantic reference. In general, cognitivists have arrived at this conviction through philosophic and legislative fiat and not as a result of any empirical investigation. As it turns out, the decision to delimit cognitive science to the study of syntactic structures may be ill-informed. In the first place it is not the sort of decision that ought to be made on the basis of philosophical reasoning alone. As John Hoaglund points out, "cognitive science rests on a profound and distinctive empirical hypothesis: that all intelligence, human or otherwise, is rational, quasi-linguistic symbol manipulation. This hypothesis might be true and it might not."[44] The empirical character of this hypothesis has not, in practice, admitted by many cognitive scientists. Instead, the computer-accessibility of intelligence is generally accepted as an article of faith. It is odd that so many cognitive scientists should persist in this conviction.

The track record of artificial intelligence over the past forty years is not what leading researchers expected. While scientists have been successful in modelling a limited range of decision procedures in such areas as medical diagnoses, geological exploration, financial investment, and robotics, they have been notoriously unsuccessful in modelling how ordinary humans make sense of ordinary aspects of experience.[45] For example, after years of study, researchers at the Berkeley Laboratory of David Wilensky are only now completing a program that can decide to dress appropriately when retrieving a newspaper lying out in the rain.[46] The outcome of this sort of research may well be to show that highly abstract intellective procedures such as those common to medical diagnosis can be modelled by highly abstract computationally accessible programs. On the other hand, such research also suggests that it takes real brains to know to carry an umbrella when it's raining! In short, there may be a phenomenology of human experience that not only accompanies cognitive processing but is fundamental to it.

A second consideration that should have made the cognitivist wary of continuing his exclusive preoccupation with syntactic modelling is the fact that some semantic elements seem to possess a *meaning* which itself determines, in part, the outcome of subsequent cogitation. On these occasions, words are used in a manner expressive of the speaker's phenomenology of experience. Communication between speakers on such occasions succeeds only to the extent that people are able to share with one another the intersubjectivity of such experience. For example, expressions of empathy by one person for the condition of another are commonly judged to be either sincere or disingenuous. Any subsequent exchange that takes place between two such persons is recognized as reflecting more than a random selection of one syntactic string from a range of permissible alternatives. In short, speech acts often have cognitively relevant meaning that transcends syntactic structure. Consequently, if one is to give an adequate account of human thinking there must be some allowance made for a phenomenology of semantic meaning. Concerns such as these have caused some cognitivists, such as Fodor, to equivocate in their commitment to an ontology of syntax.[47] And, in a much more dramatic case, the philosopher Hilary Putnam, an early champion of the cognitivist program, has directly confronted the solipsism of cognitive science and urged researchers to consider an approach to explaining human mental life that admits of three non-reductive levels of explanation, namely, the neurophysiological, the syntactic, and the phenomenological.[48]

A third challenge to the solipsistic position of cognitive science originates with those who believe that emotions do more than accompany cognitive events. These theorists believe that emotions play so central a role in human thinking that any account of cognition that omits reference to emotion fails to account for an essential and characteristic feature of thinking.[49] This challenge shares with other New Wave criticisms a concern for the phenomenology of experience that cognitivists believe to be a corrupting influence in psychological research.

The cognitivist is right in recognizing that reference to the phenomenology of experience will cause the cognitivist program to suffer a loss of its highly prized rigor. However, if the price cognitivism pays for rigor is measured in terms of less practical understanding of human mental life, then that cost is intolerably high. In what follows I will argue for a more tolerant psychology of mental life than is afforded by cognitive science. Specifically, I will limit my attention to the role certain emotive experiences play in determining the character of subsequent cognitive processing.

Minding the emotions: is there a case for tender-minded cognitive theory?

The mental events I have in mind have been previously described by Israel Scheffler as "cognitive emotions."[50] Cognitive emotions include such mental events as surprise, suspicion, and (to my way of thinking though not to Scheffler) doubt. Continued inattention to these mental events threatens to imperil the current research program of cognitive science. More important for present purposes, however, is the possibility that the terminology of cognitive science will dominate educational theorizing and practice. By the time cognitivist researchers recognize that their oversight of the cognitive emotions represents the Achilles Heel in current cognitive research, the rhetoric of cognitive science may have been transformed by educationists into a new ideology of pedagogy. Given the centrality of the cognitive emotions in the learning process, adoption of a cognitivist ideology in education could have a devastating effect on the lives of future generations of Americans and other Western, science-dominated countries. Popular conceptions of what should constitute training in critical thinking are, I believe, already beginning to reflect the myopic vision of cognitive science.

Although William James did not have post-analytic philosophy or cognitive science in mind when he spoke of the "tough-minded," tough-mindedness is today a quality much sought after by most Anglo-American philosophers, cognitive scientists and, most recently, educators. Part of what it means to be tough-minded today is that one avoids lapsing into a "mentalese" description of psychological phenomena that cannot be further subjected to precise and detailed computational modelling. So, for example, it is permissible for a cognitivist to describe a subject's saying, "It is raining today, so I will take my raincoat," as an inference, but it would be impermissible for a cognitivist to describe a subject's musing about the beauty of the rain as "dreamy" or "wishful."

As noted above, cognitive scientists are most at ease when they are modelling the structure of the I-language of a subject. Emotions, they admit, exist. Emotions no doubt influence behavior. What they do not influence is the structure of cognitive processing.

Much depends, of course, on what one counts as a cognitive process. No feeling of excitement or dread, happiness or reserve, will ever change the structural function of implication. Indeed, a variety of emotions may accompany any act of implication. In addition, emotional experiences may change throughout the process of implication and perhaps even as a result of the process. For example, Jones may think the following sequence of thoughts:

1) I have a skin cancer.
2) Most skin cancers are easily cured.
3) This skin cancer may be melanoma.
4) There is no cure for melanoma.
5) All people who get melanoma die from it.
6) If I have melanoma, I will die.

Initially, Jones may have felt worried by the fact that he had cancer (1). His subsequent belief about skin cancer may have produced in him a feeling of joy (2). His later (mistaken) belief about melanoma perhaps produced in him a feeling of fear (3). And, finally, his conclusion that if he has melanoma, he will die may have resulted in a feeling of dread or horror (6). Note that the sequence of thoughts can be identified with an invariant structure. For example, the last two sentences are an instance of a three-term propositional argument which logicians describe as modus ponens. The conclusion was, in a sense, determined before the thinker arrived at it, given the logical and (most believe) conceptual operation of implication, the invariance of subject/predicate relations, the original premises, and the uninterrupted continuation of the thinking process. In contrast, however, the sequence of feelings does not seem at all determined by the underlying structure. One can easily imagine Jones following the same line of thought on another occasion and experiencing a completely different sequence of feelings. Jones on that occasion may be especially fearful, and even the thought of *non*-fatal skin cancer creates in him intense fear. Or he may feel cavalier and uncaring: consequently, expectation of his own demise may create in him very little emotion at all.

Thus, whereas emotional sequences exhibit little by way of underlying structures, cognitive structures exhibit considerable structure. As Chomsky declares, "the language faculty involves a precisely articulated computational system—fairly simple in its basic principles when modules are properly distinguished, but quite intricate in the consequences produced. . . . This is not at all obvious property of a biological system. . . . Nevertheless, the evidence supporting it is quite substantial. . . ."[51] Since emotional sequences are variable and deep cognitive structures are not, there is no reason to believe that the two are intimately related. Even at the level of apparent surface parallelisms between emotion and thought within a given organism, such correlations seem at best coincidental. At any moment in the future an emotional sensation may fail to correlate with (say) any predicted linguistic act.

The chasm that exists between the ontology of structures identified by cognitive science and the apparently unrelated ontology of feelings and emotions abandoned by cognitivists strikes the observer as counterintuitive and scientifically misleading. There are at least three factors producing this chasm. The first has already been alluded to above. Emotions seem at best an object of study for the neurosciences, and not the cognitive sciences. At worst, talk of the emotions introduces an ambiguity into scientific discourse that ought to have been abandoned with our antiquated folk psychology.[52]

Second, in the past, talk of the emotions has been notoriously unstable. Human beings often describe their own actions as well as those of others in an emotion-laden vocabulary. Such descriptions are frequently misleading. For example, a student may describe a teacher as being angry with him or her. The teacher may respond by saying, "I am not angry with you, but I *am* very disappointed." Now, assuming that both the teacher and student are truth-tellers, we must conclude that either one or both of them are mistaken, or that anger and disappointment are names for the same emotion. This latter possibility seems most unlikely since anger is frequently cited by a person in an attempt to explain why he or she committed some outrageous act of aggression. In contrast, it is rarely—if ever—the case that disappointment would be similarly assigned such a causal role. If disappointment and anger are not two different names for the same emotion, then how is anyone to decide which speaker has mistakenly employed an emotion-term in the above example? Because there seems no way to make such fine-grained discriminations when describing emotions, emotion concepts have long been a source of irritation for those seeking a more rigorous and tough-minded science of psychology.[53]

A further source of irritation resulting from any attempt to take emotion-talk seriously is that it is not at all clear that the term 'emotion,' unlike the term 'brain,' denotes a single natural kind. There is, for example, an ordinary-language distinction to be made between feelings of the mind and feelings of the body. For example, if I say, "That principal frightens me," I am likely to deny that my being frightened is co-extensive with a set of physical characteristics such as quickened pulse, clammy hands, elevated blood pressure, and so on. By way of contrast, when I say, "I am chilly," I am perfectly happy to assent to the claim that such an expression denotes a set of physical characteristics experienced by my body. The former case is taken as a paradigm of emotional experience, or feeling of the mind; the latter is taken as a layman's way of describing physiological phenomena, or a feeling of the body. Since cognitive science was principally responsible for giving new respectability to the notion of 'mind,' there would seem to be little objection to populating the mind with mindful feelings as well as thoughts. The problem with this, however, is that as we have learned more about emotions, many have turned out to be indistinguishable from neurophysiological events.[54] For example, neuroscientists have demonstrated that the experience of fear is co-extensive with a neurochemical event. Fear in a subject can be created in an individual both by manipulating his environment, ultimately creating a neurochemical imbalance identified with the "flight response," or by directly altering the neurochemical composition of the brain. In either case, subjects unequivocally identify the feeling they experience as fear. Similarly, many of the emotions experienced by schizophrenics and other psychotics have been eliminated by manipulating the neurochemistry of the subject's brain.[55] If emotions can be so completely controlled by neuropharmacology, then, one might question, why attribute to them any causative role in cognitive processing? As the above example illustrates, the more we learn about emotions, the more they appear to be feelings of the *body* and not some sort of *mental* event. Since there is already a successful neurophysiology, there is no reason for cognitive scientists to duplicate the efforts of another promising research program.

Nevertheless, as noted above, while the term 'emotion' looks like it names a natural kind, it does not. It may be that the argument above presents a good case against including physiologically based emotions such as fear in a science of cognitive processing, but there are other mental events, the Schefflerian cognitive emotions, that are unlike fear or other "feelings of the body." The mental event of surprise, for example, is very much a *mindful feeling*.

The term 'mindful feeling' denotes a sensation which cannot occur apart from relevant cognitive activity. To be in doubt and to be surprised each involve a process of evaluation. To doubt is consequent upon some process of evaluation, a refusal to assent to the truth of a belief. To be surprised is to evaluate the consequences of an activity as unlikely and to find that its occurrence produces a sense of unsettledness. This "sense of unsettledness" should in no way be assimilated to mere startledness. None of these events can be induced chemically and none occurs void of feeling.

Of course, some philosophers, such as William Lyons, relying on experimental work completed in the 1950s and 1960s, continue to believe that *all* emotions involve the mental act of evaluation. For example, fear, Lyons argues, is experienced or at least is recognized only when the subject identifies a reason to be fearful.[56] As noted above, current neuropharmacological research simply fails to support such a conclusion.

In addition, Lyons's arguments fail to take into account situations in which fear appears, as it were, spontaneously, such as in cases of a sudden loud noise or slight auditory disturbances in an otherwise quiet and forbidding environment. Clearly, there are times when, in light of certain observations, a subject has good reason to be concerned for his or her safety. In such cases, fear is no doubt a common emotional occurrence. Nevertheless, as has been shown above, fear is equally common in situations where there is no *evident* reason for immediate concern. It is not merely a case of fear being irrational in such instances but nonetheless dependent upon an act of evaluation. Rather, it is the case that subjects may experience fear spontaneously *without* reason. Reason may be bought to bear on one's experience of fear, but it is not itself a necessary part of the experience.

While Lyons may be mistaken about the valuation content of emotions generally, he succeeds in two very important tasks of clarification. First, he draws attention to the fact that physiologically determinate feelings are not to be identified with emotions. For example, one may experience the same physiological sensation in the case of love as in the case of shame. Similarly, an observer of the same subject with extensive physiological data unique to the person at a time t, but with no information about the context the subject is in at time t or the thoughts transpiring in the subject's mind, will be in no position to identify the subject's experience as one of love, shame, or even a physiologically limited cardiac irregularity. Physical feelings are not, Lyons insists, to be identified with emotions. Emotions may often occur with feelings, but that does not make them identical to one another nor even necessarily related. It is only subsequent to an act of evaluation that a feeling becomes associated with an emotion.[57] While Lyons mistakenly concludes that emotions are never to be associated with strictly physiological events (again, fear, shock, and many other 'emotions' seem to require no further explanation beyond the physiological), it is true that many so-called emotions are distinguishable from the mere presence of feeling.

The second task of clarification in which Lyons succeeds is in noting that there is more than one meaning of the term 'emotion' as ordinarily used. For example, to use the term in an occurrent sense is a matter of associating it with the experience of a feeling. In addition, there is a dispositional sense in which the term is associated with a propensity to behave in certain ways. While neither of these captures entirely the essential features of emotions, they do reflect how people in fact seem to talk, or at least how philosophers *believe* they talk.[58] Lyons's project is to construct both a more comprehensive and a more precise sense of the term 'emotion.' For my part, I think Lyons is engaged in a quest for a holy grail. 'Emotion' is not a natural-kind term but rather a primitive and clumsy way of referring to a number of disparate classes of phenomena. Without belaboring this point any further, consider now the more limited class of phenomena I have identified as mindful feelings and Scheffler has identified as cognitive emotions.

In the case of mindful feelings there is clearly an essential act of evaluation. The centrality of the evaluative act was recognized long ago by C. S. Peirce, who repeatedly uses the word "surprise" when discussing abduction as a methodology of scientific inquiry. For example, in one particularly noteworthy passage Pierce writes, "Every inquiry whatsoever takes its rise in the observation of some surprising phenomena, some experience which either disappoints an expectation, or breaks upon some habit of expectation."[59] Here Pierce clearly notes the essential role surprise plays in disrupting an ongoing cognitive process, a habit of expectation. It is interesting to note that the cognitive scientist Chomsky does believe terms such as 'cognitive emotion' should be entered into the lexicon of cognitive science. Nevertheless, Chomsky explicitly applauds the appropriateness of the Peircian notion of abduction as a model of information acquisition and explanation.[60] As central as the process of language acquisition is to Chomsky's way of thinking, it is doubtful that he overlooked the essential role Pierce assigns to the mindful feeling of surprise in his discussion of abduction. One can only conjecture that Chomsky avoids reference to mindful feelings such as surprise because to include them would be tantamount to admitting the impoverishment of current (I-language) cognitive science.

I, for one, am not convinced that the admission of mindful feelings into cognitive theorizing would be irreparably destructive of the study of I-language processing. However, if the model of I-language processing is so vulnerable to intrusion of additional relevant phenomena, then so much the worse for the theory. In such an eventuality, it would be best to note the theory's fatal flaw and be done with it, subsequently moving on to the development of more promising research programs.

As mentioned above, however, I do not see the admission of mindful feelings as devastating to the Chomskian or to any other computational psychology. For example, one can easily imagine constructing a computer program modelling surprise by assigning Bayesian probabilities to "habits of expectation" and subsequently representing "surprising information" as a proportionate decrease or increase in previous levels of confidence. However, such a model would be a crude approximation of the actual intellective process for two reasons. First, as Alvin Goldman points out, we are as yet in no position to make such fine-grained distinctions as would be required if we were to take the proposed Bayesian model of surprise as presenting anything more than the crudest approximation of actual cognitive processing.[61] Perhaps something more like the Einhorn and Hogarth anchoring and adjustment model would reflect what we can know about the role of surprise in belief-updating.

Rather than assigning Bayesian probabilities to expectation and then increasing or decreasing subsequent probabilities in light of the system's response to new evidence, the Einhorn-Hogarth model simply indicates belief adjustment by movement along a continuum.[62] This avoids producing in the researchers an undue amount of confidence such as is likely to arise in the use of discrete Bayesian statistics in modelling belief adjustment. While such computational models allow us to incorporate more information about a mindful feeling such as surprise into a computationally accessible model of cognitive processing, it remains severely limited. Surprise is not merely a matter of adjusting "habits of expectation" in light of new evidence and in accord with some sort of algorithmic procedures. A (currently) indeterminate number of predispositions affect how the system will respond to anomalous evidence. Belief adjustment in the wake of a surprising event is a function of both the amount of new evidence presented and the intensity of the system's response to that evidence. We cannot easily give an account of how surprise disrupts or extends cognitive processing without giving a fuller account of the feeling of surprise or the intensity thereof.

The tendency among the more liberally minded cognitive scientists such as Pylyshyn might well be to explain away surprise as a primitive transducer function: that is, to adopt a computational model of belief adjustment such as Einhorn and Hogarth propose, but to assign the problem of belief intensity to the science of physiology. This maneuver would preserve computational rigor for the cognitive sciences and yet not entirely neglect the phenomenological aspects of surprise.

This bifurcation of surprise will just not do. Philosophers dating back to the time of Aristotle have championed similar bifurcated models of emotion and cognition, granting ontological reality to each and maintaining an interactive relationship between the emotions and reason.[53] Either may contribute to simultaneous or future events occurring in the other. Nevertheless, each is regarded as a separate class of phenomena.

In contrast, Nelson Goodman proposes a hybrid. "Emotion and feeling, I must repeat once more, function cognitively in aesthetic and much other experience," declares Goodman.[64] In "In Praise of Cognitive Emotions," Scheffler cites a similarly-worded passage by Goodman in his well-known *The Languages of Art*. In sympathy with Goodman, Scheffler declares, "The emotions serve not merely as a source of imaginative patterns; they fulfill also a selective function, facilitating choice among these patterns, defining their salient features, focusing attention accordingly. The patterns developed in imagination carry their own emotive values; these values guide selection and emphasis."[65] Cognitivists may read Scheffler here as confusing functions of the cognitive with functions of the emotive. But that misreading of Scheffler merely reflects the persistence of the traditional dichotomy between emotion and cognition. What Scheffler is proposing, at least as I understand him, is both revolutionary and conducive to the advancement of anything that deserves the name cognitive science. Scheffler is attempting to lay to rest forever the artificial distinction between emotion and cognition, noting that mental events often are comprised by hybrids that are indistinguishable with respect to their emotive and cognitive content. There is no ultimate substance or syntactic feature to which the term 'cognition' applies and with which 'emotion' is correlated. Some mental events are just what Scheffler and Goodman declare him to be: cognitive emotions, no more one than the other, and in no meaningful sense proportionately mixed.

The process of cognition Peirce describes in his writing on abduction could hardly occur without the existence of the hybrid phenomenon cognitive emotion, or, as I prefer, "mindful feeling." To return to the earlier passage I cited from Peirce,

> At length a further conjecture arises that furnishes a further possible Explanation. . . .. On account of this Explanation, the inquirer is led to regard this conjecture, or hypothesis, with favor. As I phrase it, he provisionally holds it to be "Plausible"; this acceptance ranges in different cases—and reasonably so—form a mere expression of it in the interrogative mood, as a question meriting attention; and reply, up through all appraisals of Plausibility, to uncontrollable inclination to believe.[66]

Scheffler was writing principally for educators, and Goodman for aestheticians. Nevertheless, their claims regarding cognitive emotion present a challenge to cognitive science. If cognitive science is to theorize in a comprehensive way about cognitive processes, fundamental cognitive events cannot be dismissed merely because they seem to contaminate the quest for rigor. The mind is not *just* a syntactic engine: it is also populated by evaluative feelings such as doubt, surprise, and so on. These feelings are so integral to cognition that to distinguish them from other feelings and emotions I have herein described them as mindful feelings. The science of mind should include all relevant mental phenomena, and this, I take it, is the great import to cognitive science of the recent work of Scheffler and Goodman.

Teaching and feeling

As noted above, Scheffler originally wrote his essay "In Praise of Cognitive Emotions" for educators. His general point in the essay is to note that education designed to enhance student cognitive skill cannot afford to become inattentive to the emotive. Reflecting upon an earlier essay by philosopher Moritz Schlick, Scheffler observes that moments of joy are of central importance in understanding scientific purpose. Specifically, it is the joy of verification that motivates the scientist to do further research.[67] On this point, I heartily agree with Scheffler and Schlick, for the joy of verification *is* of central importance to science and presumably its experience is central to science education. One must be careful to distinguish between the *joy of verification* and joy simpliciter. The joy of verification is properly understood to be a cognitive emotion; joy simpliciter is not. Clearly both the joy of verification and joy simpliciter fuel the cognitive process, but, while each is consequent upon an act of evaluation, only the joy of verification is a cognitive emotion. The reason for this is because the joy of verification is intimately a part of the act of experimental assessment, whereas joy simpliciter is conceptually distinct from any intellective process and may, in fact result from a variety of causal origins. Surprise is similar to the joy of verification. As Scheffler correctly notes, surprise is a hybrid of indistinguishable emotion and cognition.

Presumably, since emotions such as joy simpliciter and mindful feelings such as surprise may each contribute to increased individual understanding, one might be tempted to argue that each should be an educational aim. However, one can imagine a curriculum which produces no joy or any other such emotion and yet succeeds in altering—perhaps even improving—the cognitive efficiency of students. Nevertheless, I would argue that to construct with a curriculum is to attempt very little when much more could be done. For example, since the time of Plato and no doubt before, it was recognized that "youth learn best that which amuses the mind." There are, in other words, feelings that can be induced in students that will make them want to learn more and to learn more quickly. To ignore these feelings is to imperil the student's education. Thus joy simpliciter can be seen to have a certain utility. The fact that it has utility does not establish it as an appropriate aim of education in and of itself.

On the other hand, in the case of cognitive emotions, students could not acquire much in the way of improved cognitive efficiency if nothing were ever done to address the development and appreciation of cognitive emotions (mindful feelings). Apart from doubt, conviction, surprise, and so on, the student has little that will enable him or her to evaluate competing claims and arguments. Cognitive emotions are not important because they contribute to cognitive development. Rather, their development is itself a *part* of cognitive development. If education is to contribute even minimally to the cognitive development of students, it must attend to the fruitful utilization of the cognitive emotions just as it should to any other aspect of efficient information processing in humans.

There has been much ado in recent years about teaching students to think more critically. Groups such as the Informal Logic Association have been formed and treatises have been written on the need for teaching students to be more critically-minded. In the wake of such clamor, there have been an endless number of curricular programs and instructional techniques designed to teach students critical thinking. A while new testing business has developed almost overnight, producing standardized tests that claim to measure a person's ability to think critically.

Funding for innovative curriculum depends typically on the ability of theorists to show that the newly-funded program will produce the desired results. The most obvious way to show achievement is through the use of standardized tests that allow cross-group comparisons prior to beginning a new curricular program and subsequent to completing it. The construction of such tests assumes that test makers know what counts as a demonstration of newly acquired skills or information. Consequently, to test for, say, critical thinking requires that one know what counts as critical thinking. However, as has become clear in recent attempts to construct tests of critical thinking, it is not at all clear that critical thinking is a phenomenon that is well-understood. Is causal reasoning an element of critical thinking? Apparently, some psychometricians believe it is and others do not.[68] Is, as one might expect Scheffler to argue, having a well-developed sense of the cognitive emotions essential for critical thinking? If it is, then how does one go about testing for it? Once again the potential appeal of cognitive science for education surfaces. If the cognitivist is right then all mental phenomena can be modelled in algorithmic fashion. There is generally little difficulty associated with testing whether or not a student possesses algorithmically determined skills. On the other hand, if there is more to critical thinking than simply utilizing algorithms, the difficulty in testing for such things becomes overwhelming. Thus, the I-language ontology of the cognitive scientist becomes even more appealing to the psychomatrician, grantsman, and educational administrator.

On the other hand, if the development of cognitive emotions is essential to the practice of critical thinking then every effort should be made to resist any attempt to reduce critical thinking to a set of algorithms. This suggestion is of course in opposition to current trends in the critical thinking movement. With an eye to testable results, programs in critical thinking are being designed which center around sets of heuristics. While there is much debate on whether a single set of critical thinking heuristics can have crossdisciplinary application or whether heuristics must remain discipline-specific,[69] one conviction seems to be evolving, namely that whatever is to count as critical thinking, it must be comprised of discrete algorithms. While the national economy may be directed by the "visceral feelings" of one of the country's leading economists,[70] that sort of undisciplined activity will not be encouraged in the country's public schools. And why should it? When one looks at the direction cognitive science has taken in the last few years it seems evident, at least to the lay observer, that thinking and learning are simply a matter of getting the right software in place. This impression is facilitated by the claims and experimental success of the cognitive sciences. And since education has historically been so dependent on psychology for its theories, one can expect that educators too will shortly envision a computational theory of education. Students are quickly becoming, in the public imagination, the hardware units to be programmed. Teachers are viewed as the programmers. This scenario is to be avoided not because it confronts our over-romanticized image of what it means to be a person, but because it is predicated on what amounts to bad science. Should cognitive science relent in its present pursuits and consider anew the role of mental events such as mindful feelings, there may yet arise a cognitive science that will adequately support further educational theorizing.

If cognitive science continues to limit its ontology to computationally accessible evidence, we can expect one day to have a very pretty science that tells us very little about thinking and learning. If educators plod along in the wake of current cognitive science, students may shortly discover that education contains fewer surprises for them. Ultimately, the surprises that have so naturally accompanied a life of learning may altogether disappear—so much the worse for us all.[71]

Notes

1 Hugh Petrie, *The Dilemma of Enquiry* (University of Chicago Press: Chicago, 1982).

2 See for example Jonathan Baron, *Rationality and Intelligence*(Cambridge University Press: Chicago, 1985); see also Robert Sternberg *Intelligence, Information-Processing, and Analogical Reasoning* (Erlbaum: Hillsdale, N.J. 1977).

3 See for example Stephen Stich, *From Folk Psychology to Cognitive Science: The Case Against Belief* (MIT Press: Cambridge, 1982). For a history of how the cognitive revolution came about see Howard Gardner, *The Mind's New Science* (Basic: New York, 1985); see also Owen Flanagan, *The Science of the Mind* (MIT Press: Cambridge, 1984), esp. ch. 6.

4 Robert J. Sternberg, *I.Q. and Beyond* (Cambridge University Press: Cambridge, 1985); see also Roger Shank, *The Cognitive Computer* (Addison-Wesley: New York, 1984).

5 Patricia Churchland, *Neurophilosophy* (MIT Press: Cambridge, 1986): see esp. ch. 1.

6 I use the British spelling of 'programme' to distinguish reference to a set of theory and research protocols from a computer program. Also, I believe the Lakatosian sense of what constitutes a research programme is very nearly correct and it is this notion that governs my thinking in my description of cognitive science. For more on Lakatos's notion of a research programme see Imre Lakatos, "Falsification and the Methodology of Scientific Research Programmes" in *Criticism and the Growth of Knowledge*, ed. Imre Lakatos and Alan Musgrove (Cambridge University Press: Cambridge, 1972), pp. 91–196.

7   See for example Herbert Simon, *Models of Thought* (Yale University Press, 1980); see further David Waltz, "Artificial Intelligence," *Scientific American*, 247:4 (October 1983): 118–33.

8   Stich, *From Folk Psychology to Cognitive Science*, chs. 10, 11; see also Philip Johnson-Laird, *Mental Models* (Harvard University Press: Cambridge, 1983), wherein he writes, "Any scientific theory of the mind has to treat it as an automation" (p. 477).

9   Perhaps the most prominent of these is the Institute for the Advancement of Philosophy for Children at Montclair State University. Others include the Institute for Logic and Cognitive Studies at the University of Houston-Clear Lake, the Illinois Rational Thinking Project at the University of Illinois-Champain, and the Center for Reasoning and Moral Critique at Sonoma State University.

10 Gardner, *The Mind's New Science*.

11 Gardner believes the empirical study of cognitive activity dates back to the German physicist Herman von Helmholtz. My own sense of the matter is that Helmholtz lies more directly in the tradition of neurophysiology and not cognitivism. Also, as Gardner admits, cognitivism's beginning as a school of thought may be thought to have originated in the gestalt movement in psychology (see, for example, pp. 99–118). If so, there is considerable reason for describing Mach as the first gestaltist and hence the earliest forerunner of cognitivist psychology. For a discussion of Mach's claim to bring the first gestalt theorist see, Robert Blakemore, *Ernst Mach* (University of California Press: Berkeley, 1972), p. 47.

12 See for example Asa Kasher, ed., *Language in Focus: Foundations, Methods and Systems. Essays Dedicated to Yehoshua Bar-Hillel*, (D. Reidel: Boston, 1976); see also Andrew Hodges, *Alan Turing: the Enigma*, (Simon and Schuster: New York, 1983) Norbert Weiner, *I am a Mathematician* (MIT Press: Cambridge, 1956).

13 Gottlob Frege, *The Basic Laws of Arithmetic*, trans. Montgomery Furth (University of California Press: Berkeley, 1964).

14 Richard L. Gregory, *Mind in Science* (Cambridge University Press: Cambridge, 1981), p. 1–4.

15 Jerome S. Bruner, *In Search of Mind* (Harper and Row: New York, 1984); see also Jerome Bruner, *Actual Minds, Possible Worlds* (Harvard University Press: Cambridge, 1986).

16 See for example Alvin Goldman, *Epistemology and Cognition* (Harvard University Press: Cambridge, 1986).

17 Ludwig Wittgenstein, *Tractatus Logico-Philosophicus*, trans. D. F. Pears and B. F. McGuinness (Routledge and Kegan Paul: London, 1961); see also Henry Leroy Finch, *Wittgenstein—The Early Philosophy* (Humanities Press: New York, 1971).

18 See for example Ludwig Wittgenstein, *Philosophical Investigations*, trans. G. E. M. Anscombe (Macmillan: New York, 1958), pp. 175–76, 181–83; see also Garth Hallet, *A Companion to Wittgenstein's Philosophical*

Investigations (Cornell University Press: Ithaca, N.Y., 1977), pp. 91–93, 123–25, 204–6, 273–74.

19 See for example Noam Chomsky, *Knowledge of Language: Its Nature, Origin and Use* (Praeger, New York, 1986), pp. 22–24.

20 See for example Cora Diamond, ed., *Wittgenstein's Lectures on the Foundations of Mathematics Cambridge, 1938* (Cornell University Press: Ithaca, N.Y., 1976).

21 Hodges, *Alan Turing*.

22 See Ludwig Wittgenstein, *Philosophical Grammar*, ed. Rush Rhees, trans. Anthony Kenny (University of California Press: Berkeley, 1974); see also Ludwig Wittgenstein, *Last Writings: On the Philosophy of Psychology*, vol. I, ed. G. H. von Wright and H. Nyman, trans. C. Luckhardt and Maximillian Aue, (University of Chicago Press: Chicago, 1982).

23 See for example Wittgenstein, *Last Writings*, pp. 24–38.

24 Wittgenstein, *Philosophical Grammar*, ch. 9.

25 Ernst Mach, *Analysis of Sensation* (Open Court: La Salle, Ill., 1984). For an extended discussion of Mach's research into the "band phenomenon," see Floyd Ratliff, *Mach Bands: Quantitative Studies on Neuro-Networks in the Retina* (Holland-Day: San Francisco, 1965).

26 Gardner, *The Mind's New Science*, pp. 109–11.

27 See for example George A. Miller, Edward Galanter, and Karl Pribram, *Plans and the Structure of Behavior*, (Holt, Rinehart and Winston, New York, 1960); see also Jerome Bruner, *On Knowing* (Harvard University Press: Cambridge, 1962).

28 G. A. Miller, "The Magic Number Seven, Plus or Minus Two: Some Limits on Our Capacity for Processing Information," *Psychological Review*, (1956): 81–97.

29 See, for example, Stephen Kossylyn, *Image and Mind* Harvard University Press, Cambridge, 1980); see also Amos Tversky, Daniel Kahneman, and Paul Slovic, eds. *Judgment Under Certainty* (Cambridge University Press, Cambridge, 1983), Baruch Fishchoff, Sarah Lichenstein, Paul Slovic, Stephen Derby, and Ralph Kenney, *Acceptable Risk* (Cambridge University Press: Cambridge, 1981), Allan Newell and Herbert Simon, *Human Problem-Solving*, (Prentice-Hall: Englewood Cliffs, N.J., 1972), Herbert Simon, *Models of Discovery* (D. Reidel, Boston, 1977).

30 See for example, Zenon Pylyshyn, "The Imagery Debate: Analogue Media Versus Tacit Knowledge," *Psychological Review*, 88 (1981): 16–45; see also Roger Schank and R. Abelson, *Scripts, Plans, Goals and Semantic Information Processing*, (MIT Press: Cambridge, 1968), Robert Wilensky, *Planning and Understanding: A Computational Approach to Human Reasoning* (Addison-Wesley: Reading, MA, 1983), Patrick Henry Winston and Richard H. Brown, eds., *Artificial Intelligence: MIT Perspective*, 2 vols. (MIT Press: Cambridge, 1979).

31 Zenon Pylyshyn, *Computation and Cognition* (MIT Press, Cambridge: 1984).

32 See, respectively, Jerry A. Fodor, *The Language of Thought*, (Harvard University Press: Cambridge, 1979) and Chomsky, *Knowledge of Language*.

33 Chomsky, *Knowledge of Language*, pp. 22–24.

34 Joseph Weizenbaum, *Computer Power and Human Reason from Judgment to Calculation* (W. H. Freeman: New York, 1976).

35 It should be mentioned that Suppes himself does not believe that I-language study will accomplish all that Chomsky, Stich, Pylyshyn, and a host of other cognitivists believe it will. Rather Suppes remains committed to the belief that the best we can do is give a probabilistic account of linguistic activity specifically and brain activity generally. See his *Probabilistic Metaphysics* (Basil Blackwell: London, 1985).

36 Pylyshyn, *Computation and Cognition*.

37 Stich, *From Folk Psychology to Cognitive Science*.

38 See, respectively, Joseph Weizenbaum, "Once More: The Computer Revolution," in Michael Dertouzos and Joes Moses, eds., *The Computer Age: A Twenty Year View*, (MIT Press: Cambridge, 1979), pp. 439–458, John Searle, *Minds, Brains and Science*, (Harvard University Press: Cambridge, 1984), pp. 31–36, Hubert Dreyfus, *What Computers Can't Do* (Harper and Row: 1972), Hubert Dreyfus and Stuart Dreyfus, *Mind Over Machine* Macmillan: New York, 1986).

39 This example was provoked by my reading of Blaise Pascal, *Pensées*, trans. A. J. Krailsheimer (Penguin: Middlesex, 1966); see esp. Pascal's discussion of "Habit and conversion," wherein he writes, "we are as much automation as mind. . .. When we believe only by the strength of our conviction and the automaton is inclined to believe the opposite, that is not enough. We must make both parts of us believe: the mind by reason, and the automaton by habit,. . .(p. 274). In discussing this example with L. Jonathan Cohen Weizenbaum suggested that the effect of peer pressure on students in British Public Schools results in many "god-fearing" students being transformed into atheists or agnostics by the time of their graduation (personal communication, April 5, 1986). In any case, the point remains the same. One's feelings may change as a result of processing a routine sequence of thought. One's subsequent thoughts may vary from earlier repetitions. Nevertheless, and this is the cognitivist's point, the *structure* of cognitive processing, of I-language operation, will not change at all.

40 Patricia Churchland and Paul Churchland, "Functionalism, Qualia and Intentionality," *Philosophical Topics*, 12, (1981): 121–45; see also Patricia Churchland, *Neurophilosophy*, Paul Churchland, *Scientific Realism and the Plasticity of Mind*, (Cambridge University Press: 1982).

41 Pylyshyn, *Computation and Cognition*, p. 147.

42 Pylyshyn, *Computation and Cognition*, p. 148.

43 Pylyshyn, *Computation and Cognition*, p. 267.

44 John Haugeland, *Artificial Intelligence* (MIT Press, Cambridge, 1985), pp. 249–50.

45 Hubert Dreyfus and Stuart Dreyfus, *Mind Over Machine*: see esp. ch. 2, 3, 4.
46 Frank Rose, *Into the Heart of Mind* (Harper and Row, New York: 1985).
47 See for example Fodor, *Language of Thought*, pp. 79–97.
48 Hilary Putnam, "Meaning and Mental Life," forthcoming.
49 See for example Israel Scheffler "In Praise of Cognitive Emotions," *Teacher's College Record*, 79:2, (1977): 171–86; see also Nelson Goodman, *Of Mind and Other Matters*, (Harvard University Press: Cambridge, 1984), Robert Solomon, *The Passions* (University of Notre Dame Press: Notre Dame, 1983).
50 Scheffler, "In Praise of Cognitive Emotions."
51 Chomsky, *Knowledge of Language*, p. 55.
52 Stich, *From Folk Psychology to Cognitive Science*.
53 For an extended discussion of this point, see William Lyons, *Emotions* (Cambridge University Press: Cambridge, 1980), chs. 7, 8; see also William P. Alston, "Emotion and Feeling" in *The Encyclopedia of Philosophy*, ed. Paul Edwards (Macmillan: New York, 1967), pp. 479–86.
54 See for example Sir John C. Eccles, "Do Mental Events Cause Neural Events Analogously to the Probability Fields of Quantum Mechanics?" *Proceedings of the Royal Society of London*, B 227 (1986): 441–28.
55 See for example, G. Globus, G. Maxwell, and I. Savodnik, eds., *Consciousness of the Brain* (Plenum Press: New York, 1976); see also Stanley Schacter and J. E. Singer, "Cognitive, Social and Physiological Determinants of Emotional States," *Psychological Review*, 69 (1962): 379–99.
56 Lyons, *Emotions*, ch. 4.
57 Lyons, *Emotions*, ch. 4.
58 Lyons, *Emotions*, pp. 140–43.
59 Charles S. Peirce, *Collected Papers*, ed. Charles Hartshorne, Paul Weiss, and H. W. Burks (Harvard University Press, Cambridge, 1908), G. 469.
60 Chomsky, *Knowledge of Language*, p. 55
61 Goldman, *Epistemology and Cognition*, ch. 16.
62 Hillel Einhorn and Robin Hograth, "A Contrast Model for Updating Beliefs," University of Chicago, Center for Decision Research (1984); see also Robin Hogarth, "Beyond Discrete Biases: Functional and Disfunctional Aspects of Judgmental Heuristics," *Psychological Bulletin*, 90 (1981) 197–17.
63 See for example, Aristotle, *De Anima* Books II and III, trans D. W. Hamlyn (Clarendon Press: Oxford, 1968); also, see Jerome Bruner's *Actual Minds and Possible Worlds* (Harvard University Press: Cambridge: 1976), wherein he discusses at length the "question of how emotion and cognition interact" (p. 111). It is surprising that Bruner talks that way since he seems influenced by Goodman: see for example ch. 7.
64 Goodman, *Of Mind and Other Matters*, p. 8.
65 Scheffler, "In Praise of Cognitive Emotion," p. 178.
66 Peirce, *Collected Papers*, G. 469.

67 Scheffler, "In Praise of Cognitive Emotion," p. 180; see also Moritz Sch-
    lick, "The Foundations of Knowledge" in A. J. Ayer, ed., *Logical Positiv-
    ism* (Free Press: New York, 1959).
68 The theorists who constructed the New Jersey Test of Reasoning did not
    include items designed to test student skill at causal reasoning. Test sponsor
    philosopher Matthew Lippman wisely argued that it is not at all clear yet
    what should count as good causal reasoning. Consequently, one should not
    attempt to test for it. Apparently, psychometricians associated with other
    critical tests are not troubled by the widespread uncertainty surrounding
    current discussions of the notion of causality. (personal conversation with
    Virginia Shepman, senior research psychologist with the Educational Test-
    ing Center of Princeton, New Jersey and author of the New Jersey Test of
    Reasoning, April 22, 1985). This strikes me as a classic example where
    the appeal of a testable algorithmic structure as the goal of education won
    the day. This, despite the fact that one of the best tests of causal reasoning
    available to the individual is the ability to be surprised on the one hand and
    to appreciate the joy of verification on the other.
69 See for example Richard Paul, "McPeck's Mistakes" *Informal Logic*, 7:1,
    35–44; see also John McPeck "Paul's Critique," *Informal Logic*, 7:1, 45–
    54, Israel Scheffler, *Of Human Potential*, (London: Routledge and Keagan
    Paul, 1985), pp. 85–91, David Perkins, *The Mind's Best Work*, (Harvard
    University Press, Cambridge, 1985).
70 David Stockman, "The Triumph of Politics" *Newsweek*, April 21, 1986,
    p. 52.

Index